ISRAELI FOREIGN POLICY

Israeli Foreign Policy

South Africa and Central America

by Jane Hunter

South End Press   **Boston, MA**

Copyrights are required for book production in the United States. However, in our case it is a disliked necessity. Thus, any properly footnoted quotation of up to 500 sequential words may be used without permission, so long as the total number of words does not exceed 2,000. For longer quotations or for a greater number of total words, authors should write to South End Press for permission.

The charts on pages 110, 133, and 141 are reproduced with the kind permission of Bishara Bahbah, from his book *Israel and Latin America: The Military Connection* (New York: St. Martin's Press, in association with Washington, D.C.: Institute for Palestine Studies, 1986).

Typesetting, design, and layout by the South End Press collective
Cover by Todd Jailer
Manufactured in the U.S.A.

Library of Congress Cataloging-in-Publication Data

Hunter, Jane, 1943-
    Israeli foreign policy.

    Includes index.
    1. Israel—Foreign relations—South Africa.
2. South Africa—Foreign relations—Israel.
3. Israel—Foreign relations—Central America.
4. Central America—Foreign relations—Israel.
I. Title.
DS119.8.S6H86   1987   327.5694068   87—13024
ISBN 0-89608-286-5
ISBN 0-89608-285-7 (pbk.)

South End Press   116 St. Botolph St.   Boston, MA 02115

96 95 94 93 92 91 90 89 88 87   1 2 3 4 5 6 7 8 9

To my children
Charlie and Jenny
with love and affection

Table of Contents

Introduction ....

Another Man's Genius

"This will always be our response to international boycotts and threats against us," said President P.W. Botha as he unveiled the Cheetah, South Africa's advanced combat aircraft. The South Africans said that the plane was a secret project of the government's Armaments Corporation.[1]

Claiming the new aircraft was more than a match for neighboring Angola's MiG-23s, Gen. Magnus Malan, the white government's defense minister, told the assembled industrialists and foreign press corps that the Cheetah "signaled a new era of self sufficiency and enhanced operational capability for the South African Air Force." It was proof of the technological leadership of the South African arms industry, asserted President Botha.[2]

The Cheetah was also the one major item an international arms embargo had managed to deny South Africa. The South Africans, who in July 1986 were anxiously following the progress of sanctions legislation in the U.S., lost no time in driving that point home.

In its nightly broadcast to North America, Radio South Africa said the "futility" of the UN's 1977 arms embargo

> was recognized 18 months ago by the UN General Assembly, which called on member countries to stop importing arms from South Africa. After all, they were supposed to be applying an arms boycott against the country...The arms embargo has achieved the opposite of what it was intended to achieve. In the

last two decades the country has built up the tenth largest arms industry in the world and this achievement was the direct response of the misguided attempt to isolate South Africa and make it more vulnerable to outside pressures.[3]

In all their jubilation, the South Africans omitted one key detail: Israel Aircraft Industries (IAI) had played a major role in creating the Cheetah out of the carcass of an aging Mirage III-C. The Cheetah was the latest of a number of projects on which the state-owned IAI and other Israeli weapons manufacturers had collaborated with the South Africans.

Vanunu and Hasenfus

On October 5, 1986 the London *Sunday Times* carried a front page account of Israel's nuclear capability. The information had been provided by dissaffected Israeli technician Mordechai Vanunu, who had worked at Israel's secret plutonium plant in an underground facility in the Negev Desert. The account astonished leading nuclear scientists—some of whom had been called in to challenge Vanunu, and to verify the photographs he had smuggled out of Israel—who were forced to revise their estimates upward and declare Israel to be the world's sixth largest nuclear power.[4]

Over the years bits and pieces of Israel's nuclear weapons development had emerged: a series of tests on weapons and delivery systems with the French in Algeria;[5] Francis Perrin, for many years head of the French atomic agency, recently admitted that France built Israel the nuclear reactor at Dimona in the Negev, and also that between 1957 and 1959 the two governments had been working together on an atomic bomb;[6] the discovery in 1965, just after the Dimona plant came on line, that as much as 130 pounds of enriched uranium was missing from the NUMEC enrichment plant (which the CIA believed was largely financed by Israel) in Apollo, Pennsylvania;[7] the preparation of nuclear-tipped Jericho missiles for use in the early days of Israel's 1973 war;[8] a joint program with Iran under the Shah to build and test long-range, nuclear-capable missiles;[9] the test with South Africa of a nuclear missile in the South Atlantic in September 1979; and reports in 1985 that Israel had deployed nuclear-armed Jericho II missiles in the Negev Desert and perhaps also in the occupied Golan Heights.

All this, coming as it did in fragmentary reports over a period of 30 years, did not add up to alarm. The October 5, 1986 story which for the first time portrayed all the megatonnage at Israel's disposal and described, in the words of leading nuclear scientists, Israel's ability to produce sophisticated thermonuclear warheads, did not rouse much reaction from disarmament activists or from most Western governments. A report by a small newsletter that South African scientists had habitually worked at the secret plant in Dimona was put on the desk of every member of Congress. It was ignored.

Had it not been for the continuing drama surrounding the fate of Mordechai Vanunu, the matter might have been completely forgotten. On September 30, 1986, Vanunu disappeared in London. The following November 9, the Israeli government announced it had him in custody and would try him for treason and espionage. Vanunu later made it known to journalists that he had been kidnapped in Rome. Although smeared by the Israeli media as a traitor and a money-grubbing opportunist, through a hunger strike and messages delivered through his lawyer, a friend, and his brothers, Vanunu contended that he had acted out of principle. His travails sparked Israel's first ever anti-nuclear effort. Support for him began to grow in the U.S.[10]

Also on October 5, 1986, a U.S. mercenary was captured when Nicaraguan soldiers shot down the plane in which he had been ferrying arms to the anti-Nicaragua contras. The admissions made by load master Eugene Hasenfus to the press in Nicaragua sparked investigations that revealed a network of high U.S. officials and former military and intelligence officers put together to circumvent the will of Congress and aid the counterrevolutionary bands assembled by the CIA in the early days of the Reagan Administration. It soon emerged that financing for the supply operation—it had been called, with a wink and a nod, "private aid"—had been obtained by shaking down Egypt and Israel for kickbacks on their U.S. aid. Even greater amounts of money had been squeezed out of Saudi Arabia, as an expression of thanks for administration support of the kingdom's purchase of AWACS aircraft against the wishes of the pro-Israeli lobby in Congress in 1981.

The Hasenfus scandal was soon transcended by the discovery that Israel had led a small group within the Reagan Administration into a complicated morass where Israel sold U.S. arms to Iran (persuading the Iranians to ransom U.S. hostages held in Lebanon) and applied a part of the profits from those arms deals to the purchase (from Israel and other sources) of weapons for the contras. Known as the Iran-contra affair, this imbroglio riveted the national attention to several areas of policy which had long been ignored.

However, in their understandable—if belated—lust to pin these crimes on the President, the Congress and the media blithely ignored the intellectual author of the intricate disaster—Israel.[11]

The Perfect Coup d'Etat

The coup came off like clockwork. Since 1981, the young officers had been meticulously planning their move. On March 23, 1982, soldiers of the Mariscal Zavala Brigade ran through the streets of Guatemala City to take up positions around the Presidential Palace. So secret had been the preparations—by one account even the CIA and the U.S. embassy were taken by surprise—that in order to identify one another the participants had, at a coded signal, rolled up the right sleeves of their combat fatigues.

While helicopters flew above the palace, other participants took over radio and television stations and closed the national airport. Outside Guatemala City, garrison by garrison, the military declared its allegiance to the young officers' revolt. At four in the afternoon, head of state Gen. Romeo Lucas Garcia quietly surrendered.

The man chosen by the young officers to succeed him, Gen. Efrain Rios Montt,[12] told ABC News that he attributed the success of the coup to the training of "many of our soldiers" by Israelis.[13] As they had assisted Lucas Garcia, Israeli advisers would help Rios Montt's scorched earth fight against the insurgency that was sweeping the rural highlands. They would help with the implementation and design of a forced resettlement program in that largely Mayan Indian area.

Rios Montt was a Protestant Evangelical affiliated with a U.S. fundamentalist sect—the first non-Catholic head of state in Guatemala's history. During his tenure, right-wing fundamentalists from the U.S. flooded into the Indian highlands and began to take an active part in the "pacification" activities underway there.

In August 1983, Rios Montt was overthrown by officers offended by "the aggressive and fanatic religious groups" which had access to the highest levels of his government (and by his promotion of young officers).[14] He was then spirited away to Miami by an Israeli adviser.[15] Both Israelis and right-wing U.S. Christians continue to work in the resettlement program, where Indians must often eat food donated by right-wing religious organizations while they are forced to grow crops for export.

*

In each of these instances Israel acted autonomously, directing its own foreign policy for the sake of its own objectives. Yet in all of these instances—and they are not selective, but rather illustrative of the many occasions on which Israel has intervened in the course of another nation's history—the United States was party to Israel's action.

Israel's presence in Guatemala cannot be divorced from the historical process begun when the CIA overthrew that country's elected government in 1954. Regarding South Africa, the Carter Administration gave Israel a green light to continue its relationship with apartheid, asking only that the Israeli Kfir aircraft and the Merkava tank, developed with substantial U.S. funding, not be suplied to the white government[16] and, as shall be seen, turned a blind eye when Israel and South Africa tested a nuclear weapon in 1979. It can be safely assumed that the Reagan White House was wholeheartedly in support of the continuing growth of Israeli-South African ties. But even some of the most ardent progressives within the U.S. Congress went out of their way to avoid confronting Israel over its support of South Africa at the same time they were fashioning sanctions against the apartheid state.

Of the instances cited, and of those to be mentioned in the following pages, there is not a single one that does not cry out for the attention of those who oppose the course of post-war foreign policy from a progressive perspective.

There is also a special responsibility for U.S. activists to make themselves heard regarding Israel's ambitious involvement in repressive situations. Throughout the world Israel is perceived as acting as a representative of the U.S., whether or not, in any given set of circumstances, this is actually the case. When the victims of Israeli weapons hear no outcry from the opponents of U.S. policies, they are justified in wondering by what set of criteria progressives operate.

In fact, it is the very reluctance of the progressive movement to turn its critical focus on Israel that has led to the growth of Israel's role as an adjunct to some of the most inexcusable undertakings of U.S. foreign policy.

Ratcheting this irony yet another turn is the indisputable correlation between progressive foreign policy achievements and Israeli intervention: the latter cancels the former out, almost every time. When Congress, pressed by constituents, cut off aid to the anti-Nicaraguan contras, Israeli aid to the contra mercenaries increased. When Congress warned that a rightist coup in El Salvador would result in a cancellation of U.S. aid, Salvadoran rightists propitiated Israel.

To cite a more current—and retrievable—example, when the South Africans carry on about the bracing effect of sanctions they are bragging mainly for domestic consumption, to reassure anxious whites. They are also providing their supporters abroad a last-ditch argument: sanctions don't work. However, sanctions do work and the South Africans are very nervous about their actual and psychological effect. The U.S. anti-apartheid measures are particularly frightening to the South Africans, but they will only have their desired effect if their enforcement by the administration and Congress is monitored vigilantly—and if Israel is prevented from making a mockery of them.

The U.S. has had a reasonably functional arms embargo against South Africa for a decade—during which time Israel, as shall be seen, helped South Africa establish an indigenous arms industry.[17] Months before the 1986 anti-apartheid legislation was passed, Israeli officials were urging South African businessmen to ship their products to the U.S. via Israel to take advantage of Israel's special duty-free trade agreement with Washington.

Thus, our hard won victories regularly turn to ashes. The congressional intention built so laboriously by grassroots activism is cynically subverted. The obvious corrective would be for Congress to accompany each of its anti-intervention and anti-apartheid actions with a postscript enjoining Israel to adhere to the spirit of the action. In a pointed (if unintended) message to activists, a small step was taken in this direction when an amendment requiring that South African dealings of U.S. allies be scrutinized was tacked onto the anti-apartheid legislation of 1986 (see Conclusion). Authored by retiring Republican Senator Charles McC. Mathias, it raised the hackles of not a few Congresspeople.

It is clear, however, that no sustained initiative will come spontaneously from Congress, and that without vigorous pressure Congress will go on as it has for so long considering Israel to be beyond reproach.

Indeed, Congress is the last body that might be expected to reassess its no-questions-asked support of Israel. In the process of cultivating the U.S. support so critical for its survival, Israel and its domestic support system have, logically enough, made Congress, with its powers of appropriation, the central focus of their efforts. (The executive branch of government and the media have been a secondary, but by no means insignificant, focus.)

The enormous amount of U.S. aid that Congress regularly bestows upon Israel—$3 billion for 1987—is a testament to the success of those efforts. So large has Israel's aid package become, by any standard of comparison, that it is commonly considered to be indebted to the U.S. Many, upon hearing that Israel has taken over the task of propping up this dictator or that despot, simply assume that Israel has taken over in situations which Congress (or, as in the case of the Carter White House and its human rights policies, the President) has declared out of bounds for the U.S., as a *quid pro quo* for the aid it receives—that these are the invisible strings attached to Israeli military and economic assistance. But this perception is not entirely accurate, nor is it very useful in understanding the dynamics of Israeli interventionism in the framework of U.S.-Israeli relations.

How the U.S.-Israeli Relationship Evolved

There are two important historical threads to follow—Israel's search for an international backer and its quest for political independence. Out of their ostensibly contradictory meanderings is woven the stark fabric of Israel's reality.

Israel was established in part by a plan drafted by the United Nations and in part by "facts on the ground," territory in Palestine occupied by Jewish forces in fighting during the final days of the British Mandate and immediately following the departure of the British from Palestine.

A United Nations plan passed in 1947 for the partition of Palestine into Jewish, Arab, and international states conferred legitimacy on the concept of a Jewish state. The partition plan was approved by the USSR, the U.S., and France. In its early days Israel—which declared independence in May 1948 while claiming sovereignty over a territory already well outside its UN-drawn borders[18]—would turn to both of the latter for support.

France was the most immediately forthcoming, supplying the new state with weapons and technical support. Then, in June 1967, the Israelis received the back of de Gaulle's hand. Just as Israel commenced its attack on its neighbors, the French president blocked the delivery of all arms to Israel, an embargo which included an already-paid-for fleet of 50 Mirage aircraft and a number of missile boats.[19]

It was at that point that Israel turned the full force of its attention to the U.S. If the 1967 war had repelled de Gaulle, it had the opposite effect on U.S. Jews, inspiring them into devoted support for Israel. The U.S. had soon replaced France as a reliable international backer for Israel.

From the Ruins, an Israel Lobby

The history of American Jews and their interactions with the government in Washington is complex, as were Jewish communal politics in the first half of this century. There were then, as now, progressive Jews, many of whom came to the U.S. from Eastern Europe during the mass migrations of the late nineteenth and early twentieth centuries. There were also the self-styled aristocrats, mostly German Jews, who had arrived in the U.S. throughout the course of the nineteenth century and who had prospered. In a very general sense the progressive Jews participated in the broad popular movements of the day, while the aristocrats—in their organized manifestation represented by B'nai B'rith, a fraternal order, and the American Jewish Committee, an exclusive organization constituted to combat anti-Semitism—appropriated the role of sometime ethnic advocates, practicing a quiet diplomacy with highly-placed officials to whom they had access by virtue of their wealth and power.[20]

With the rise of Hitler, the divisions in the Jewish community became apparent. The aristocrats counseled quiet approaches to those in power— the U.S. was, until well after World War II, an unabashedly anti-Semitic society and many Jews believed it was best not to have too high a profile— while those Jews identified with popular causes participated in strenuous efforts to warn of the dangers of German fascism. Preeminent among these efforts was a boycott campaign against Hitler, spearheaded by Rabbi Stephen Wise of the American Jewish Congress.[21] The attempted 1933 boycott was undercut in its initial stages by the American Jewish Committee and B'nai B'rith who feared a backlash against Jewish assertion.[22]

The protest drive against Nazi Germany started with a March 27, 1933 rally in New York's Madison Square Garden that drew tens of thousands and received international support.[23] The ground was soon cut out from under this early opposition to Hitler when several (competing) Zionist factions began negotiating with the Third Reich to ransom the Jews of Germany.

> Zionist leaders, during April 1933, sought to cooperate with the Nazi Reich to arrange the orderly exit of Jewish people and wealth from Germany. But during the very same weeks, Jewish groups throughout the world were struggling to resist and topple the Reich to keep Jews in Germany as citizens.[24]

Ultimately a "Transfer Agreement" was worked out, under which the funds of wealthy German Jews were shared between the Reich, the Jewish authorities in Palestine, and, on arrival there, by the emigrating Jews. It was, as intended, a way of rapidly building Zionism during a period when the movement for a Jewish national homeland had a small and divided following.[25]

Relatively few organized American Jews were Zionists until after the shock of the Holocaust, Hitler's murder of 6 million Jews. News of Hitler's genocide against the Jews was confirmed by the governments of the U.S., the UK, and the USSR in 1942.[26] A shaken Jewish community came together to issue a statement that included endorsement of a Jewish state in Palestine.[27] However, the ascendancy of Zionism during the critical period 1942-44 had the overarching side-effect of blunting efforts to rescue European Jews. Bound up in political contention, very few Jewish leaders responded forcefully to the plight of the Jews in Europe.

An unavoidable conclusion is that during the Holocaust the leadership of American Zionism concentrated its major force on the drive for a future Jewish state in Palestine. It consigned rescue to a distinctly secondary position.[28]

After the war Jews intensively lobbied the Truman Administration, first to back the UN partition plan, and then to recognize the newly established state of Israel. Facing an uphill fight for reelection in 1948, Harry Truman ignored the counsel of the State Department, the Department of the Navy, the War Department and the Joint Chiefs of Staff[29] and responded instead to a flood of letters and personal approaches, recognizing Israel in May 1984.[30] There was bitterness in the State Department, where it was remembered that the recently deceased President Roosevelt had promised Arab leaders to consult with them before taking such a step.[31]

Suddenly moved by the Holocaust, both houses of Congress also responded to the political onslaught mounted by Jewish activists with resolutions supporting recognition of Israel.[32]

Dwight D. Eisenhower was the only President to resist pressure from the pro-Israeli lobby, as the incresingly well organized Jewish community was coming to be known. On three occasions Eisenhower withheld U.S. aid from Israel: to force it to stop diverting water from Jordan in 1953, to force it to cease its attack on Egypt (the Suez crisis of 1956) and to force it to withdraw from Egyptian territory occupied during its 1956 war. In the face of militant opposition from a Congress already swayed by Israeli lobbying efforts and supportive of Israel's determination to hold the land it had seized, Eisenhower maintained his hardnosed approach, asking, "Should a nation which attacks and occupies foreign territory in the face of the United Nations disapproval be allowed to impose conditions on its own withdrawal?"[33]

Israel received more solicitious treatment from the next two presidents, Kennedy and Johnson. U.S. arms sales began under the Kennedy Administration.[34] The Johnson Administration secretly helped Israel prepare for its 1967 war, and when the French cut off Israel's arms supplies, the Johnson Administration kept Israel in equipment[35] long enough for Israel to increase the territory under its control by 200 percent.[36] President Johnson courted the Jewish community by calling attention to the aid his administration was giving Israel.[37] Johnson also strongly urged Israel to extend diplomatic recognition to the puppet government his administration was backing in South Vietnam and to send a health team there. Israel refused, agreeing only after months of requests to accept under conditions of complete secrecy eight Vietnamese agricultural trainees in Israel.[38] Almost two decades later, this scenario would be repeated, when Israel refused to be the lead player with the contras.

Richard Nixon was a strong supporter of Israel and was generous with aid during its 1973 war, although as Watergate engulfed him he was reportedly toying with the idea of suspending military aid to Israel as a way of forcing it to approach its Arab neighbors for peace.[39] Nonetheless, with the exception of some elements of Reform Judaism, no major Jewish organizations took a stand against Nixon, and when it became clear that Nixon might have to surrender the presidency, some Jewish leaders expressed a preference for him over Vice President Gerald Ford.[40] Ford actually did suspend aid to Israel, during a 1975 "reassessment" of U.S. Middle East policy.[41] Reassessment was a euphemistic way of expressing extreme displeasure with Israel's intransigent refusal to vacate several positions in Egypt. In response to the Ford cutoff, pro-Israeli forces worked the Congress until Ford relented.[42]

Jimmy Carter is remembered for knocking together the heads of Menachem Begin and Egyptian president Anwar Sadat to achieve the 1978 Camp David accords. But his administration was very susceptible to Israeli pressure, both directly and through the Congress, where AIPAC (the American Israel Public Affairs Committee), Israel's registered lobbyist, was making its power felt. Carter fired his UN Ambassador Andrew Young after Young met with the PLO representative to the UN. Unwilling or unable to order Israel to stop its dealings with South Africa, Carter presided over a cover-up "investigation" of a nuclear weapons test conducted by Israel and South Africa in 1979.

While all of the administrations since Eisenhower were obliging to one degree or another, the Reagan Administration seems to have made Israel the object of cult worship. It is known that the President subscribes to the superstition propounded by right-wing Christian fundamentalists that

Israel will be the site of the battle of Armageddon which precedes the end of times.[43] To help Israel prepare for more immediate battles, the Reagan Administration has increased its military and economic aid to the highest levels ever. It was also Ronald Reagan that allowed his administration to be directed by Israeli officials and Americans partial to Israel in the sale of arms to Iran and funneling of funds to the war against Nicaragua. But even with Reagan, a president with whom Israel enjoyed a "virtual honeymoon that existed over most of...six years,"[44] the pro-Israeli lobby often felt compelled to intervene, through Congress and with other government agencies, in the fashioning of Middle East policy and other matters it considered to be within its realm of interest.

Several years into the Reagan Administration it was common knowledge that the Israeli government had "friends" placed in every nook of the vast bureaucracy of the executive branch of the federal government.

> The [pro-Israeli] lobby's intelligence network, having numerous volunteer "friendlies" to tap, reaches all parts of the executive branch where matters concerning Israel are handled. Awareness of this seepage keeps officials—whatever rung of the ladder they occupy—from making or even proposing decisions that are in the U.S. interest.[45]

Whereas the State Department, with its history-conscious bureaucracy and its seasoned professionals had once acted as a counterbalance to the political suasions of the pro-Israeli forces, under Reagan it seems to have succumbed. Even the Secretary of State, George Shultz—formerly with the large Bechtel construction company and close to Arab governments—has become a wholehearted supporter of Israel.

While relations with each administration had their high and low points, Israeli influence with the Congress was plotted on an ever-ascending curve. Besides cultivating the legislative branch as the source of financial assistance, Israel mastered the craft of using Congress to overcome political opposition from the executive branch. In legislation concerning Israel, Congress has set numerous precedents: a Free Trade Agreement; a resolution demanding the relocation of the U.S. embassy in Israel from Tel Aviv to Jerusalem (having been advised by State Department officials that such a move would ignite anti-U.S. protests in Muslim nations as far distant as Indonesia, the President did not act on this); permission to spend military aid on development of weapons in Israel.[46] Although it has empowered itself to do so, Congress has never called Israel to account for its nuclear weapons program. Members of Congress seem to compete to speak at pro-Israel events (many of which include honoraria).

The incredible success of Israel's lobby argues strongly that rather than progressively obligating Israel, the astronomical rise in aid is a product of Israeli influence on the Congress. That much of the influence is gained by pressure, browbeating, and intimidation rather than the presentation of a convincing case—Congress, for example, routinely appropriates billions for Israel's "defense" rather than pressing it to conclude a just peace with its neighbors and with the Palestinian people—suggests that as it wins more concessions from Congress, Israel is simultaneously entrenching its position in a never-never land called "beyond reproach."[47]

The Development of Israel's Arms Industry

De Gaulle's halting of the arms flow at such a critical juncture also provided Israel with the impetus to embark on a crash program to develop an arms industry.

In this endeavor, Israel was not starting from scratch. As early as 1921, Jewish settlers in Palestine had made hand grenades and explosives for use against Arabs protesting their presence.[48] The history of the Jewish state's foundation is laden with tales of weapons obtained abroad by hook or by crook, and of secret workshops in British-ruled Palestine where primitive small arms were constructed.[49]

After the establishment of Israel in 1948 these munitions factories were brought above ground and incorporated into a government-owned military industry. As the great powers, for varying geopolitical reasons, were slow to sell arms to the new state, the Israelis pressed ahead, producing the Uzi submachine gun in 1952, and by 1965 had developed the rudiments of aviation, munitions, and electronics industries. Israel's objective was a guaranteed source of supply, but as early as 1954 it also began marketing weapons.[50]

In 1967, shaken by de Gaulle's abrupt cancellation of major contracts for aircraft and patrol boats, the Israelis embarked on a crash effort to lower their future political vulnerability by striving toward self-sufficiency in weapons production.[51] They opted to invest funds that had previously been earmarked for purchases overseas into the indigenous arms industry.[52]

> In keeping with the decision immediately after the war to proceed with an intensified effort to develop and enlarge Israel's own weapons industry, cost-benefit calculations were set aside in favor of producing essential items in Israel.[53]

With some critical technological inputs from abroad—some arriving in the form of foreign investment and purchase of foreign technology,[54] some pilfered, such as plans for the Mirage combat aircraft which were stolen by Mossad, Israel's secret service, from the French Dassault company's Swiss licensee,[55] making possible the task of designing and building the Mirage-copy Kfir jet fighter—the arms industry expanded rapidly. Israeli determination was further spurred by displeasure with the amount of time it took the U.S. to resupply Israel during the 1973 war.[56]

By the end of the 1970s, the Israeli military industry was supplying 40 percent of Israel's military needs.[57] But production runs solely for the domestic market resulted in high costs per item. The longer production runs necessary to lower unit costs created an imperative to export.

The government began a concerted marketing campaign, through diplomatic and military contacts, as well as news releases and exhibits at fairs.[58] In later years a sales force of retired military officers eager for commissions fanned out over the globe.[59] While the secrecy of the Israeli government makes it impossible to exactly calculate the volume of Israel's weapons sales abroad, the general consensus of analysts of the international arms trade indicates that between 1972 and 1980 Israel's arms exports soared, particularly in the latter part of that span, rising from $50 million[60] to top $1 billion,[61] and, with the possible exception of 1983,[62] have remained over $1 billion annually. A 1986 estimate puts annual sales at "more than $1.25 billion."[63] Since 1982 Israel has been ranked among the world's top ten arms producers.[64]

The importance to the overall economy of the arms manufacturing sector also increased, with weapons exports estimated to have comprised 31 percent of industrial exports in 1975, up from 14 percent in 1967[65] and more recently 30 to 40 percent of Israel's industrial output.[66] The arms industry employs "anywhere from 58,000 to as many as 120,000 Israelis," or, taking the lower figure, 20 percent of the industrial labor force,[67] with the biggest unit, Israel Aircraft Industries, the nation's largest employer, carrying 20,000 on its payroll.[68]

The export imperative, in turn, brought its own set of problems, these centering on the overseas markets available to Israel and on its choice of customers from that list. For varying reasons, Israel was largely shut out of the Eastern Bloc, the Arab world and NATO countries. That left its potential clientele to be found on the peripheries: pariahs such as South Africa and Guatemala, the strong-man regimes of Taiwan, Zaire, and Chile, and the occasional government wary of strings-attached arms purchases from the superpowers. Over the years Israel has sold weapons—and often along with the weapons come Israeli advisers—to Costa Rica, Dominican

Republic, El Salvador, Guatemala, Haiti, Honduras, Mexico, Nicaragua (under Somoza), Panama, Argentina, Bolivia, Brazil, Chile, Colombia, Ecuador, Paraguay, Peru, Venezuela, Cameroon, Ethiopia, Ghana, Kenya, Liberia, Morocco, Nigeria, Rhodesia, South Africa, Swaziland, Tanzania, Uganda, Zaire, Australia, China, Indonesia, Malaysia, New Zealand, Papua-New Guinea, Philippines, Singapore, Sri Lanka, Taiwan, Thailand, Iran, and a number of European countries and several non-governmental factions.[69] Sometimes even the least desirable customers have required some softening up: "Greatly detailed stories abound of the huge bribes Israel has used to suborn defense ministries, with the sole objective of nailing down arms deals."[70]

As time went on an additional problem arose: arms sales became the motor driving Israel's foreign policy. In times of economic crisis it became the supreme exigency. In September 1986, the Israeli defense minister explained to a press conference what was behind a raft of scandals involving Israeli arms exports and technology thefts (these last, most frequently from the U.S., have been an inevitable hallmark of a small country attempting to sustain a full-scale armaments industry). "...We cut our orders in our military industries..." he said, "and I told them quite frankly: 'Either you'll fire people or find export markets.'"[71]

The export markets open to Israel are frequently among the world's most unsavory; indeed, to be off limits to the superpowers they often are located inside the very gates of hell. Already under international censure for its oppression of the Palestinians in the territories it occupies, Israel's dealings with the scum of the world's tyrants—including the white clique in South Africa, Somoza of Nicaragua, Gen. Pinochet of Chile, Marcos of the Philippines, Duvalier of Haiti, Mobutu of Zaire, the allegedly cannibalistic Bokassa of the Central African Republic[72]—invariably result in its further exclusion from more "respectable" circles. "A person who sleeps with dogs shouldn't be surprised to find himself covered with fleas," comments the military correspondent for Israel's major daily newspaper.[73]

Israeli critics, who term the phenomenon "arms diplomacy," warn that the export imperative has motivated a sequence of ad hoc, opportunistic decisions that have precluded the development of a coherent foreign policy, which, in turn, might over the long term mitigate Israel's isolated position in the world. Yet these critics are far from sanguine about the ability of Israel to set itself on a different course.

They point to the power of the "security establishment lobby," comprised of the upper echelon of Israel's political leadership (this has remained remarkably constant since the founding of the state), the top levels of the military, and the officials of the parastatal arms industries. As in the U.S., there is a "revolving door" in Israel, with many of the top figures serving successively in two or all three of these sectors. It is these men who find the clients and have insider access to the Ministerial Committee on Weapons Transfers (MCD)—its members are the prime minister and the ministers of defense, foreign affairs, and trade and industry—which will make the final decision on every sale.[74] Such decisions are made secretly— the Israeli parliament, the Knesset, excluded. The cabinet, too, is often excluded. Critics of the hegemony of the arms export business say it has relegated the foreign ministry to a subordinate role in Israeli foreign policy making, and they see in its wake grave social and political consequences.

A sector has evolved in Israel, headed by an elite with identical social characteristics and marked by a fairly high degree of cohesiveness, whose decisions and actions have a significant effect not only on the country's economy and its foreign and defense policy but also on its social and value systems. No less important, however, is the issue of whether a closed system has been created whose activities and decisions undergo less public supervision and scrutiny than any other area of life in the country.[75]

A Co-equal Type of Proxy

Israeli analysts often argue that Israeli arms sales are dependent on U.S. approval;[76] in a limited sense this is true. The U.S. has blocked—at the behest of Britain—the delivery of A-4 Skyhawks to Argentina, and it has in the past vetoed the export of the Kfir aircraft, leverage it is able to exert because of the Kfir's U.S. engine. However, the Carter Administration was unable to prevent Israeli nuclear cooperation with South Africa, and the Reagan Administration was unsuccessful in persuading the Israelis to halt their arms sales to Iran in the early 1980s (assuming it wanted to). The Israeli success in persuading the Reagan Administration to incorporate Israeli arms sales to the Islamic Republic into a bizarre and controversial series of contacts with Iranian leaders is probably more typical of the operative U.S.-Israeli dynamic.

On the other hand, Israel has often obliged this or that sector of the U.S. government, selling arms where it would be embarrassing or illegal for the U.S. to do so: the contras, the Peoples Republic of China in the early 1980s,[77] and the Derg government of Ethiopia[78] are examples. In 1975,

Israel followed Secretary of State Henry Kissinger's advice and helped South Africa with its invasion of Angola.[79] Even after the passage the following year of the Clark Amendment forbidding U.S. covert involvement in Angola, Israel apparently considered Kissinger's nod a continuing mandate.

Given the export imperative under which the Israeli government operates, this 1981 proposal from the chief economic coordinator in the Israeli cabinet, Yacov Meridor, should be taken with great seriousness:

> We are going to say to the Americans, "Don't compete with us in South Africa, don't compete with us in the Caribbean or in any other country where you can't operate in the open." Let us do it. I even use the expression, "You sell the ammunition and equipment by proxy. Israel will be your proxy," and this would be worked out with a certain agreement with the United States where we will have certain markets...which will be left for us.[80]

Part I

Israel and South Africa

History ....

Israel and South Africa

Israel's ties with South Africa seem to be especially disturbing to many who follow Israel's international activities. Perhaps it is natural that Israel has been castigated more harshly for its arms sales to South Africa than for its sales to other countries: first, because there has been for a decade an arms embargo against South Africa; and second, because of the unsurpassed criminality of the white regime and the uses to which it puts the Israeli-supplied weapons.

It has also been said that those arms sales are understandable, given the striking similarities between the two countries in their day-to-day abuse and repression of their subject populations, South African blacks and Palestinians under Israeli rule; in their operating philosophies of apartheid and Zionism; and in their similar objective situations: "the only two Western nations to have established themselves in a predominantly non-white part of the world," as a South African Broadcasting Corporation editorial put it.[1] That understanding, however, is somewhat superficial, and the focus on similarities of *political* behavior has somewhat obscured the view of the breadth and depth of the totality of Israeli-South African relations and their implications.

Israel's relations with South Africa are different than its interactions with any of its other arms clients. That Israel gave South Africa its nuclear weapons capability underscores the special nature of Tel Aviv's relations with the white minority government and begins to describe it—a full-fledged, if covert, partnership based on the determination of both countries to continue as unrepentant pariahs and to help each other avoid the consequences of their behavior.

For South Africa's sake the partnership is designed to thwart international efforts against apartheid. What South Africa is expected to do for Israel is not as easily delineated; some Israeli critics, in fact, have argued that nothing South Africa can do for Israel is worth the price Israel has paid in international opprobrium.

> Israel has become embroiled in an unequal relationship with ambiguous returns. The scope of exchange, though diverse, is meager. The benefit Israel derives from these interchanges is unclear; in any event it is in no way commensurate to that reaped by the other partner in the equation.[2]

Beyond the guessing game (due to the strict secrecy maintained by Israel and to a lesser extent by South Africa) into which discussions of Israeli-South African links frequently deteriorate, it is certain that something of value is being received in Israel. To Naomi Chazan, the Israeli critic whose words appear above, that value received might be worthless, even negative, as she is holding it up to a standard she describes as "the nature and development of an Israeli ethos" out of what she views as Israel's contradictions.[3]

Chazan's image of a liberal, beneficent state of Israel is also the dominant one in the minds of many North Americans. However, during its not quite 40 years, the liberal, or socially progressive state of Israel has existed mostly in the blandishments of fundraisers and the flatterings of the U.S. media, where it has existed at all.[4] The Israeli leadership, from the start, were hardened people, who took a hard lesson from the Holocaust and the centuries of Jewish travail that preceded it. The current leadership, where it differs from the founders, almost all of whom have come through the higher ranks of the Israeli military, have not softened.

> Their understanding of modern Jewish history, with its themes of the Holocaust and powerlessness, reinforced by long professional military training, causes these elites to be impressed by visible manifestations of power and strength at the same time as they are inclined to be cynical toward false standards of international conduct.[5]

Whatever the large and small incentives to be found in links with South Africa, Israel's leaders have pursued them avidly.

An Early Zionist Outpost

Fifty years before the Holocaust, utterly determined Zionists began going to South Africa to enlist support for a Jewish national home in Palestine. They found support in the flourishing Jewish community and access to leading figures in the British empire.

Small numbers of Jews had arrived in South Africa in the beginning of the nineteenth century—when non-Christians were first allowed to settle in the Cape Colony.[6] In the wake of pogroms in the late nineteenth and early twentieth centuries a great migration from Eastern Europe—mainly Lithuania—brought the major part of the present day Jewish community to South Africa. A small number of the new immigrants were socialists who considered the idea of a Jewish national home in Palestine a backward notion; the large majority of South African Jews were rapidly won over to Zionism[7] decades before their co-religionists in the U.S. or Europe.

Early in this century South African Jews began to lobby leaders of the South African government to "persuade them to intercede on behalf of Zionism with the British Government which controlled the fate of Palestine." At the request of Theodore Herzl, considered the founder of Zionism, the South Africans approached Cecil Rhodes, the Cape Colony premier who took personal responsibility for extending Britain's grasp on Africa, and other prominent figures. A 1916 approach to General Jan Smuts, who would later lead the South African government, bore spectacular fruit. As a member of the British War Cabinet, Smuts supported the drafting of the 1917 Balfour Declaration, a statement of Britain's commitment to a Jewish homeland in Palestine. Through the years, though British commitment to the declaration wavered, Smuts' support was constant.

> He consistently maintained that the strategic safety of Britain's main line of imperial communication through the Suez Canal would be best assured if there were a British-sponsored Jewish homeland adjacent to it...[W]hen the Balfour Declaration was being drafted, his immediate consideration was to find "a formula to which the Great Powers would agree," for staking Britain's claim "to the main role in the future of post-war Palestine in cooperation with the Jews."[8]

In London Smuts befriended Chaim Weizmann, who would become Israel's first president. In 1943, Weizmann wrote a memo to Smuts outlining a plan to develop industry and agriculture in Africa and the Middle East capable of competing with U.S. industry. The scheme was "of great importance," Weizmann stressed, "and it is doubtful whether there exists any other scheme of equal importance for the future of the empire."[9]

Although the British Empire through which Weizmann and Smuts foresaw the realization of their peoples' futures was about to collapse, their contacts, and Smuts' continuing attachment to Zionism—as premier, the South African leader would remain a stalwart supporter of the Zionist movement, often acting as a fundraiser for Zionist organizations— generated significant momentum for the drive for Jewish statehood.

Many other South African leaders were attracted to the Zionist cause. In 1962, the cabinet of the Union of South Africa passed a resolution pledging support in international forums for "a National Home for the Jewish People in Palestine—an object which it regards as an important contribution to peace and civilization."[10]

In 1934, South African Jews formed Africa-Israel Investments to buy land in Palestine. Now owned by Israel's Bank Leumi, Africa-Israel Investments owns choice residential and industrial real estate. South Africans remain as minority shareholders and company debentures are sold in South Africa.[11] Bank Leumi itself has about 1,000 South African stockholders. At the height of the civil turmoil in 1986, the Africa-Israel Company was negotiating a $50 million contract with the white South African government and a West German firm to build 1,700 units of housing for blacks near Capetown "in order to calm hostilities there."[12]

In the late 1940s, Prime Minister Smuts permitted South African Jews to send money and supplies to the Jewish forces in Palestine, as well as permitting a great number of enthusiastic South African volunteers to join the fight to establish the state of Israel. South African Jews have long been the highest contributors to Zionist causes and Israel on a per capita basis.[13] In May 1948, Prime Minister Smuts extended *de facto* recognition to the new state.[14]

The Founding of the State: Jews Should Go "Thither"

In 1948, the end of the British mandate—and the concurrent establishment of the state of Israel—coincided with the accession of a new set of leaders in South Africa. These were the Afrikans-speaking Nationalists who had supported the Nazis in the recent war and whose defeat of the Smuts government was greatly worrying to South African Jews. However, the Nationalist Premier, Daniel Malan, publicly assured Jews that there would be no discrimination against them.[15] Malan allowed the money and supplies sent by South African Jews to Israel to continue and even turned a blind eye to the departure of Jewish volunteers.[16] He extended *de jure* recognition to Israel in 1949, and in 1953 became the first foreign head of state to visit Israel.[17]

There was a cynical side to all this good will, which would haunt the South African Jewish community in following years. The centerpiece of the Afrikaner Nationalists' campaign platform was apartheid, and they moved quickly to institutionalize the racial segregation that had always been a feature of South African life. According to James Adams, Malan's cordiality to the Jewish community was "a shrewd move." Not only did the Nationalists realize that persecution of the Jews would have sparked both international repercussions and a flight of capital from South Africa, writes Adams, but their granting of concessions:

> bought off the Jewish hierarchy who were now faced with a very delicate issue of divided loyalty...the Jews were well aware that a vociferous campaign against apartheid might well result in the Malan government or its successors abandoning previous agreements...[and] possibly introducing discrimination in some form against the Jewish population.[18]

However, the Transvaal branch of the Nationalist Party continued for several years to bar Jews from membership.[19] And although (spurred by their dislike for the British) Afrikaners had begun in the late 1940s to identify with the establishment of a Jewish state, as the Afrikaner press expressed it, their well-wishing was the kind of support so often given to Zionists by anti-Semites. At a time when the displaced person camps in Europe were flooded with homeless Jews, *The Transvaaler* editorialized that it "grant[ed] the Jew his ideals in Palestine but, at the same time, desire[d] an increasing exodus of Jews thither and not their increase here."[20]

Gen. Yigal Allon, who would later be Israel's Foreign Minister, got a warm reception from South Africa's Defense Minister F. C. Erasmus in May 1956. He warned the South Africans of the Egyptian leader Col. Nasser and said, "it would not be many years before South Africa would have to ask permission to cross the Red Sea."[21] This did not grab the Afrikaner imagination, as South Africa was developing trade ties with Arab nations and did not have a great deal of use for Israel in the 1950s. South Africa did not reciprocate the Israeli establishment of a consulate (in 1949) until 1971,[22] ten years after it was forced out of the Commonwealth of Nations and eight years after the first serious round of UN sanctions against it.

Although Israeli Foreign Minister Moshe Sharrett visited in 1951[23] and war hero (later Defense Minister) Moshe Dayan in 1957,[24] just as South Africa was being internationally ostracized because of its apartheid system, Israel's interest in closer ties had diminished as it began to successfully court the emerging nations of Africa with creative development assistance programs.

The approach to Africa reflected Israel's decision in the late 1950s to leapfrog over its immediate—hostile—neighbors in its search for diplomatic and economic contacts. Africa, where many nations were just receiving independence, was a natural choice. A friendship cultivated by Israeli Premier Ben Gurion with Kwame Nkrumah, Ghana's founding leader, facilitated the approach. During the 1960s, Israel signed cooperation agreements with 20 African nations.[25] By 1970, 2,483 Israeli experts had completed assignments in Africa in fields ranging from rural development to banking and construction; and 6,623 African trainees had come to Israel for training.[26]

Israel and its assistance programs were well received in Africa. Africans identified with Israel as a fellow graduate from British colonialism, and Israel's shirt-sleeve instructors were welcome for their egalitarianism. The Israelis brought none of the political baggage that the former colonizers inevitably carried. Then too, many African leaders admired the rapid progress Israel had made in the social and technological integration of new immigrants, as well as its agricultural achievements. Along with the civilian expertise, military assistance was frequently given to friendly African governments.

Ironically, one of the major fields of emphasis was trade unionism. Israel's labor federation, Histadrut, played a leading role in training African unionists and members of cooperatives.[27] Evidence is now beginning to mount which indicates that during its halcyon African days, Israel served as a conduit for money from the CIA.[28]

During its Africa phase Israel dipped deep into South Africa's reserve of goodwill. A joint communique criticizing apartheid was issued in 1961 by Ben Gurion and the president of Upper Volta (now Burkina Faso). That same year Israel voted to censure remarks made at the UN by South Africa's foreign minister. It aligned itself against the West on a General Assembly vote for sanctions that almost passed. These actions deeply offended the white regime—and alarmed the South African Jewish community which came under Afrikaner pressure to condemn the Israeli actions. (The ensuing backlash to this pressure was of utmost significance, as will be discussed below.) Even before Israel committed a still graver provocation, siding with African states on a 1962 UN vote to impose sanctions on South Africa—Israel, then led by Golda Meir, was hoping to win African support for a UN resolution calling for direct Arab-Israeli negotiations—the South African Treasury had refused to approve a routine transfer of Jewish donations to Israel. When Jewish officials appealed the denial, the minister of finance said the currency export privilege had been withdrawn because Israel had "slapped South Africa in the face and ganged up with her enemies."[29]

Leaders of Israel's Labor government argued that reasons of state, specifically the necessity of pleasing Israel's African allies, took precedence over the exigencies of the South African Jewish community.[30] In 1963, Israel lowered the level of its diplomatic mission in South Africa, and in 1966 it voted at the UN to revoke South Africa's mandate over Namibia, the colony formerly known as Southwest Africa.[31]

Israel and South Africa Draw Together

Although Israel would continue to step on Pretoria's toes in its pursuit of African governments—a 1971 Israeli attempt to make a $2,000 contribution to the Organization of African Unity's (OAU) Liberation Committee triggered another South African cutoff of Jewish funds[32]—Israel's 1967 war delivered a telling blow to its relationships with African nations. Coming at a time of strengthened African-Arab links, the resulting Israeli occupation of Arab and African territory (i.e. Egypt's Sinai) brought about the beginning of a shift in African perceptions: Israel was no longer viewed as an embattled underdog, but a powerful aggressor.[33]

Israel's 1967 war had the opposite effect on South Africa, eliciting its admiration. A team of South African military observers is reported to have flown to Israel "to study tactics and the use of weapons." Israel's war (which resulted in the occupation of substantial areas of Jordan and Egypt) would become one of two battles taught in South Africa's "maneuver schools."[34] In October 1967, the Chief of Staff of the Israeli Air Force, General Mordechai Hod, lectured the South African military on the conduct of the war.[35]

The drawing away from Israel of independent African states provided South Africa with a political opportunity. Almost totally bereft of friends itself by the late 1960s, South Africa demonstrated its interest in closer ties by coming quickly to Israel's aid. Currency-hoarding Pretoria permitted South African Jews to transfer immediately an extra $20.5 million to Israel. The white government itself sent replacement weapons and aircraft.[36] After the French embargoed arms shipments to Israel, South Africa, which had also received a great part of its arsenal from France, "ran an emergency service, supplying Israel with just about all the components it wanted."[37]

These gestures generated a response in Israel. In 1968, Israeli politicos formed the Israel-South Africa Friendship League.[38] Menachem Begin was president of this organization when he became prime minister of Israel in 1977.[39] Simcha Erlich headed the League during the time he served as Israel's finance minister.[40] In 1969, former Prime Minister Ben Gurion paid a high profile visit to South Africa and met there with Prime Minister John Vorster.[41] Accompanying Ben Gurion was Chaim Herzog, currently the president of Israel.[42] In 1972, South Africa opened a Consulate General in Israel.[43]

After the June 1967 war—four years after the UN's first embargo on arms sales to South Africa—Israel began to sell weapons to the white minority government. Israel was said to have offered South Africa both its Arava short-take-off-and-landing aircraft[44] (used by other customers for counterinsurgency warfare, see chapter on Guatemala) and plans for the Mirage III aircraft, stolen by Mossad in Switzerland.[45] James Adams in *The Unnatural Alliance* noted reports that the Arava had been tried in Namibia.[46] Israel was also said to have offered the apartheid regime weapons captured during the 1967 fighting.[47] By 1971, South Africa was manufacturing the Uzi submachine gun under a license arranged through Belgium.[48] In 1971, it was reported that a Greek freighter had brought high explosives from Eilat to Durban.[49]

During this period Israel's relations with independent African nations continued to deteriorate. Finally, the October 1973 war hastened a mass rupture of diplomatic relations. Between September and November 1973, 22 African governments severed ties with Israel, leaving only 4 independent African nations with diplomatic relations with Tel Aviv.[50] (All four, Swaziland, Lesotho, Malawi, and Mauritius, also have relations with South Africa.[51])

During the 1973 war, South Africa again came to Israel's aid. Defense Minister (later State President) P.W. Botha said that practical ways would be found to manifest South Africa's moral support for Israel.[52] It was reported that the South Africans' sympathy extended to Mirage jet fighters and that these were piloted by South Africans eager for combat experience. The Egyptians claimed that they had shot down a South African Mirage.[53] The war also drew 1,500 Jewish volunteers from the white-run state.[54] Also, the Pretoria government permitted South African Jews to send over $30 million to Israel.

Israel responded with the appointment of an ambassador to Pretoria in June 1974—a move reciprocated by South Africa the following year.[55]

Starting shortly before Israel went to war in the fall of 1973, the frequency of visits back and forth between Israel and South Africa increased in status, as well as in number. Yitzhak Rabin, between stints as Israel's ambassador to the U.S. and prime minister, arrived on a fund-raising mission in 1973; and Moshe Dayan was hosted by the South Africa Foundation in 1974.[56] Other Israeli visitors to South Africa in 1973 and 1974 included the former Israeli ambassador to Denmark, Israel's Deputy Minister for communications, and Israel's Chief Rabbi Shlomo Goren, who met President J.J. Fouche, Defense Minister Botha and other military brass. South Africans travelling to Israel included the head of BOSS (the since disbanded Bureau of State Security), Hendrik van der Bergh, and the Mayor of Johannesburg and a team of 15 housing officials led by the director of the building branch of the South African Council for Scientific and Industrial Research.[57]

Far from being irrelevant, or, in another sense, comparable to counting dogs frequenting a favorite fire hydrant, this matter of visits for "pariah" countries is immensely important. Both the Israeli and the South African state-run media go on at great length about foreign visitors—especially ranking officials—or trips abroad by their own dignitaries, whose welcomes are recounted in great detail. This we-are-not-alone syndrome also explains the frequent and almost always baseless predictions that this or that African nation is about to renew diplomatic ties with Israel. That the Israeli visits were more "diplomatic" is explained by the presence of the South African Jewish community and the greater degree of South African isolation. That the South African visits to Israel during this period appear to have been more "business-oriented" is readily explained by Israel's slightly stronger international standing and its concomitant lack of interest in parading South African political figures before its populace.

Recalling Israel's sea change, South Africa's first ambassador to Israel wrote:

> The latent support for South Africa, which we knew existed but which had been difficult to quantify came to the surface. Why, it was asked, had Israel been supporting resolutions in the United Nations which were hurtful to South Africa, when South Africa now stood revealed as one of the few countries to stand up and be counted when Israel was in peril?[58]

A number of circumstances propelled the bonding process. The lessons of Israel's recent war took on new significance for South Africa as

Portugal was forced to give up its African colonies and South Africa worried about a military threat from the newly independent Mozambique and Angola.[59] Moreover, the Nonaligned Movement, then coming into its own as a force of the developing world, was bringing increasing pressure to bear on South Africa.

Because of its intransigent refusal to negotiate a withdrawal from the territories it had occupied since 1967 and the brutality of its occupation of them, Israel was also the object of intense international criticism. In November 1975, the United Nations General assembly passed Resolution 3379 declaring Zionism a form of "racism and racial discrimination." The resolution also condemned "the unholy alliance between South African racism and Zionism."[60] Also in 1974 the UN began steps that would result in the conferral of observer status on the Palestine Liberation Organization.

In late 1974, Israel's resistance to the U.S. peacemaking efforts led the Ford Administration to declare an aid moratorium to all countries in the Middle East while Washington "reassessed" its policy in the region. The anxiety this caused Tel Aviv was considerable. (A letter signed by 76 Senators that urged continued U.S. support for Israel "was a blunt reminder to the President...[that] should cause [him] to think twice before making any rash move on the Middle Eastern scene,"[61] reflected the level of Israel's consternation at the time.) A scandal breaking in 1975 over CIA "dirty tricks" in Angola led Secretary of State Henry Kissinger to suggest to Israel that it help South Africa with its invasion of Angola.[62] Israel complied with Kissinger's request by sending counterinsurgency weapons and instructors. In July 1975, a former Israeli intelligence chief said that senior Israeli military officers were giving South African troops counter-insurgency training.[63] *The Economist* said Israel had stopped short of sending the troops which Kissinger had wanted, but that the Israelis took his suggestion as a green light for developing a closer relationship with South Africa.[64]

Conspiracy Opens Up a Whole New Phase of Relations

In June 1975, Connie Mulder—his star was then rising and, as heir apparent to the prime minister, he had been made Information and Interior Minister—and Information Secretary Eschel Rhoodie made a secret trip to Israel. Their meetings with Prime Minister Yitzhak Rabin, Defense Minister Shimon Peres, and six other members of the Israeli cabinet was arranged by Oscar Hurwitz, a Jewish South African and an instrumental figure in the plot that would become known as the "Muldergate" scandal.[65] Les de Villiers, the South African Deputy Information Minister who also attended that meeting, asked the Israelis to recommend a "lobbyist." The name of New York public relations man Sydney Baron was mentioned and the South Africans retained him.[66] Baron, who had past connections to New York political boss Carmine deSapio, would funnel $200,000 of South African money into the 1976 U.S. senatorial race of Republican S.I. Hayakawa in a successful attempt to defeat South Africa's nemesis, California Senator John Tunney, a Democrat. In 1978, Baron would repeat the process with a $250,000 South African donation to Iowa Republican Roger Jepson in his successful challenge to Democratic Senator Dick Clark (the author of the Clark Amendment, forbidding CIA involvement in Angola).[67]

These deals were only a fraction of the influence-buying of the secret "information project" set up by the South Africans in the early 1970s. Eschel Rhoodie and Connie Mulder spent at least $100 million in at least half a dozen countries—buying newspapers, setting up front organizations, running junkets for politicians or buying them outright—all in a fruitless attempt to improve South Africa's image. The Mulder gang was ultimately charged with flagrant "financial irregularities" and forced out of office in a 1978 power play that won P.W. Botha the right to succeed the retiring Premier John Vorster.[68]

In the 1975 meetings in Israel, the Labor government under Yitzhak Rabin agreed to play a consultative role in the Mulder-Rhoodie disinformation offensive.[69] (They also apparently agreed to let the South Africans operate Project David in Israel, which funded propaganda and brought South African sports teams to Israel.[70]) They recruited Arnon Milchan, an Israeli arms dealer—he would also be used to funnel weapons to South Africa—to launder the funds. Milchan has admitted that he agreed to play this role and said that on one occasion he put 66,000 pounds sterling into a Swiss bank; the money was then withdrawn and used to purchase the London-based magazine *West Africa*, later sold.[71]

In March 1976, then Defense Minister Shimon Peres made a secret visit to South Africa and invited the South African prime minister to visit Israel. John Vorster arrived in Israel the following month, eager for his first official visit to a democratic state.[72]

The visit by John Vorster was certain to be provocative, but the isolated Israelis must have felt they had very little to lose, and, in South Africa, with its gold and minerals and its complement of transnational corporations, they must have seen a possible substitute for the U.S.

Arms Industry ....

The 1976 Accords

Israel received Vorster warmly, with a red carpet running to the door of his plane. At the other end Israeli Prime Minister Yitzhak Rabin headed the pack of dignitaries waiting to greet him. Vorster met with Foreign Minister Allon, with President Ephraim Katzir, and numerous other Israeli leaders. Half the cabinet turned out to a farewell banquet for Vorster hosted by Rabin,[1] this despite a formal communication from the Netherlands warning that the visit would make it more difficult for "Israel's friends abroad to persuade the world that there is no connection between Zionism and racism."[2] Vorster, who had been jailed for 20 months during World War II by the British for his pro-Nazi activities and had never repudiated his Nazism,[3] had last been made welcome in Paraguay.[4]

At the state banquet Prime Minister Rabin turned to his South African counterpart and said,

> We here follow with sympathy your own historic efforts to achieve detente on your continent, to build bridges for a secure and better future, to create coexistence that will guarantee a prosperous atmosphere of cooperation for all the African peoples, without outside interference and threat.[5]

When the head of the apartheid regime was not being received or visiting religious sites or climbing to the Masada fortress where Jewish rebels made a last stand against the Romans in the first century, or,

31

incongruously, laying a wreath at the Yad Vashem Holocaust memorial, Vorster spent his four days in Israel touring military installations, including the state-owned Israel Aircraft Industries (IAI).[6]

These visits gave rise to reports that the South Africans were shopping for Israeli arms. Both Israeli and South African officials denied that this was the case.[7] Yet obviously, at least from the Israeli standpoint, there was more to receiving Vorster than a provocative and defiant political statement. It is generally accepted that among the comprehensive set of bilateral agreements announced as having been concluded during Vorster's trip to Israel—covering commercial, trade, fiscal, and "cooperative" arrangements[8]—were secret pacts covering arms sales and nuclear cooperation.[9] All of the agreements, the departing Vorster told reporters, would be overseen by a joint cabinet-level committee which would meet annually to review and promote Israeli-South African economic relations. Vorster also spoke of a "steering group" to coordinate the exchange of information and encourage the "development of trade, scientific and industrial cooperation and joint projects using South African raw material and Israeli manpower."[10]

What Israel and South Africa had accomplished was a strategic meshing of strengths and weaknesses: South African capital and raw materials to Israel, counterpoised against the transfer of Israeli weapons and advanced technology to South Africa.[11] The 1976 agreements have been periodically renewed. As the years progressed the strength generated by Israeli-South African cooperation would be turned outward to sanctions-busting, allowing South Africa to fend off internal and external pressure for reform.

Israel has also reaped benefits from the relationship—in the tangible sense for the development of its arms industry, and in a not altogether ephemeral sense, politically: as long as South Africa remains the focal point of international outrage, Israel escapes the brunt of that attention; moreover, as long as it can be shown that sanctions are ineffective against South Africa, there is less chance they will be imposed on Israel.

Nuclear Apprentice

There are few areas where the respective needs and advantages of Israel and South Africa dovetailed so perfectly as in the field of nuclear cooperation.

"The most powerful reason for Israeli willingness to bear the undesirable consequences of expanded and more open trade with South Africa may be her desire to acquire material necessary to manufacture nuclear weapons," wrote a military analyst in 1980.[12] To that must be added Israel's great desire to test the nuclear weapons it already had, and the attractions of South Africa's vast territory and proximity to even vaster uninhabited spaces—the Atlantic and Indian Oceans.

Then at the point in its nuclear development where it was fashioning sophisticated bombs (devices which use less nuclear material but have infinitely greater explosive force than the "primitive" bomb dropped by the U.S. on Hiroshima), Israel would find it particularly helpful to observe the performance, explosive force and fallout of a detonated weapon.[13]

Since 1984, Israel had been operating a plutonium extraction plant in a secret underground bunker at Dimona in the Negev Desert. Built by the French in the late 1950s, the Dimona plant also included facilities for manufacturing atomic bomb components.[14] At the time of the 1976 accords, Israel was preparing to build an adjoining plant for the extraction of lithium 6, tritium and deuterium, materials required for sophisticated thermonuclear weapons.[15]

Israel's reasons for devoting what had to have been a significant portion of its scant resources to such an ambitious nuclear weapons program—nuclear experts have recently ranked it as the world's sixth nuclear power, after the U.S., the USSR, Britain, France and China[16]—have been variously offered as the desire to develop a credible deterrent to attack by its neighbors and the desire to substitute that deterrent for at least part of the costly conventional arsenal that Israel, with one of the world's most powerful military forces, maintains, and also (with much less frequency) as an "umbrella" over a partial withdrawal from the occupied territories.[17]

However, these are by way of superficial rationales. The decision to develop nuclear weapons was taken in the earliest days of the state and has been doggedly pursued for over a quarter of a century.[18] Israel's determination suggests that it has always been directed toward establishing, perhaps expanding, its borders by force and has always believed that its existence can only be guaranteed by maintaining the entire Middle Eastern region in a state of fearsome disequilibrium.

There is no consolation to be found in a search for an element of responsibility in the Israeli nuclear program. The Middle East as tinderbox has become a cliche, while Israel's own track record of flagrant aggression—since 1981 Israel has bombed Iraq's nuclear reactor, invaded Lebanon, bombed Tunisia, and tried to persuade India to conduct a joint raid on Pakistan's nuclear research facility[19]—does not recommend Tel Aviv as a mature guardian of the ultimate weapon. Moreover, it is quite possible that Israel has accumulated an estimated 100-200 warheads for political purposes. Dr. Francis Perrin, the head of the French nuclear program from 1951-1970, during which time France collaborated with Israel on building an atom bomb and built the Dimona reactor/plutonium plant, recently explained:

> We thought the Israeli bomb was aimed against the Americans, not to launch it against America but to say "if you don't want to help us in a critical situation we will require you to help us, otherwise we will use our nuclear bombs."[20]

South Africa is not thought to have been as highly motivated as Israel to acquire nuclear weapons capability. Given its—reasonable—expectation of a domestic uprising perhaps aided from neighboring states, South Africa's first priorities were Israeli weapons and Israeli technological input for its conventional weapons industry. Yet South Africa is magnificently endowed with uranium and during the 1970s was striving to manufacture enriched uranium for export. To the South Africans a nuclear bomb was something of a bonus.[21]

They are thought to have achieved the requisite techniques in 1980 and since then have incorporated nuclear weaponry into their bluster, and perhaps into their military doctrine. In 1977, Information Minister Connie Mulder said, "If we are attacked, no rules apply at all if it comes to a question of our existence. We will use all means at our disposal whatever they may be."[22] In 1979, Prime Minister P.W. Botha said, "we have military weapons they do not know about."[23] In 1985, the South Africans let it be known that they were capable of building two bombs a year.[24]

South Africa's nuclear position roughly parallels Israel's. There is the deterrent factor against a threat from the outside, which has become somewhat more credible than Israel's with talk among members of the OAU of establishing a pan-African force to aid the liberation struggle in South Africa;[25] this is a somewhat sad turn of events for an organization which made its first demand that Africa be a nuclear weapons-free zone in 1963.[26] There is the notion of regional dominance, to which Nigeria has already begun to react by broaching for consideration the idea that it, or Africa, must develop a nuclear counterdeterrent.[27] There is South Africa's history of brazen attacks on its neighbors. There is the possibility that "by threatening *use* of the bomb, Pretoria could effectively block international efforts to impose sanctions on it for its racist policies."[28]

There is also the distinct possibility that the white minority government has developed detailed plans to use neutron-type bombs (low-yield devices that kill people without widespread devastation of property) on the domestic black majority. A set of maps in the possession of the African National Congress (ANC) appears to show population concentrations and fallout radii.[29]

In conjunction with its nuclear weapon "option," the Pretoria regime is apparently aiming to enrich uranium for export at its Palindaba plant, due to start operation in 1987. Although the South Africans have refused to put the plant under international safeguards,[30] it might well be that they cherish hopes of establishing lines of communication with potential Western customers through sales of uranium for nuclear power plants.[31]

During the 1950s, when "peaceful" atomic energy was in vogue, Israel and South Africa had both participated in U.S. atomic energy programs. South Africa has had help from Britain, West Germany and France, as well as the U.S. Over the years, though, it has become more and more difficult for both Pretoria and Tel Aviv to obtain nuclear technology because both refuse to sign the Nuclear Nonproliferation Treaty, and each has refused to open all its nuclear facilities to inspection.

In 1965, after South Africa brought its Safari I safeguarded reactor on line, Israeli scientists began advising South Africa on their Safari 2 research reactor.[32] In 1968, Prof. Ernst Bergmann, the "father" of Israel's nuclear program, went to South Africa and spoke strongly in favor of bilateral cooperation on the development of nuclear technolgy.[33]

According to the authors of a novelized treatment of Israel's nuclear program—barred from publication by the Israeli censor—as early as 1966, South Africa had invited Israel to use its land or ocean space for a nuclear weapons test. Led at that time by Prime Minister Levi Eshkol, Israel declined the invitation. However, according to the Israeli authors, whose sources included Shimon Peres, an enthusiastic intimate of the Israeli nuclear program, and Knesset Member Eliyah Speizer, during his April 1976 visit to Israel Premier Vorster again extended the invitation to Israel to conduct a nuclear test.

It is commonly held that Israel wanted a test venue far from the Middle East in order to uphold its longtime position that it would not be the first to introduce nuclear weapons into the region.[34] This "position," hinging on some arcane reading of the word "introduce," is as meaningless as the endlessly heard term "peace process."

The following year, a Soviet satellite picked up unmistakable signs of preparation for a nuclear test in the Kalahari Desert. Fearing that such a test "might trigger an ominous escalation of the nuclear arms race," the U.S., Britain, France and West Germany joined the USSR in pressuring South Africa to abort the test.[35] As to the bomb that was to be tested, " 'I know some intelligence people who are convinced with damn near certainty that it was an Israeli nuclear device,' said a high-ranking Washington official."[36]

At three o'clock in the morning on September 22, 1979, Israel and South Africa conducted a nuclear weapons test where the South Atlantic and Indian Oceans merge.[37]

A newly recalibrated U.S. Vela intelligence satellite[38] recorded the characteristic double flash of light. It was a small blast, designed to leave very little evidence.[39] The CIA told the National Security Council that a two- or three-kiloton bomb had been exploded in "a joint South African-Israeli test."[40] A Navy official revealed that U.S. spy planes over the test area had been waved away by South African Navy ships and forced to land secretly in Australia.[41] The CIA knew (and later told Congress) that South African ships were conducting secret maneuvers at the exact site of the test.[42] The South African military attache in Washington made the first ever request to the U.S. National Technical Information Service for a computer search on detection of nuclear explosions and orbits of the Vela satellite.[43]

Almost immediately the Carter Administration convened a special panel to conduct an investigation of the incident. The panel heard reports from the U.S. Naval Research Laboratory, the Defense Intelligence Agency, and the CIA; and representatives of the Los Alamos National Laboratory, the Department of Energy and the State Department presented evidence to the panel supporting the occurrence of a nuclear explosion. Their findings were summarily dismissed by the Carter White House, which after a delay of seven months declared:

> Although we cannot rule out the possibility that this [Vela] signal was of nuclear origin, the panel considers it more likely that the signal was one of the zoo events [reception of signals of unknown origin under anomalous circumstances], possibly a consequence of the impact of a small meteroid on the satellite.[44]

Moreover, as new information became available, it was simply ignored. In one critical instance, evidence of radiation observed in the thyroid glands of Australian sheep was discounted. The initial lack of this "smoking gun," traces of radiation, suggested to a Los Alamos scientist that the low-yield weapon tested had been a neutron bomb. However, the Carter panel had used the absence of radiation as a prime excuse in its cover-up.[45]

Many who had been involved with the investigation were aghast and wondered why the Carter White House was "equivocating."[46] Some within the government said that the Carter Administration was hiding behind the "zoo" theory to avoid dealing with the political headaches that would accompany acknowledgement of the test. An affirmative report might have affected the ongoing negotiations over the creation of Zimbabwe in which South African cooperation was needed and upset the just negotiated Camp David accords between Israel and Egypt. Carter also had reason to fear "complications in garnering Jewish votes during the upcoming Democratic Party primary campaign against Sen. Edward Kennedy."[47]

But beyond that, as a State Department official explained, coming clean on the test "would be a major turning point in our relations with South Africa and Israel if we determined conclusively that either had tested a nuclear bomb. It makes me terribly nervous just to think about it."[48] Of course by deciding to ignore reality the Carter administration—and following in its footsteps, the Reagan Administration, which went on record May 21, 1985 as upholding the Carter "verdict"[49]—destroyed the already tattered credibility of the nonproliferation posture of the U.S. There was no challenge forthcoming from Congress. Quite the contrary: in 1981 Representatives Stephen Solarz and Jonathan Bingham withdrew legislation they had introduced calling for a cutoff of U.S. aid to nations manufacturing nuclear weapons after they learned from the State Department "that such a requirement might well trigger a finding by the Administration that Israel has manufactured a bomb."[50] The U.S. government turned its back on the potential victims of Israeli and South African nuclear aggression, and stuck its head in the sand like an ostrich.

Five years later, the Washington Office on Africa Educational Fund in cooperation with Congressman John Conyers (D-MI), the Congressional Black Caucus Foundation and the World Campaign Against Military and Nuclear Collaboration with South Africa issued a report on the 1979 nuclear weapons test. Based on documents obtained from the government under the Freedom of Information Act, the report detailed scientific evidence not taken into account by the Carter panel. It demonstrated conclusively that a cover-up had been perpetrated by the Carter Administration. Written by Howard University Professor Ronald Walters, the report warned that the cover-up, "coupled with the Reagan Administration's subsequent allowance of an increase in nuclear aid to South Africa has serious implications for international peace and security."[51]

The sponsors of the report urged that the investigation be reopened under the auspices of the National Academy of Sciences and the National Academy of Engineers, and also called for a Congressional investigation and "the release to the public of all pertinent information."[52]

Although it came at a time of heightened anti-apartheid activity, the report was largely ignored. Small, dutiful articles about a Conyers press conference appeared but generated none of the official (or activist) response that might have kept the issue alive.

In July 1985, during debate on the 1986-87 Foreign Aid Authorization bill, Rep. Conyers offered an amendment stipulating that "United States foreign assistance may not be provided to any country having a nuclear relationship with South Africa." Howard Wolpe, Chair of the House Foreign Affairs Subcommittee on Africa persuaded Conyers to withdraw the amendment, promising instead that upcoming hearings on nuclear proliferation would consider the implications of South Africa's nuclear capability.[53] As 1985 wore into 1986, and while Congress spent itself in a literal orgy of anti-apartheid legislation, the promised hearing was never scheduled.

Congress may succeed in shelving the problem of the 1979 test for another few years, but despite the refusal of the U.S. political monkeys to see, nuclear collaboration between Tel Aviv and Pretoria continues. A second test in December 1980 was reported in the same area, with another CIA sighting of South African ships nearby. A British authority on nuclear weapons, Dr. David Baker, said that the weapon fired in this test was probably a 155 mm nuclear shell fired from a special howitzer which the Israelis had helped the South Africans acquire[54] (see below).

In 1981, it was reported that South Africa had hired Israeli consultants "to advise on the safety aspects of its first two commercial reactors." As those reactors were being built by the French company Framatome, some thought it odd that Israeli, rather than French, scientists would be hired.[55] The Israeli advice, which according to intelligence officials "could assist the Government there to acquire the technological expertise to build nuclear weapons," came in exchange for uranium.[56] Although South Africa has its Koeberg commercial reactor under international safeguards, these are lax, "making diversion of materials for nuclear weapons possible if a government so chooses."[57]

In 1986, Mordechai Vanunu, a technician who had worked nine years at the Dimona installation, told reporters that South African scientists and metallurgists had regularly worked at Dimona.[58]

In 1985, the BBC reported that Israel and South Africa had tested an Israeli-made Jericho II (nuclear-capable) missile in South Africa.[59]

Late in 1986 South African scientists working on remote Marion Island, halfway between Antarctica and the southern coast of South Africa, disregarded Pretoria's orders to remain silent and reported that Israeli and South African military officers had been visiting the island. Experts said that the two nations were undoubtedly in the process of developing a nuclear missile-testing range in conjunction with a $6 million mile-long airstrip South Africa was planning to build on the island and that this "important military asset" could also be used as a base for anti-submarine warfare. The scientists said they had gone public out of fear that their meteorological station would be used to cover such activities. They discounted South African excuses that the airstrip would be useful for resupply, medical evacuation and rescue activities. The scientists said there was little shipping, fishing or aviation in the area.[60]

The environmental organization Greenpeace, at the time setting up a research station to monitor the large Antarctic wildlife population, issued a statement opposing the airstrip. A Greenpeace spokeswoman at the organization's Washington office said the organization was also opposed to use of the island for military purposes by Israel and South Africa. (The Greenpeace statement notes that Marion Island is near the site of their 1979 nuclear test). If work was begun on the runway, she said, "it will definitely engender a response."[61]

Collaboration on Weapons

Although the 1976 Vorster agreements marked the beginning of a large and systematic commerce in arms, it by no means launched the sanctions-busting commerce in weapons between Tel Aviv and Pretoria. Israel had already sold South Africa an assortment of military gear, and, by one account, had *imported* Chieftain-type tanks from South Africa.[62] By 1971, South Africa was building the Uzi submachine gun under license.[63] In fact, shortly before the signing of those agreements, the Israelis, acting in concert with "retired" CIA agents and cooperative European companies, played an important role in an elaborate deception that resulted in the delivery of one of the most sophisticated weapons ever to reach South Africa. This was the Space Research Corporation (SRC) 155 mm howitzer, acknowledged at the time to be the most advanced long-range artillery piece in the world. Originally developed by Canadian-American Gerald Bull to launch satellites, the SRC howitzer is also capable of firing miniaturized nuclear shells.

After failing to secure production rights to Bull's invention for themselves (and for resale to South Africa), Israel served as the official "end user" on U.S. papers accompanying conventional 155 mm shells through their production process in the U.S. and Canada.[64] According to Britain's Independent Television, the Israeli Cabinet discussed the deal.[65]

In a welter of phony addressees and illicit shipments, the conspirators also accomplished the transfer to South Africa of the SRC howitzer blueprints and the machine tools necessary for its production. South Africa now produces and markets the howitzer as the G5 and G6; it is this artillery piece with its 250 mile range[66] that was apparently used in the 1980 nuclear test mentioned above.[67]

As in the SRC case, as Western nations came under pressure to abide by the UN arms embargo of 1963—and the subsequent United Nations Mandatory Arms Embargo of 1977—Israel began to act as a funnel for shipments from other Western countries. One notorious case involved the shipment of 11 U.S.-made Bell helicopters from Haifa to South Africa (and thence to Rhodesia) using Singapore as a phony destination.[68] Another concerned the shipment from Italy of Oto Melara naval cannon through Israel to South Africa. South Africa installed the guns on Reshef patrol boats, which by then it was making under Israeli license (see below).[69] In 1983, authorities in Copenhagen stopped a shipment of 400 pistols for South Africa. The pistols were then taken to Vienna—Austrian law permits export to South Africa of "sports and civilian weapons"—and from there were to "be dispatched to South Africa via Israel."[70]

Although it is difficult to pinpoint precisely the date of sale of Israeli weapons to South Africa, following the Vorster agreements Israeli military sales to South Africa increased dramatically. Israeli equipment deployed in South Africa includes mortars,[71] electronic surveillance equipment, radar stations, anti-guerrilla alarm systems and night vision devices,[72] high technology equipment for a squadron of South African helicopters,[73] "a large number of Soviet-made artillery pieces"[74] and eight Reshef long-range missile boats, two of which were supplied with helicopter decks and sophisticated electronic gear.[75] South African navy personnel, about 50 by one account, were brought to Israel to train on the boats.[76]

South Africa also bought six Dabur patrol boats (for $300,000 each) and equipped them (and its own German-built corvettes) with Gabriel surface-to-surface missiles for the Israeli craft.[77] South Africa is also thought to have bought Israeli Shafrir (heat-seeking) missiles some time around 1978.[78]

It is equally difficult to try to pinpoint the amount of money involved in these transactions. A 1976 assessment by the London International Institute for Strategic Studies said that Israel and France were South Africa's "primary suppliers."[79] A 1977 report said Israel had received $100 million worth of orders from South Africa that year.[80] More recent reports have varied between $50 million and $800 million annually.[81]

Nonetheless, with the official curtailment of British and French weapons transfers to the white government, Israel became a lifeline for the apartheid regime—and apartheid became a gold mine for Israel. In its 1981 Yearbook, the respected Stockholm International Peace Research Institute (SIPRI) lists South Africa as the major customer for Israeli arms, taking 35 percent of the total prior to 1980.[82]

After the well documented sales of the 1970s, and especially with the imposition of the UN's 1977 mandatory arms embargo, secrecy on arms shipments remained nearly absolute until 1986-87 when a great deal became known (see below). Although the statistics suggest the sale of numerous weapons systems in great quantity, very little is known about what has actually changed hands. This is because of the overarching secrecy observed by all facets of the Israeli arms industry[83] and the obvious need of the South Africans to avoid revealing the source of their imported arms—every so often they can't resist a gleeful reference to "friendly countries"—and thus drying it up.

Despite this decade of secrecy, a few sales have become known. The South Africans have been steady purchasers of Israeli electronic "security" fencing. This is the early warning barrier Israel has strung around its own borders. Microwave devices and infra-red devices alert soldiers to those intruders who are not snared by the anti-personnel mines which are part of the package.[84] The South Africans call the system a "ring of steel" and have said that other border areas near Mozambique and Angola are "riddled with anti-personnel mines manufactured in Israel."[85]

Although the Israelis have variously insisted that they scrupulously respect the 1977 UN embargo, or that their arms sales to South Africa do not include weaponry that could be used for internal repression, a 1986 report on National Public Radio proves them wrong on both counts. Listeners to "Morning Edition" on January 13 heard a tape of Israeli military industries salesmen making a sales pitch to two delegations of South African "security men." Tear gas and smoke gas grenades were being demonstrated. During its almost perpetual state of emergency, South Africa has used a great deal of tear gas.[86]

During the broadcast an Israeli professor told "Morning Edition" that none of South Africa's other trading partners "is quite as intimately involved in security matters, in the preservation of apartheid through force," as Israel is.[87]

Israel has sold South Africa one or more "drones" (remotely piloted spy planes). In 1983, one of these camera-laden aircraft shot down over Maputo, Mozambique still bore its IAI factory markings.[88]

Indications of Magnitude

Two news leaks about arms shipments in 1986 (three, counting the Cheetah—see Introduction and below) might well be indicative of what has been passing between Israel and South Africa on a regular basis. One arms shipment included 50 Gazelle helicopters, armored cars, cannons, mortars, 20,000 automatic rifles and 12,000 machine guns purchased from Egypt on Israel's behalf by Adnan Khasogghi, the infamous international arms dealer, after Egypt rebuffed a direct Israeli attempt to purchase them. They were shipped to Israel and from there immediately sent to South Africa. (Another ten helicopters from Zaire were also included in this shipment.[89]) While the South Africans are probably eager for the helicopters it is likely that the small arms will be passed along to one of the mercenary forces, Unita, or the "Mozambican National Resistance," attacking the Frontline states.

Late in the year, converted Boeing 707 aircraft appeared in South Africa.[90] There were four to six in all, and Israel had outfitted them as dual in-flight refueling platforms and flying electronic warfare stations.[91] Far beyond anything available to any other African government, these aircraft gave South Africa command of the entire continent.[92]

There is no way of gauging the frequency and magnitude of similar sales which escape detection. The transfer of ready-to-use weaponry, however, is overshadowed by other aspects of Israeli military collaboration with South Africa which have been instrumental in South Africa's achieving a high degree of immunity from the effects of international sanctions, in part through an extensive weapons industry of its own.[93]

The South African publication *Interconair* stated, "thanks to the friendship which binds us to Israel...we have succeeded in creating a nucleus of modern ships based on fast-attack and missile craft derived from the Israeli Reshef."[94] This appreciation was not merely for Israeli willingness to sell missile boats; nor was it simply to buy and sell weapons outright that Israel and South Africa hammered out their 1976 agreements. Instead, the agreements

> centered on South Africa's willingness to finance some of Israel's costlier military projects. Israel was to reciprocate by supplying weapon systems and training... Israel was asked to fill [South Africa's] needs for naval, armored, electronic and counterinsurgency equipment.[95]

In the case of the Reshef patrol boats, after selling the first three outright and training South African officers, the Israelis licensed the South

Africans to produce nine.[96] The South Africans call their Reshef the Minister, or Minister of Defense (MOD). Israel also licensed South Africa to produce the 65-foot Dabur patrol boat.[97]

In addition to the famous Uzi submachine gun, the apartheid government produces the Israeli Galil assault rifle under license as the R-4.[98]

Both the Dabur and the Reshef carry Gabriel missiles, the Israeli-made equivalent of the French Exocet. South Africa now produces these under license, calling them the Scorpion.[99] It was with a Scorpion that the South Africans sank a Cuban food ship during a June 1986 attack on the Angolan port of Namibe.[100] These licensing agreements include the future transfer of any Israeli modifications of the systems.[101]

There have been persistent reports of other licensing arrangements between Tel Aviv and Pretoria, including submarines and a new Israeli guided missile patrol boat, but none have been definitively confirmed. Reports of collaboration on the missile boat go back to 1977, when it was described as "a miniature aircraft carrier."[102] James Adams calls this the Q9 corvette.[103] A more recent report says South Africa is "considering buying several new corvettes from Israel."[104]

A four-way deal to construct submarines seems in the making. South Africa is planning to build submarines at its own yards in cooperation with Chile.[105] Meanwhile, Israel has been negotiating with Washington over a submarine to be built jointly by Israel and West Germany[106] while a West German state-owned shipyard has sold blueprints for submarines to South Africa (resulting in a fairly severe scandal in Bonn, when it was determined that Chancellor Kohl and other top officials discussed the sale).[107] If there is any substance to the reports of an Israeli-South African submarine project, then in all probability the ship will be a three-way project including Israel, South Africa and Chile. (Israel is performing the same Mirage update for Chile that resulted in the South African Cheetah.[108]) Israel's submarine project is being financed by its U.S. military aid.[109] South Africa could be a direct recipient of the benefits of U.S. military assistance to Israel. It is a pattern that marks other purported licensing deals as well.

There have been frequent reports that South Africa is a silent partner in the next generation Israeli fighter, the Lavi. The Israelis embarked on this ambitious project in 1977, hoping to advance their own technological base a giant step with copious helpings of the latest U.S. technology.[110] Israel also wanted to produce an aircraft without any U.S. parts, which would make the export of the Lavi not subject to a veto by Washington.[111]

As the evolving design incorporated features of a vastly more sophisticated aircraft, Israeli leaders sought and won U.S. financing for rising costs of the Lavi's development. By the end of 1986, Congress had earmarked $1.3 billion of Israel's U.S. military assistance for the Lavi.[112] Furthermore, Congress allocated $700 million of that sum to be spent in Israel on the Lavi's development.[113]

As early as 1977, it was reported that Israel was helping South Africa develop a fighter plane within the framework established in 1976: South African financing and Israeli technological input.[114] A top secret trip by Israeli Defense Minister Ezer Weizman to South Africa in March 1980[115] is thought to have been "to discuss, among other things, the joint Lavi fighter project."[116] Weizmann definitely reached agreement with the South Africans over financing the development of the avionics—the computerized flight systems—for the Kfir aircraft, which the South Africans later obtained for their Cheetah.[117]

An IAI marketing document in the early years of this decade spoke of an outright sale of the Lavi to South Africa. It projected selling 407 Lavi aircraft to South Africa, Chile, Taiwan and Argentina.[118] In 1984 it was reported that "South Africa is known to be prepared to invest in the...Lavi."[119]

An objective analysis of the Lavi's current status would appear to rule out the possibility that South Africa still hopes to be cut in on the deal. As the project and the Israeli economy ran into trouble in the mid-1980s, Israel was forced to contract an increasing amount of the work on the Lavi to U.S. firms,[120] and thus the amount of leverage the U.S. has over any potential export deals has risen. The Lavi's avionics have been developed by Israel, and hence are not subject to a U.S. export veto.[121] At one point, the Israelis sought a U.S. partner for the Lavi.[122] The Bet Shemesh engine plant, which was to co-produce the first batch of Pratt and Whitney engines for the Lavi, went into receivership, presumably eliminating the possibility that Israel could pass along the engine for the Lavi to South Africa. Yet the situation surrounding the transfer of Kfir technology to South Africa to produce the Cheetah (see Introduction) may be instructive. It had long been suspected that Israel was about to let South Africa build the Kfir under license (or sell the aircraft outright to the white regime).[123] Israel eventually passed along pieces of Kfir technology and also gave South Africa assistance in producing the engine. It is not out of the question that South Africa would receive plans for building the Lavi power plant; nor is it out of the question that another country might be drawn into the scheme, increasing the opportunities for *legerdemain*.

Minister Without Portfolio Moshe Arens—as Defense Minister, head of IAI, and Ambassador to the U.S., Arens made the Lavi his personal "obsession"[124]—recently went to Japan and proposed that Israel share its

Lavi technology with Tokyo, which is contemplating co-producing a fighter plane with the U.S.[125] Arens has called the Lavi "the most potent new jet fighter in the Western world."[126]

While these scenarios of the Lavi's future are speculative, they are nonetheless germane. For all the $1-plus billion it has designated for the Lavi—"with such alacrity that it initially provided $150 million more than Israel could spend"[127]—Congress has ignored a number of problems associated with the plane, as well as the reports of South African collaboration. It has not dealt with the prospects of the Lavi as an export, even though it had been pointed out repeatedly that the Lavi would compete with the U.S.-built Northrop F-20 Tigershark. The F-20, which had no federal funds for its development, was abandoned in November 1986 after failing to find U.S. or foreign buyers.[128]

The Israelis have assured Washington "categorically" that they were not developing the Lavi for export, but some U.S. officials remain skeptical.[129]

Pentagon efforts to persuade Israel to scrap the Lavi project because its rising costs would impair other Israeli military programs—the Pentagon said the finished aircraft would cost $22 million per plane, the Israelis claimed it would be $15 million[130]—were ignored by Congress. Instead, eight U.S. Representatives wrote a letter to the Departments of State and Defense and to the White House urging that the next installment of $70 million for the Lavi be released.[131]

In an editorial calling into question the fiscal soundness of the Lavi project, the *Oakland Tribune* also suggested: "...If Congress does extend further aid, it should insist on guarantees that none of the technology will leak out to South Africa."[132]

In the face of general knowledge on the hill of Israeli-South African military cooperation, shouldn't Congress' lack of interest in possible South African access to the Lavi be interpreted by Israel as "a wink and a nod"?

In 1979, the U.S. allowed Israel to use $107 million of its military aid to develop its main battle tank, the Chariot, or Merkava, in Israel. (This precedent, spending foreign aid outside the U.S., would later be used to justify the far larger sums the U.S. permitted Israel to convert to its local currency for the Lavi.[133])

Meanwhile, South Africa's help was enlisted in the production of the armor plating for the tank. Israel obtained rare steel alloys from South Africa, and also—in a rare turnaround—South Africa's advanced steel manufacturing technology. In return Israel supplied the formula for fabricating the plating and refitted all of South Africa's tanks and armoured vehicles.[134] The armor is said to be the hardest in the world. The production was handled by Iskoor,[135] a jointly owned steel company located in Israel.

Arms Sales and Policy ....

Toward Arms Self-Sufficiency

In addition to permitting South Africa to build its systems under license, Israel has given South Africa direct assistance in the establishment of its arms industry:

> The Haifa shipyard helped establish South Africa's virtually non-existent shipbuilding industry by supplying personnel to the Sandock-Austral yard [in Durban] and advising on the organization of an efficient production line.[1]

Representatives of Israel's major military electronics producers, Tadiran, Elbit and IAI helped South Africa establish its own electronics sector. South Africa now produces—and smugly claims credit for developing—a range of military communications gear.[2] As it is clear that in their daily routines the South African police and military, the enforcers of apartheid, benefit directly from state of the art Israeli electronic technology, it is equally clear that the so-called "dual-use" communications gear used by the police and military must be included in the category of military goods that should be denied to South Africa (by both the U.S. and Israel).

Many of the 20,000 Israelis now living in South Africa[3]—a number that has increased from 5,000 in 1978[4]—are believed to be involved in the high tech and military sectors. In 1981 South Africa began recruiting Israeli engineers, and electronics and computer specialists.[5]

47

From surrounding a township to mounting an invasion of Angola, the white government has had the advantage of sophisticated and secure communications. In May 1985 a South African commando captured by Angolan troops while preparing to bomb the Gulf Oil installation in the enclave of Cabinda explained how an emergency escape into neighboring Zaire would have been handled:

> If the situation arise that we have to go to Zaire, then by means
> of that radio over there, we can talk to Pretoria, who will then
> exactly tell us which people will meet us there.[6]

South Africa's capacity for havoc and destruction is underscored by continuing speculation that a sophisticated decoy radio signal was responsible for the crash of the airplane carrying Mozambican President Samora Machel from Zambia to Mozambique on October 19, 1986 at 9:15 in the evening. Coming in for a landing at Maputo, the plane instead flew into a mountain just over the South African border.

Machel, revered within and far beyond his own nation, lay dying in the wreckage, while South African police and soldiers, who arrived immediately after the crash, drove off medical volunteers and prowled through the wreckage, trampling bodies, searching by flashlight for documents (the South Africans later displayed notes from the meeting which they said discussed a plan to overthrow the government of Malawi, where South African backed mercenaries attacking Mozambique have found refuge) and asking "Where's Samora?" The foreign minister himelf, Pik Botha, came to the crash site. Later, recounted one of the passengers who lay in the wreckage with both legs broken, South African vehicles and helicopters arrived. The vehicles ringed the crash site and then turned off their headlights, their drivers joining the search with flashlights. It wasn't until the following morning that the first survivors were taken to a hospital.[7] Later the South Africans would say that Machel's heart and brain were "not present due to the violence of the accident."[8]

Amidst a consensus that South Africa was generally to blame—according to President Kenneth Kaunda of Zambia "because apartheid is responsible for all our distress in this region"[9]—it was quickly established that South Africa had the ability to send decoy radio signals.[10] Careful studies of the flight's last moments led analysts to believe that a decoy beacon from South Africa led it astray.[11] The South Africans themselves said that the pilot was "disoriented" by a powerful omnidirectional beacon transmitting from Swaziland,[12] a nation completely in the thrall of South Africa (and also a country where Israelis are made to feel at home).

It is also, perhaps, worth noting that Zairian President Mobutu was at the meeting Machel was attending on the southern shore of Lake

Tanganyika, in a remote area of Zambia.[13] Mobutu's personal guard has been trained by Israelis.[14] And what the South African Foreign Minister said the day of Machel's funeral, as he expressed regret that South Africa had not been invited: that his government's presence at the crash site showed "clear evidence of the respect shown for President Machel," and South Africa's willingness to "ben[d] over backwards."[15]

The area where the crash occurred is a restricted South African military zone, and unusual army activity had been observed there in the days immediately preceding the crash. Eyewitnesses said a camp was dismantled immediately after the crash.

An investigation under the control of South Africa (in which Mozambique did not participate) revealed that the cockpit voice recorder contained exchanges among crew members over whether the beacon signal they were receiving indicated a turn in the proper direction. They followed a signal that led them 37 degrees off course.[16]

Whether or not South Africa acquired the specific technology capable of bringing down Samora Machel's aircraft from Israel, after a decade of formalized cooperation with Israel, the white-ruled outlaw state has the ability to manufacture all kinds of advanced equipment. The apartheid government brags it has accomplished this itself:

> The arms boycott failed for a perfectly simple reason: white South Africans refused to commit political suicide. The price that had to be paid in buiding up a local armament industry had to be paid. There was simply no alternative.[17]

While Pretoria might be correct in touting itself as the world's 10th largest exporter of arms,[18] it is far less self-sufficient than it pretends to be.[19] It is dependent on Israel for access to developing technology and thus it is critical that Israel be prevented from providing South Africa any further updates.

This question came up as Israel, facing unprecedented Congressional scrutiny, and possibly a forced curtailment, of its military commerce with South Africa, wondered (through the media) whether "semi-military systems" might also provoke Congressional objection. This was only one of the questions Israel raised, indirectly through leaks and in private talks with the Reagan Administration and on Capitol Hill, as the day (April 1, 1987) approached when the President was to submit to Congress a report on U.S. allies' military dealings with South Africa.

That report had been mandated by a provision of an amendment to the 1986 Comprehensive Anti-Apartheid Bill, passed by Congress on October 2, 1986. Drafted not by anti-apartheid activists but by two Republican senators (Charles McC. Mathias of Maryland and Dan Evans of Washington) and appearing as Section 508 of the final bill, the provision required the President to conduct a study "on the extent to which the international embargo on the sale and exports of arms and military technology to South Africa is being violated," and, 180 days after passage of the anti-apartheid bill, to submit a report to Congress containing "a detailed assessment of the economic and other relationships of other industrialized democracies with South Africa." The report was to identify "those countries engaged in such sale or export with a view to terminating United States military assistance to those countries."

Had it not had such serious ramifications, the whole episode could be appreciated as a farce. When it was introduced in the Senate Foreign Relations Committee, some of Israel's special friends there scrambled to delete it from the larger amendment offered by Mathias and Evans. The committee took three separate votes on the measure: first accepting, then rejecting, finally, after adjourning to a back room where several Democratic senators were made to realize how hypocritical their attention-getting opposition to apartheid was if they weren't willing to act against Israel's violations of the arms embargo, it was rejected. On the final vote Senators Pell (D-RI, who in 1987 became chair of the committee) and Cranston (D-CA, who had greatly pleased his progressive constituents by introducing in the Senate the very stiff sanctions bill authored by Rep. Ronald Dellums (D-CA) and passed by the House) stood firm, voting against the provision with a minority comprised of ultra-rightist Jesse Helms (R-NC) and other anti-sanctions Republicans.

While Israel's lobby could normally have had the amendment deleted, in this case the legislation sped along so quickly AIPAC was never able to catch up with it. Debate was limited in the full Senate to prevent filibustering. The House immediately abandoned its own previously-passed anti-apartheid legislation (the Dellums bill) and passed the Senate's version without debate. After the President (who never saw a racist he didn't try to help) vetoed the measure, both houses of Congress passed it over his veto—again, without debate. AIPAC never had a chance.

In the end, Congress, the administration, and, most of all, Israel, were faced with a responsibility that none of them wanted.[20] In January and February, Israel worked to achieve an understanding with the administration over what "gesture" might satisfy the Congress—constituents, who might have been harder to satisfy, were, unfortunately, silent. When Prime Minister Yitzhak Shamir visited Washington in mid-February, the subject of how much Israel needed to change its relations with South Africa was high on the list of matters discussed.

After announcing through official sources that to precipitously end existing contracts with South Africa would cost $500 million (over several years) and many million more in possible lawsuits, not to mention "hundreds, if not thousands, of jobs in Israeli military industries,"[21] Israel's friends raised questions in the press about whether Congress might accept the continuation of licensing deals and sales of "semi-military" items.[22] With a deafening silence from both the White House and Capitol Hill, Israel decided on a:

> "deprofilization" of [its] presence in South Africa. In other words, the special relationship between the two nations—particularly in what is called "strategic affairs"—will continue, but in a much less visible manner and with less direct involvement of the military so as not to clash with the will of Congress.[23]

Defense Minister Yitzhak Rabin was dispatched to South Africa—the South Africans were threatening to "tell all" about some yet undisclosed aspect of Israeli collaboration[24]—where he gave reassurances[25] and urged the Boers to keep their heads down. Shamir told U.S. reporters that Israel would keep its "commitments" to South Africa.[26]

The impression was left floating—through intentional newsleaks—that Israel might phase out existing agreements and not enter into new ones,[27] but there was no evidence of any intention to put that offer into effect. Moreover, six weeks before the report was due to be submitted to Congress it was clear that Congress would not cut off Israel's $1.8 billion annual military aid, and Israeli officials had begun concentrating on preventing

> political backlash [that] could nonetheless be very damaging. Shamir and his colleagues hope that both the Reagan Administration and Congress will stop short of any public condemnation of Israel based on assurances that it will gradually end its military relationship with South Africa.[28]

Was Israel to end its nuclear collaboration with South Africa "gradually"? Before Section 508 of the Anti-Apartheid Act of 1986 fortuitously pried out the information that Israel did hundreds of millions of dollars per year of military business with South Africa, Israel always denied any arms dealings at all. What assurance is there that Israel is now accurately portraying the extent of its trafficking, not just half or one-quarter? The assertion of Defense Minister Rabin, that "whatever happens Israel has to maintain its credibility with the U.S. and Israel has never played tricks with the U.S.,"[29] is less than satisfying after the Iran-contra revelations and the Pollard spy case.

There was no voice in Congress to question Israel's word, much less to wonder aloud if the people of Southern Africa were not owed some kind of reparations from the people of the U.S., whose client Israel has contributed so greatly to their death, suppression and suffering. Instead, Israel's efforts to keep the lid on its continued lethal supply lines to South Africa and Congress' efforts to keep its own dereliction of duty out of the minds of its constituents are both greatly assisted by the almost blanket censorship imposed by the South African government.

The notion of South Africa's "self-sufficiency" should not obscure the degree of integration between the two arms industries. James Adams calls it their "joint arms industry."[30] Iskoor, the steel partnership, is one example of this integration. A joint Scorpion[31] helicopter operation involves initial construction in South Africa at the Cape Town firm of Rotoflight Helicopters and then final assembly at Israel's Chemavir-Masok.[32] Yet another example is Israel's permitting South Africa construction companies to bid on a military complex in the Negev Desert.[33]

Coordinated Exports

The integration of military industries also appears to have led to some degree of integration of foreign operations. Tadiran and the South African firm Consolidated Power have established an electronics enterprise in Guatemala.[34]

It seems the two might also be coordinating their weapons exports to a certain extent. A 1982 report noted that South Africa was delivering rush orders of parts for Israeli Gabriel missiles and the Nesher (an early version of the Kfir) to Argentina, then engaged in the Malvinas/Falklands war with Britain.[35]

Although the full extent of coordination between Tel Aviv and Pretoria is impossible to know, both Israel and South Africa have been supplying arms to the governments of Sri Lanka,[36] Iran and Morocco.

Israel, which had counted the Shah of Iran its most important arms customer, had been selling arms to the Islamic Republic since its war with Iraq began in 1980,[37] and in 1985 brought the U.S. into partnership in this enterprise, later known as the Iran-contra affair. South Africa followed Israel into the Iranian market with an oil-for-arms swap reportedly concluded in 1985, under which Iran received $750 million worth of weapons. The only weapon known to have been involved in that deal was the G-5 howitzer,[38] the South African version of the SRC 155 mm howitzer which Israel helped South Africa obtain from the U.S. (South Africa cut the same deal with Iraq.[39]) There is an international embargo on oil shipments to South Africa, and Israel has often used violations of the embargo by Middle East governments to support its claim that it should not be singled out for its dealings with South Africa. Although many of the shipments to South Africa that originate in the Gulf are purveyed to the apartheid regime by private dealers such as fugitive financier Marc Rich, it appears (although the news accounts seem mainly to emanate from the London newsletter *Euromoney Trade Finance Report*) that Iran and Iraq are directly involved in such deals.[40]

Visitors to the Sahrawi Arab Democratic Republic have seen South Africa weapons which the Polisario Front has captured from Morocco in its battle for control of the formerly Spanish Western Sahara. Polisario also charges that South Africa is training Moroccans. Following a visit of Prime Minister Shimon Peres to Morocco in July 1986—described in terms of the (interminable) "peace process"—Israel reportedly pledged to provide Morocco with sophisticated arms and training.[41] In the past, Israel has sold Morocco tanks and armored personnel carriers.[42] Israeli officers have been sighted near the wall[43] King Hassan II is building to try to maintain the fiction that he controls the territory claimed by the SADR, and taking part in the "African Eagle" military exercises staged by the U.S. and Morocco in November 1986.[44]

Discouraging as these developments may seem to advocates of sanctions against South Africa, our continued efforts to curtail the flow of military technology to Pretoria still matter: preventing the white regime from producing state-of-the-art weaponry will make its export offerings less attractive, hence depriving it of further income to pursue its aggressive domestic and external policies.[45]

Southern Africa: After the Israeli Model

In these foreign operations, which strengthen both countries and challange the confines of their international isolation, Israel has generally been the facilitator, possessing the entre to such adventures as Guatemala and Sri Lanka. As it came snarling and hissing into the 1980s in its own region, South Africa has also looked to Israel for help and inspiration.

Many parallels in the tactics and strategies employed by Israel and South Africa have been noted.[46] Partly this is a result of collegiality: the military attaches of Israel and South Africa "consult frequently on counterinsurgency tactics."[47] Yet there is an unmistakable teacher-student pattern in the communication of the very techniques which have brought down international criticism on both. As in the direction of the technology flow between the two nations, the imparting of repressive techniques usually casts Israel in the mentor's role.

The South Africans greatly admired the Israeli raid on Entebbe airport.[48] "South African generals now consciously emulate the flamboyance of the Israeli generals," wrote a specialist on the South African military.[49] Even before 1976 South Africans had looked to Israel for techniques they might adapt. Describing the lecture given by Air Force General Mordechai Hod during his 1967 visit to South Africa, a member of the select military audience said, "It was an intensely interesting lecture, which made it apparent that the tactics employed by the Israeli Air Force were brilliant. The Israelis seem to have been as clever as a cartload of monkeys."[50]

The South Africans began teaching the lessons of Israel's 1967 war at their maneuver school,[51] and Israeli advisers began teaching the Boers the arts of suppressing a captive population and keeping hostile neighbors off balance.[52] In the Vorster agreements discussed earlier, Israeli advisory services for South Africa were institutionalized.

> Senior army officers in Israel have confirmed that IDF [Israeli Defense Forces] personnel have been seconded to all branches of the South African armed forces, and according to senior sources in the Israeli defense establishment, there are currently some 300 active Israeli servicemen and women on secondment in South Africa. These include army, navy and air force personnel who help train the South Africans, border security experts...counter intelligence experts... and defense scientists who cooperate on the development of new weapons systems. In addition, there are several hundred South Africans in Israel at any one time, being trained in weapons systems, battle strategy and counter-insurgency warfare.[53]

The white government's practice of domestic counterinsurgency combines outright military brutality with the extensive use of informers and collaborators. It is impossible to know how many refinements of these age-old techniques have been borrowed from the Israelis' occupation of the West Bank, Gaza, and the Golan Heights. The Israeli system of village leagues is obviously comparable to the hated town councils imposed on segregated townships by the apartheid government. The collective punishment employed by the Israelis, such as the destruction of a whole family's home when one of its members is arrested as a *suspect* in an act of resistance, has lately been matched by the recent South African practices of sealing off townships, and assaulting entire funeral processions. What is perhaps more salient is the South African victims' perceptions of Israel's involvement in their oppression and how readily that perception is communicated.

At a party in Santa Cruz, California, a South African student passes around a photograph of a street scene in Soweto, the large black township outside Johannesburg. Somewhat reproachfully he calls attention to the white policeman in the picture and the Uzi he's holding.

Nobel laureate Archbishop Desmond Tutu, was more direct when he told guests at a San Francisco breakfast sponsored by the American Jewish Congress that he was troubled by reports of Israeli collaboration with South Africa, "with a government whose policies are so reminiscent of Nazis."[54] (While quick to point out the contributions of individual Jews to the struggle against apartheid, Tutu has in the past lambasted Israel for its "monopoly on the Holocaust."[55])

Even those South African blacks willing to cooperate with Israel have publicly called on Tel Aviv to stop selling arms to South Africa. Chief Gatsha Buthelezi, a great favorite of Israel, told reporters there that he favored an international arms embargo against South Africa.[56] One member of a group of black South African "activists" brought to Israel for a training program (see below) told the press that Israel was "among the countries that sell weapons to South Africa, which kill [sic] blacks with them, including three-year-old children."[57]

"Israel," wrote a reader to the *City Press*, a black South African paper, "has chosen to support the South African Government—thereby sanctioning the brutal suppression of our people."[58]

It should also be noted that South Africans—with other people around the world—regard the activities of Israel as an extension of U.S. policy.

If Israel's role in the internal repression meted out by South Africa (including the active Israeli role in the bantustans—see below) is a matter of perception, evidence is accumulating, despite strenuous attempts to maintain a lid of secrecy, of Israeli involvement in South Africa's foreign aggressions against Namibia and the Frontline states.

Namibia

Israeli specialists have been "permanently based" along South African border areas for over a decade. Numbering "more than fifty" in 1984, their assigned task is to advise the South Africans on preventing cross-border infiltration.[59] In the late 1970s, uniformed Israeli soldiers were reported active in Namibia, the former colony of Southwest Africa which South Africa has refused to relinquish, against fighters for SWAPO, the South West Africa Peoples Organization, which has an extensive following in Namibia. One of these reports noted that uniformed Israelis had been seen in the capital, Windhoek, and that "they were constructing an electrified barrier the length of the [Namibian] frontier with Angola."[60]

In 1981, Ariel Sharon, at the time Israel's Minister of Defense, spent 10 days with South African troops in Namibia on the Angolan border.[61] Uri Dan, a close associate of Sharon who accompanied him on that visit, wrote of his experience:

> 36-year-old Col. Lamprecht does not talk as an army man, but as someone in charge of civilian administration in an area under military rule...When I look at the South African officers, talking Afrikans or English, and during operations, I get the feeling that they will soon begin giving orders in Hebrew. Their physical appearance, their freshness, their frankness, their conduct on the battlefield, remind one of Israeli officers. And I didn't say this about the American and South Vietnamese officers I met 11 years ago in Vietnam...
>
> "Don't underestimate the influence the example of the Israeli army as a fighting army has on us," a senior officer told me in Pretoria."[62]

In the guise of development assistance, Israel has also helped the South Africans establish control of the long-suffering population of Namibia.[63]

In 1984, at a time when even South Africa's staunchest Western supporters took a hands-off position in response to a South African challenge to take Namibia off its hands[64] the Israeli Ambassador to Pretoria went to Windhoek and told South African radio that "Israel would not insist on a precondition that the territory first become independent before agreeing to help it in its economic development."[65]

In response to the ambassador's invitation a team of high ranking officials of the South African colonial government paid a twelve-day visit to Israel the following April. They were there to look at what Israel had to offer in the field of "agriculture, water management and water supply, community development and regional planning."[66]

A second visit to Israel the following year brought the puppet government's Health and Education ministers to Israel. They issued a long report when they returned to Namibia, prattling on about Israeli integration of peoples from "non-industrial cultures into an industrial and technical culture, including the accompanying social, language and unemployment problems" and the Israeli labor unions and health systems. Their report promised specific proposals for Namibia.[67] Namibian recruits were taking courses in Israel at Histadrut's Afro-Asian Institute in early 1986.[68]

The true definition of "community development" programs in contested areas is, of course, "pacification," as practiced unsuccessfully by the U.S. in Vietnam—and as practiced with increasing effect by Israel. As elsewhere, the object of these programs in Namibia is to destroy indigenous and/or revolutionary forms of social organization and to construct a repressive, regimented system that monopolizes provision of social services and compels participation—"winning hearts and minds," it is called—and thereby establishing political control. In the case of Namibia, much of which is under a dusk-to-dawn curfew and occupation by more than 100,000 South African troops (compared to a white Namibian population of 76,000)[69] the benefits to South Africa of long-term control of the population are obvious. South Africa, which established a puppet regime in Namibia in June 1985, clings to the former German colony both for its wealth of natural resources and as part of its drive for dominance over Africa.

Israel's doctrine of pre-emptive attack has served as a model for South Africa. Its 1982 invasion of Lebanon—Israeli officers briefed the Afrikaners on their operations there[70]—inspired South Africa to attack Mozambique in 1983 and to invade Angola in 1984. A somewhat imprecise term, "invade," as South Africa has occupied part of Southern Angola almost constantly for the last decade. (As with Israel's wars, South Africa's constant aggressions have enabled officials to boast that their export weapons are "battle-tested."[71])

The Frontline States

The South Africans noted that their May 1983 aerial attack (dubbed "Operation Shrapnel") on Mozambique's capital, Maputo, was analogous to Israel's attack on Beirut the previous summer. One analyst, Joseph

Hanlon, believes that one of South Africa's objectives in the attack was to see how its version of events would play in the media. It was received very well indeed, according to Hanlon, with the Western press accepting South Africa's claim that its attack was in "retaliation" for an ANC attack and that ANC "bases" were hit.

Instead, the South African Air Force hit a childcare center and private houses with "special fragmentation rockets," leaving 6 dead and 40 wounded.[72] This follows the Israeli practice in Lebanon of speaking about PLO installations while civilians are the actual targets, and attacking with particularly heinous anti-personnel weapons—cluster bombs and phosphorous bombs.[73]

The victims of South Africa's angst are not blind to the similarity of attacks—or motives.

> President Samora Machel likened the Israeli Government to the Pretoria regime. He said that because of its inability to contain the fury of the Palestinian people led by the PLO, the Zionist regime is trying to transfer the war to other regions.

So reported Mozambican radio shortly after Israeli aircraft bombed PLO headquarters in Tunisia in October 1985.[74]

The model provided by Israel, which punishes every internal act of resistance and violent act outside its jurisdiction with a bombing raid on Palestinian targets in Lebanon—almost always refugee camps cynically identified by the Israelis as "terrorist bases" or "headquarters"—has served South Africa well. In January 1986, the white government's radio delivered a commentary on "the malignant presence" of "terrorism" in neighboring states and said "there's only one answer now, and that's the Israeli answer." Israel had managed to survive "by striking at terrorists wherever they exist."[75]

In May 1986, South Africa demonstrated that it had assumed the right to attack its neighbors at a time and on a pretext of its own choosing. The chosen time was during a visit by the Eminent Persons Group of the Commonwealth of Nations, which was attempting to establish negotiations between the apartheid regime and its opposition. The victims—Zambia, Botswana and Zimbabwe, all Commonwealth members—were chosen for their alleged harboring of "terrorists"; the real victims were South African exiles and an employee of the government of Botswana. The South Africans said they had attacked "international terrorism" and compared their raids to the Israeli attack on Tunisia and the U.S. attack on Libya in April 1986.[76]

The attack was similar in style to Israel's 1985 attack on Tunisia. Initially, the Israelis had been threatening Jordan[77] and perhaps because

King Hussein of Jordan was at the time on an official visit to the U.S., the Israelis chose to take revenge for the killing of three Israelis (believed to be top Mossad agents) in Larnaca, Cyprus on the PLO in Tunisia.[78]

Two weeks after its three-pronged attack on its Commonwealth neighbors, South Africa attacked the Angolan harbor of Namibe, firing their version of the Israeli Gabriel missile.[79]

Israel has also been connected with the mercenary forces deployed by South Africa against Angola and Mozambique. In the 1970s Israel aided the FNLA (Angolan National Liberation Front) proxy forces[80] organized and trained by the CIA to forestall the formation of a government led by the MPLA (Popular Movement for the Liberation of Angola—now the ruling party of Angola). John Stockwell, who ran the CIA operation against Angola, recollected three arms shipments Israel made in cooperation with the CIA: a plane full of 120 mm shells sent via Zaire to the FNLA and Unita; a shipment of 50 SA-7 missiles (all of which were duds); a boatload sent to neighboring Zaire in a deal that the Israelis had worked out with President Mobutu, even though the Zairian strong man had broken ties with Israel two years earlier.[81]

When Israel reestablished relations with Zaire (in 1982) and began to train Zairian forces in the Shaba border province, Angola had cause for concern. The leader of the FNLA had been Holden Roberto, brother-in-law of Zairian president Mobutu, Israel's new client.[82] In 1986, it would be established that Zaire acted as a funnel for "covert" U.S. military aid for the Unita forces of Jonas Savimbi.[83]

In 1983, the Angolan News Agency reported that Israeli military experts were training Unita forces in Namibia.[84] Since Zaire began receiving military aid and training from Tel Aviv, Angola has been ill at ease. Its worries increased after discovering that:

> Israeli Defense Minister Ariel Sharon was personally involved in the organization, training and equipping of "commando" units of the army of Zaire, especially organized for missions along the borders of the RPA [Angola].[85]

In 1984, the *Financial Times* (London) wrote of "joint Israeli-South African support for Unita forces."[86] Other sources also report the transfer of Israeli arms and financial support to Unita.[87]

In 1983, Angola's President Jose Eduardo dos Santos told Berkeley, California Mayor Eugene (Gus) Newport that an Israeli pilot had been shot down during a South African attack. The Angolan President showed Newport pictures of captured Israeli weapons. The following year, Luanda reported the capture of three mercenaries who said they had been trained by Israeli instructors in Zaire.[88]

Israel has also been involved with the Mozambican "contras," the South African-backed MNR (Mozambique National Resistance or "Renamo"), which has brought great economic and social distress to Mozambique. Renamo has a particular reputation for ideological incoherrence, being regarded by most other right-wing insurgencies as a gang of cutthroats. For several years there have been stories coming from Southern Africa of captured mercenaries of Renamo who say they were trained in neighboring Malawi—one of the four nations to maintain relations with Israel after the Organization of African Unity (OAU) declared a diplomatic embargo in 1973—by Israelis. And more than one report has told of "substantial Israeli aid" to the MNR, thought to have been funded by the CIA and Saudi Arabia as well as South Africa and former Portuguese colonialists.

In late 1986, "intelligence reports" from Southern Africa confirmed the reports of Israeli training and attributed the MNR's "greatly improved tactics" to the Israeli trainers.[89] Around the same time, found among a number of white men left dead after an attack on Zimbabwean troops on duty in Mozambique was a man wearing a Star of David.[90]

There are at least two earlier reports of Israelis captured in Mozambique. One, a pilot captured in the late 1970s, might have been included in an east-west spy swap in 1978.[91] The other, 27-year-old Amikam Efrati of less certain occupation, was held for three months by Mozambique and released after Israeli Laborites asked members of the French Socialist Party to intervene. A warm welcome was prepared for Efrati on his Golan Heights kibbutz.[92]

Economy ....

Economic Cooperation

In addition to South Africa's cash and strategic mineral contributions to Israeli-South African military undertakings, the two have forged economic links that are as strategic as they are profitable. They are almost as well concealed as the military commerce between the two nations, enabling Israel to claim that its trade with South Africa is insignificant.[1]

However, well before grassroots campaigns in the U.S. and Britain prompted the exodus of big business from South Africa and, in the case of the U.S., the imposition of economic sanctions, Israel qualified in many ways as South Africa's most important trading partner. This determination was reached by adding the undisclosed amounts of the weapons Israel sells to South Africa and the diamonds it obtains from the white-run state.[2]

Because the diamonds are sold from a London office by the South African DeBeers syndicate, the Central Selling Organization, which has a lock on the world market for uncut stones, they do not appear in statistics of two-way trade between Israel and South Africa. Polished diamonds are Israel's largest single export item, accounting for over $1.5 billion in 1986.[3] There is very little value added in the polishing: imports for 1986 were $1.25 billion.[4]

Also invisible in the published statistics of trade between the two nations are revenue from joint military and civilian enterprises of Israel and South Africa. The known civilian undertakings are Zimcorn, a shipping company,[5] and South Atlantic Corporation, a fishing enterprise.[6] A range of business activities are carried out by one in the economy of the other. Iskoor, the Israeli-South African steel company which makes tank armor, is owned by South Africa and Israel's Histadrut trade union federation, and operates in Israel.[7]

Thus, although the revealed statistics of trade between Tel Aviv and Pretoria seem rather paltry—$66.4 million Israeli exports to South Africa and $187 million exports from South Africa to Israel[8]—it is important to bear in mind that they reflect only trade in items both sides are willing to make public. These include coal, steel, base metals, timber, tobacco, hides, wool, paper, minerals, and foodstuffs from South Africa and from Israel finished products such as computer software, agricultural and other types of machinery, textiles, pharmaceuticals, electrical goods, and "safety and security products."[9] Although trade grew by a multiple of ten between 1970 and 1979 (from $20.9 million to $199.3 million)[10] the numbers on paper certainly do not seem large enough to explain the existence of dynamic Israel-South Africa Chambers of Commerce in Tel Aviv and Johannesburg, or the annual meetings of finance ministers[11] under the framework of the ministerial committee set up during the 1976 Vorster talks. By contrast, Israel exported $2.2 billion worth of goods and services to the U.S. in 1985.[12]

What *is* truly remarkable is the unrevealed and hence uncalculated scope of Israeli-South African economic cooperation. It goes well beyond weapons and diamonds, falling under the broad category of investment in each other's economies, but it is most notably directed to helping South Africa escape the rigors of the sanctions which, in an effort to force the white minority government to dismantle apartheid, the international community has begun to impose.

South Africa has a significant interest in the Israeli economy, providing 35 percent of all non-U.S. investment in the three years prior to 1984.[13] This South African investment, "tens of millions of dollars...has been an important source of new funds for Israeli industry and construction."[14]

Although originally an exception to South Africa's extraordinarily tight currency and trade laws, the export of Jewish contributions to Israel, (see above) was expanded under the 1976 bilateral agreements as a unique dispensation for South African citizens to invest in approved projects in Israel.[15] In 1980, the white minority government also gave permission for Israeli government bonds to be sold in South Africa.[16] While Israelis trying to minimize the extent of their country's economic relations with South Africa will often explain that dealing with Pretoria enables South African

Jews to get their capital out of the country, a South African newspaper points out:

> ...investors in Israel today include names off the company boards of the [Johannesburg Stock Exchange]. For the individual or smaller corporate investor, there exists a handful of Israeli companies whose specific business is to attract [South African] and other foreign investment in joint ventures.[17]

In fact, raising funds from the Jewish community and boosting business links with South Africa go hand in hand. In 1982, on one of the annual meetings established under the 1976 agreements, Israeli Finance Minister Gideon Pat visited South Africa and:

> [took] part in 17 meetings of the emergency [a reference to Israel's invasion of Lebanon that June] bonds fundraising group, will meet with economic officials and will see to increasing investments by South African companies in Israel.[18]

South African capital has contributed to major Israeli infrastructural projects: development projects in the Negev desert, a coal loading facility, a Mediterranean-Dead Sea water diversion project, a major insurance company, tourist and sports facilities and commercial and residential real estate as well as a railroad linking Tel Aviv with the Red Sea port of Eilat.[19] Other approved areas for South African investment include film production, oil exploration, and the purchase of shares in Israeli companies to increase production capacity,[20] all areas of obvious benefit to South Africa.

The Springboard

Although Israel's economy hit the skids in the 1980s, South African businessmen have had a compelling motive for continuing to invest their money in the Jewish state: Israel provides a tried and true "springboard" into markets where South African products are unwelcome. Since the late 1970s South Africans have been establishing joint ventures in Israel where their cheap-labor products are brought for final assembly and marked with a "made in Israel" label.[21] Shipped abroad, these products enter U.S. and European markets under Israel's duty free entitlement. Israel has a Free Trade Agreement with the U.S. under which all tariffs will be removed by 1995; a similar agreement with the EEC allows duty-free entry for all Israeli nonagricultural products.

In the 1970s and early 1980s, such an opportunity was particularly attractive to South African businessmen, as their own highly protected economy was faced with steep tariffs by Western trading partners. In 1977, in conjunction with the South Africa-Israeli Chamber of Commerce, the Universities of Tel Aviv and Stellenbosch presented a series of seminars in South Africa entitled "Israel: Crossroads of International Trade," to acquaint South African businessmen with the benefits of exporting via Israel.[22]

In 1979, South African industrialist Archie Hendler, whose joint venture in Israel manufactured kitchenware, noted that "the main reason for going into Israel is to gain access to the Common Market" on Israel's favorable terms.[23]

In the mid 1980s, as sanctions began to threaten South African exporters, the use of Israel as a springboard or back door into Western markets became even more attractive. In 1983 the Israeli Finance Minister went to South Africa with specific proposals for joint industrial ventures that the South African Government could establish with Israel.[24]

How effective has this bilateral conniving been? What is the actual amount of goods Israel has helped South Africa sneak into the market baskets of unwitting consumers? That, of course, is difficult to determine—especially since no one has tried very hard to unearth the facts. It has been known for a decade that Iskoor has been representing the South African steel industry in the European Economic Community.[25] It was reported in 1980 that the Israeli government's agricultural marketing board, Agrexco, was selling South African fruit in the U.S.[26] South Africa's large electronics firm (owned by the Oppenheimer holding company Anglo American) Control Logic mated with the Israeli Elron group to form Conlog, whose business is to springboard South African products from Israel.[27] The United Nations, in 1981, published a report containing the names of several companies and their products—Koor, owned by Histadrut, and Sentrachem, a South African fertilizer and chemical concern;[28] Israel's Polichrom and South Africa's Chemtra, exporting chemicals for the paints and plastics industries; Transvaal Mattresses, exporting with Israel's Greenstein and Rosen; and Israel's Muenster foods, selling the South African brands Honey Crunch, Epol and Vital[29]—but this did not contain the brand names under which South African products were sold abroad.

In one more recent case, products were sold with no labels. The Hanita kibbutz, which is affiliated with the labor movement

> buys drills and other small tools from South Africa and re-exports them to Japan, South Korea, the European Economic

Community and the United States... The products are sold with no marks to identify them as either Israeli or South African.[30]

Histadrut, the parent of Koor, is involved in a great deal of the South African trade[31] and the Hanita Kibbutz is no aberration.[32]

What is certain is that as the antiapartheid movement in the U.S. gathered force via local and union boycotts of South African products, and local and institutional divestment from corporations involved in South Africa and, in 1985 and 1986 pushed sanctions legislation to the top of the Congressional agenda, Israel and South Africa both stepped up efforts on this type of sanctions busting.

In September 1985, the South African Ministry of Trade and Industry released an *Export Bulletin* reminding exporters:

> [Companies] can use Israel as a production base from which they can export their goods duty-free to the U.S. provided value added in Israel is at least 35% of the article's value when it enters the U.S.

A Johannesburg daily said that "Local companies...say they are being encouraged by senior Israeli officials." [33] A November 1985 report noted a 53 percent increase of South African exports to Israel between the previous January and May.[34]

Also in November 1985, the white South African government set up an office to coordinate "nonconventional trade" through "other countries."[35] Several months earlier an Israeli businessman, Amnon Rotem, had offered himself to the South African government as "a middleman in channeling [South African] exports to European and American markets... duty free" and said the scheme would require "a large investment" by the government.[36] By year's end, "new strategies to counter the challenge on sanctions and boycotts by overseas political lobbies" were in place, and South Africa's exports had risen 44 percent in the first 10 months of the year over the corresponding period the previous year.[37] During the first two months of 1986, South African exports increased again by 25 percent over the first two months of 1985.[38] Although it is not possible to establish a direct relationship with the increased South African exports, Israeli imports of merchandise did register a gain of 11.4 percent in the first five months of 1986 over the corresponding period in the previous year.[39] In August 1986, the South African minister of trade and industry urged censorship of trade statistics, which "could easily be used by our adversaries..."[40]

South Africa has tried to organize businessmen in a number of western countries and to establish front companies in dependent African countries.

For instance, a joint South African-Israeli operation called Liat has recently set up shop in the West African nation of Sierra Leone[41] and a number of South African companies operate in Swaziland.[42]

A great portion of South Africa's sanctions busting strategy has involved Israel. As early as July 1984, the senior general manager of Iscor Ltd., the South African partner in Iskoor, met with Israeli leaders to discuss the consortium of South African companies and banks proposed to finance—to the tune of $250-$300 million—the completion of the Eilat rail road. "The railway to the Red Sea port city would spark new life into the flagging port facilities and would help speed South African exports to their destinations in Israel."[43]

Despite mounting pressures from international circles and within its own ruling establishment—a former director-general of the Israeli Foreign Ministry urged Tel Aviv to downplay "the public aspect of the South Africa connection" and also to resist "the pressures [of] some South African businessmen" and their Israeli counterparts "who have their links with influential politicians here" to act as an export conduit for South Africa[44]— Israel has continued to respond to the white government's needs as if helplessly in its thrall.

The grim news for anti-apartheid activists is that South Africa, 54 percent of whose trade is already clandestine, would only need to boost its sanctions-busting by 16 percent to compensate for the U.S. sanctions now on the books.[45]

In late 1986 both Israel and South Africa were embarrassed by an advertisement placed in the Johannesburg paper *Business Day* offering "unconventional trade" services including "trans-shipments, re-invoicing, document recertification, temporary warehousing, bartering and buy-backs." The Voyager Corporation in Tel Aviv placed the ad. Its South African agent said it had been placed in error by U.S. associates![46]

In June 1986, in an effort to head off demonstrations marking the 10th anniversary of the Soweto uprising, the apartheid government instituted its most brutal state of emergency to date. At the last moment, Israel followed other Western governments in a 24-hour closure of its Pretoria embassy. The Israeli Knesset took the opportunity to issue some elegant statements condemning apartheid. One of these claimed, "Israel as the state of the Jewish people is commited to stand at the head of those who negate apartheid and fight for human rights."[47] Prime Minister Peres said, "We know it is impossible to compromise with racial discrimination."[48]

Less than two months later, with one official privately warning "In the end, we're going to have to pay a heavy price for this," a delegation departed for South Africa, under the leadership of the director general of the Finance Ministry.[49] The director general said that the annual agreements with South Africa were about to expire[50] and Israel justified the trip by pointing out that the delegation was for the first time not headed by the finance minister himself.[51]

The talks were said to concern Israel's fishing rights in South African waters, a better deal on credits for its coal imports, and, most significantly, increased South African investment in and trade with Israel. The talks "highlight[ed] Israel as a potential weak link in the chain of international sanctions against South Africa."[52]

The trip, taken when South African authorities were jailing and torturing thousands of anti-apartheid activists, made international headlines and prompted intense speculation on the role of Israel (and the South African Jewish community) as "South Africa's insurance policy against isolation."[53] A statement issued after the talks said they had been held in "a friendly atmosphere" and "were fruitful and continued trade and financial cooperation is considered to be in the interest of both countries."[54] It was also announced that South African investment in Israel would be allowed up to about $15 million during the coming year.[55]

Meanwhile, to revive its beached economy, Israel is banking on a more sophisticated and aggressive marketing campaign for its exports to the U.S. and specialization in high technology development and exports,[56] another area of vital concern to South Africa, which will be discussed below.

It is worth contemplating whether protection for Israel is embedded in the agreements the two governments have signed, should international attention some day turn from South Africa to focus on Israel's human rights abuses. One known area of such cooperation is the coal which Israel receives from South Africa.

Israel was badly traumatized by the oil price rises of the 1970s, and by the abrupt cessation of its oil supply when the Shah of Iran was overthrown in 1978. It later returned the Sinai oilfields to Egypt under the Camp David Accords. Although Israel's oil supply is guaranteed by the U.S. and Mexico,[57] and it is therefore not subject to the threat of boycott, there is no guarantee that the price won't go through the roof again. Because of its refusal to sign the Nuclear Proliferation Treaty, Israel has also been unable to find a country willing to help it build nuclear power plants. South African coal companies have not only signed a series of contracts to deliver increasingly large allotments of coal to Israel for power generation,[58] but South Africa has promised to join Israel in a naval escort should there be a problem with making deliveries.[59] Israel has built a new coal-fired generator and unloading facilities and is "aggressively moving" toward coal-fired powerplants.[60]

Israel's Stake in South Africa

Israel obviously does not compare in size of investment to U.S. and European participation in the South African economy, as the latter occurs through national and multinational corporations. However, Israeli investment in South African enterprises has shot up recently; excluding the United States and Western Europe, Israeli investment in 1983 and 1984 trailed only Taiwanese investment and included investment in South African steel enterprises,[61] with ten new Israeli enterprises reported in 1984.[62] A 1985 report said Israeli investment in South Africa had grown "tenfold" in two years.[63] Meanwhile, U.S. and European firms are leaving South Africa in droves.

What the Israeli investment might lack in volume, it makes up by being concentrated in two key areas: high technology and the bantustans, the austere tribal reserves to which the white government has exiled more than half of the black majority.

Scientific cooperation—in the civil as well as the military sphere—was a major element in the 1976 Vorster agreements, and what has been provided on a commercial basis (with either private or parastatal enterprises) seems to have been in close conjunction with the bilateral undertakings. As time goes by and one of the most powerful effects of international sanctions—that South Africa will be left by the wayside of technological progress[64]—does not come to pass, the significance of the Israeli contribution will be understood, perhaps lamented.

Visiting Israel in the fall of 1986, S. Kruger, the director of the South African Department of Trade and Industry, noted that "Israel could provide much of the high-technology needed by South Africa."[65]

Although much of the collaboration in technology has seen South African money going to the Israeli industrial sector, some energy has been directed toward providing the Boers with their own industrial applications. The 1983 agreement, according to the South African Finance Minister Owen Horwood,

> covered joint projects already tackled and still to be tackled by the two countries. It also made provision for the freer flow of money between the two countries and the setting up of mutual trade and credit and cooperation in the spheres of agriculture, technology and research.[66]

Out of that agreement was born the Israel/South Africa Industrial and Agricultural Research and Development Programme. Working under the direction of Saidcor (South African Inventions Development Corporation) and the Israeli Ministry of Trade and Industry, the program establishes bi-national partnerships for specific projects. To date the projects have included educational software, computerized water management systems, and an enhancement of the capability of South Africa's Posts and Telecommunications Department. Under consideration are a laser-material processing center and a pilotless (drone) crop spraying plane.[67]

In 1984, the Israeli minister of science and development and South Africa's ambassador to Israel met and announced that Israel and South Africa would strengthen scientific and research ties.[68] In early 1985, a South African delegation concluded a visit to Israel by secretly signing yet another agreement with Tel Aviv for cooperation in science and technology. According to similar reports in *Jane's Defense Weekly* and the Israeli daily *Ha'aretz*, the "joint ventures and projects in high technology fields" stipulated by the contract were worth $5 million. The agreement was negotiated by the Israeli ministries of finance and trade and industry. It was then approved by the Israeli cabinet.[69]

(That two such articles should evade Israeli censorship is highly unusual. It might even be that the story was floated as an attempt at *a priori* damage control. Thus, the suspiciously low figure of $5 million might have been given with the idea that later on it could be cited to prove the "minimal" nature of Israel's dealings with South Africa.)

The inclusion in the trade delegation that visited South Africa in August 1986 of a representative from the chief scientist's office[70] points to yet another increase in Israeli cooperation with South Africa in the sphere of civilian technology. Israel and South Africa have held 14 joint scientific symposiums, nine in Israel and five in South Africa. The last one was held in 1984 at Ben Gurion University in the Negev.[71] South African money has also been poured into Israel's Technion, the country's major scientific university. In 1984 the South Africa Advanced Manufacturing Systems Building and Laser Laboratory, financed by $1.5 million from South African, was dedicated.[72]

It is in this institutional context that Israeli investment in South Africa must be regarded. At least a dozen major Israeli companies have invested in South African operations,[73] among them the military electronics firms noted above. Afitra, one of many companies owned by the Israeli labor federation Histadrut, whose giant Koor is a major player in South Africa, markets some of Israel's most sophisticated products (advanced software, computerized milling machines, emergency lighting systems, etc.) as well as products of Israel's *kibbutzim*,[74] or collective farms. Another Israeli firm, Agri-Carmel, brings the latest Israeli agricultural developments to South Africa. Agri-Carmel is a partnership of the Israeli parastatal Agridev and the South African company Gerber Goldschmidt.[75]

The Bantustans ....

The Bantustans

A critical element of Israeli investment in South Africa is a rapacious "private enterprise" interest in the bantustans, the barren pseudostates that warehouse much of the black majority. The centerpiece of apartheid, the bantustans were envisioned as "tribal homelands," putting forth the fiction of South Africa as a number of diverse tribal groups. The "white" tribe, which did the geographical engineering, just happened to have the homeland with all the industrial infrastructure, rich farmland and access to transport.

The Israeli government provides development and military aid and a measure of political recognition for the bantustans accorded by no other government. This has been especially evident in the case of Ciskei, an enclave of 600,000 near Cape Town, which has been described as "one of the most economically underdeveloped areas in the world and also one of the poorest in Africa."[1]

During the 1983 Israeli-South African bilateral economic meeting, the Israeli radio reported: "It was...decided that close ties will be established between Israel and Ciskei, one of the puppet states set up in South Africa for the blacks." The radio quoted South African reports that Israel would also supply weapons to Ciskei.[2] The Israeli government denies it now, but it was reported to have signed an arms contract with Ciskei in 1982.[3] A twin engine jet once used by Israeli Prime Minister Begin was sold at a nominal cost, and "special weapons and knowhow" was also transferred to Ciskei.[4]

71

Included in the deal was the gift of a police dog to Charles Sebe, security chief and the brother of bantustan "President" Lennox Sebe.[5] During the summer of 1984, a group of farmers from Ciskei studied on Israeli kubbutzim and moshavim (communal and cooperative settlements, respectively).[6]

In late 1982, Ciskei had established a trade mission in Tel Aviv.[7] It appointed Yosef Schneider and Nat Rosenwasser as representatives. Schneider had previously served as an aide to extremist Knesset Member Meir Kahane.[8] Rosenwasser was a member of the Herut Party Central Committee.[9] Herut is the dominant component of the Likud coalition. Schneider and Rosenwasser had arranged a number of tours to Ciskei for Israeli notables.[10] Undoubtedly their work encouraged Israeli entrepreneurs, some of them former officials, others with close connections to the highest echelons of the Israeli governing establishment, to avail themselves of the cornucopia of investment incentives offered by the minority government in Pretoria to lure employers to Ciskei and the other bantustans.[11]

By July 1984 there were 60 Israeli entrepreneurs operating in Ciskei.[12] Ephraim Poran, former Prime Minister Begin's military secretary, went in with two other major Israeli industrialists to establish the Ciskatex textile factory. Other enterprises taking advantage of Ciskei's cheap labor were a plant of the apparel company Indian Head, Oren Toys[13] and Classic Cars, an establishment belonging to former Finance Minister Yoram Aridor, which manufactures vintage automobile replicas.[14]

In 1985, there were 200 Israelis—advisers and technicians as well as entrepreneurs—in Ciskei.[15] Ciskei presented special opportunities because of the exalted level of brutality of its leader Lennox Sebe, and his consequent insecurity. Bisho, the "capital" of Ciskei was "rife with stories of the 'fast buck' approach of Israeli entrepreneurs."[16] An explicit look at their activities was provided in 1985, when a scandal burst into the international press as the "authorities" of Ciskei announced—via large advertisements in the Israeli press—that it had closed the bantustan's trade mission in Israel and fired its Israeli representatives.

The scams in which many of the Israeli investors became involved were auctioning, or subcontracting, of contracts—many of these were awarded without bids, often far above actual cost—to South African companies. Many of the Israelis participating in these deals did so through shell companies.[17]

A key contact for the Israelis was Dr. Hennie Beukes, the only white "minister"—his portfolio was "health"—in Ciskei's "cabinet," who was said to have acted as intermediary in many Israeli activities in Ciskei. These included two hospitals built by the Gur Construction Company which Ciskei rejected. (In their off hours, Gur's workers built a bar and swimming pool at Beukes' residence.)

Buekes also arranged for a $10 million pilot training project, which sent 18 trainees to Israel to receive training that critics charged was inferior and overpriced.[18] It is unclear whether the training was for commercial or military aviation. A South African paper noted that Ciskei had two air bases and said Israeli Air Force instructors were to give preliminary training to Ciskeians before they attended pilot classes in Israel.[19]

Beukes also arranged the contracts for Israeli military advisers to work as bodyguards and military trainers in Ciskei. One company, Tammus—its owner a former Israeli artillery officer—made $300,000 a year providing security advisers to Ciskei "President" Sebe.[20] Tammus was one of the first Israeli firms to have its Ciskeian contracts canceled.[21]

Ira Curtis, the Israeli owner of the flight school, also bribed the Ciskeians to choose U.S. aircraft, which he attempted to smuggle into the South African tribal reserve, over superior French aircraft.[22] The planes were bought for Ciskei by listing Israel on the sale documents.[23]

In 1984, the Israeli government was forced to reassure Pretoria that it was not involved in a scheme for cheap Israeli flights from Ciskei to Israel and on to Europe. Word of the flights, which would compete with the **government-owned South Africa Airways, had sparked a South African** government protest to Israel. The apartheid regime warned that it would not be liable for Ciskei's debts for projects that were not in the category of "urgent development" and expressed its unease "over the intrusion of Israeli entrepreneurs and paramilitary advisers into its sphere of influence in the black homelands."[24] The Israeli government then denied landing rights in Israel to Ciskei—even though Israeli entrepreneurs had convinced Ciskei's rulers to build an airstrip.[25]

Ciskei is not the only bantustan in which Israel and Israelis played a role. In 1985, the president of the Development Bank of Southern Africa— former South African finance minister Owen Horwood—visited Israel and told reporters that he had come "to evaluate Israel's role in facilitating the economic development of the southern African independent states (i.e. bantustans)."[26]

Israel has invested $45 million in Bophuthatswana agriculture, and is training youth in that tribal reserve after the model of its own "Nahal" (a program combining military training with agricultural development).[27] Israel has also developed a television service for Bophuthatswana.[28] An Israeli, Ilan Sharon, served as a "special adviser" for the bantustan authorities. Israeli architects have signed contracts for major public edifices.

An Israeli company has also moved into Bophuthatswana to manufacture sports shoes.[29] When Bophuthatswana opened a Tel Aviv office, Israeli officials were embarrassed.[30]

Israeli security mercenaries also guard the casino tables at Sun City, the "interracial" gambling resort attached to the pseudo-state of Bophuthatswana.[31]

In early 1983 the entire "chamber of commerce" of another bantustan, Venda, visited Israel.[32]

The Israeli government is pulled two ways over the bantustans. On the one hand, there is a powerful "lobby" comprised of former officials and their associates who have investments in the pseudostates. To this must be added the obvious sympathy most Israeli officials must feel for the South African dilemma: no government in the world recognizes the benighted bantustans as the independent countries the racist regime has declared them to be. Israel has the same dilemma, in that not one government (including the U.S.) recognizes its claim to the occupied West Bank, to which it has given the spurious names Judea and Samaria, or, for that matter, (with the exception of Costa Rica and El Salvador) to East Jerusalem, which Israel captured from Jordan in 1967 and annexed as its capital in 1980.

In 1984 during ceremonies held in the Israeli-occupied West Bank town of Ariel, twinning that settlement with Ciskei's "capital" Bisho, Ciskei's Israeli representative Yosef Schneider said, "It is symbolic that no country in the world (except South Africa) recognizes Ciskei, just as there is no country in the world that recognizes the Jewish settlements in Judea and Samaria."[33]

On the other hand, the Israelis are well aware that recognition of the bantustans would be an unbearable offense to the many African nations, which they have courted assiduously during the 1980s. They tread a fine line.

In its decision in August 1985 to establish close working ties with Mangosuthu Gatsha Buthelezi, chief minister of the KwaZulu bantustan, a patchwork of settlements in Natal, Israel seems to have ignored his status as the leader of the entity designated by Pretoria as the "tribal homeland" of the Zulu people. In the West this is also frequently overlooked.

When such heads of state as Ronald Reagan and Margaret Thatcher receive the urbane, wealthy and ambitious Buthelezi—he is a frequent visitor to the West, where he argues against the imposition of sanctions and badmouths the mainstream liberation organizations—they present him as a "moderate" black leader, opposed to the "violent" methods of the outlawed African National Congress (ANC).

Chief Buthelezi speaks eloquently and sincerely against apartheid. According to a longtime friend of the descendant of Zulu royalty, Buthelezi (along with many of his Western promoters) sees himself as leader of a post-apartheid government. Presumably to further this goal, Buthelezi has developed ties across the entire spectrum of white South Africa. He has close links with the white opposition Progressive Federal Party, with which he tried in 1986 to design a multiracial government for Natal Province. Their plan called for a complex system of racial checks and balances, with overweighted guarantees for the white minority—Buthelezi has always promised to give whites a veto, as opposed to the ANC demand for universal suffrage—but the Pretoria government rejected it out of hand.[34]

Although his disagreements with the Botha government have been widely heralded—Buthelezi has refused "independent" status for his bantustan and has refused to participate in "negotiations" over South Africa's future with the Botha regime—he has certainly been the witting instrument of the minority government, both during his trips abroad and during the turmoil of the past several years.

In 1981, the *Economist* noted that

Shrewd white strategists know that, sooner rather than later, the Afrikaner government will have to negotiate with the only coherent tribe larger than its own, the 5 million-strong Zulu... The tolerance of the political activities of Chief Buthelezi has deepened into private contacts between his Inkatha movement and the secret Afrikaner Broederbond.[35]

The Broederbond has been the acknowledged manipulator of the ruling Nationalist Party. Inkatha is Buthelezi's political vehicle and means of patronage distribution. As polls taken over the years have shown, Buthelezi's following is trifling, even in Natal province, compared to that of the ANC, the United Democratic Front (UDF), or Nelson Mandela. Membership in Inkatha, which Buthelezi claims has one million members, is supposedly voluntary, but "strongly recommended for those living in Zululand."[36]

In 1983, the year the UDF was created, the murder of five University of Zululand students was traced to supporters of Buthelezi, in marked contrast to his "nonviolent" label.[37] Inkatha thugs, organized in bands called *impis* have frequently been reported to have attacked and often killed UDF protesters against the white government.

Visiting South Africa in June 1986, Denis Healey, the British Labor Party's spokesman on foreign affairs, refused to meet with Buthelezi. Instead Healey cited sworn affadavits from vigilante attack victims in the

Durban area and showed newsmen a photograph of a member of the Zulu royal family (to which Buthelezi is related) leading *impi* vigilantes.[38] Later that month, with the nation under a lock-down that forbade any gathering, Pretoria allowed Buthelezi to hold a rally in Soweto, the black township outside Johannesburg. Thousands of Buthelezi's followers, some armed with traditional Zulu weapons, were bused in from Natal for the event.[39]

In December 1986, Inkatha members were blamed for abducting and then shooting to death a shop steward of the Metal and Allied Workers along with another union member and the daughter of a third.[40]

During the period in which these incidents took place, no Israeli leader moved to dissociate the Tel Aviv government from the close ties it had established with Buthelezi in 1985. Indeed, Buthelezi's official visit to Israel began the day before a mob of armed *impis,* under the complacent eyes of government police, began an attack on their opponents in KwaMashu township in Natal. In the week of strife that followed, 66 blacks died, of which the police admitted to having shot 36. The others, "stabbed and mutilated," were assumed to be victims of Inkatha.[41]

That was in August 1985. Israel was at the time casting about for a way to deflect mounting criticism of its ties with South Africa. The criticism came from liberal Israelis who worried that Tel Aviv's South Africa policy was becoming noticably out of line with other Western states, and, more quietly, from the U.S., where South Africa's links with Israel were increasingly discussed on campuses and within anti-apartheid organizations, causing dismay on the liberal wing of organized Jewry. A poll of the Congressional Black Caucus underway at the time was revealing that those members of Congress and their constituents believed that Israel was a major backer of South Africa.[42] On August 5 Prime Minister Shimon Peres had been queried by Rep. Howard Wolpe (D-MI) and had assured him that Israel was against apartheid. In a separate meeting Yitzhak Shamir, then foreign minister, also assured Wolpe of Israel's "objections" to apartheid.[43]

It was never clear exactly who took the initiative for the Buthelezi visit—the South African embassy made phone calls to the Israeli media, asking them to go easy on the chief minister, and the *Jerusalem Post* responded with particular alacrity, in one case crediting him for preventing a revolutionary explosion in South Africa and asserting that "the wrong South African [then Bishop Desmond Tutu] won the Nobel Prize for peace"[44]—but for the Israeli government, his arrival was a godsend, even though he perpetuated his critical motif, calling for enforcement of the UN arms embargo against the white government.[45]

A wide range of the Israeli leadership held official meetings with the Zulu chief: Prime Minister Peres and Foreign Minister Shamir; former

Labor Foreign Minister Abba Eban hosted a luncheon in his honor; Foreign Ministry Director-General David Kimche, Israel's most persistent critic of links with South Africa, agreed to help him.[46] The Israeli government and the Histadrut labor federation eagerly responded to Buthelezi's requests for assistance for KwaZulu, regarding the connection as "a new door into African development."[47] Israel offered agricultural aid and a range of training including "leadership and trade union training in Israel, and assistance for women's organizations and cooperatives."[48] Buthelezi said he had been assured that Israeli specialists would soon visit his bantustan.[49] Yehuda Paz, director of Histadrut's Afro-Asian Institute, made plans with Buthelezi for the establishment of links between Histadrut and labor unions affiliated with Inkatha.[50]

The connection was somewhat odd, even for a labor aparatus like Histadrut, whose companies are active in South Africa, and whose unequal treatment of Arab workers is legendary. Buthelezi has made no bones about running his bantustan for the convenience of those who invest there. Although there is a KwaZulu labor bureau and a labor relations act, the average wage in 1985 was 100 rands a month (at the time less than $100), and workers who complain to the bureau find themselves blacklisted.[51] In March 1986 the KwaZulu "government" announced that the "United Union of Workers of South Africa," widely perceived as a challenge to the powerful Congress of South African Trade Unions, or COSATU, would be launched that May.[52]

Israel presented its new relationship with Buthelezi as a look toward the future and a connection with South Africa's black majority. "Buthelezi's visit will give a boost to Israelis who would like to criticize apartheid without breaking off political and diplomatic relations with Pretoria," announced the Israeli government radio. Buthelezi, explained the state radio, "is more than a puppet. While he accepted the chief ministership of the KwaZulu homeland, he refused to have it declared independent like Ciskei or Bophuthatswana."[53] Few critical observers find the distinction a meaningful one.

A Weapon Against the ANC

Nonetheless, Israel's newly forged links with Buthelezi provided its supporters in the U.S. with fresh ammunition to use against critics of Israel's relations with South Africa. *Near East Report,* the weekly publication of AIPAC, celebrated Buthelezi's visit as "the first by a leading

South African opposition leader," and quoted Buthelezi's parting words: he was "encouraged and inspired by the complete abhorrence which...the Israeli people have for apartheid, and the commitment of the Israeli people to its destruction."[54] For AIPAC, which often sets the pace for other U.S. Jewish organizations, the quote was welcome relief from the old chestnut from Andrew Young, which has been used unremittingly for years:

> It is unfair to link Israel to South Africa. If there is a link, you must compare Britain, Germany, Japan, and the United States. All of them have links with South Africa. Israel becomes a too easy scapegoat for other problems we have."[55]

Unlike Young, who left the Carter Administration (only several weeks before Israel and South Africa detonated a nuclear weapon) with the Israeli government in hot pursuit after he had met with the PLO's representative to the United Nations,[56] Buthelezi continued to provide valuable copy. "Israel is indeed a land of miracles," he told a Jewish Telegraphic Agency (JTA) reporter, who tagged the KwaZulu leader as a possible first black president of South Africa.[57]

The interview Buthelezi gave JTA served to justify Israel's linkage with South Africa, and, as it consisted mostly of a hot diatribe against his sworn rival, the ANC, it delivered the message of the white government in Pretoria to the U.S. Jewish community on the respectable pages of such publications as the Washington DC *Jewish Week*.

"I would say that Libya's Col. Muammar Qaddafi is today part of the ANC," offered the Zulu chief, *a propos* of nothing in particular.

"The ANC describes itself as anti-Zionist, not anti-Semitic, like many African groups. But anti-Zionism and anti-Semitism are one and the same thing, I have always found," propounded Buthelezi. In a lengthy aside, interviewer Levine informs his American readers that

> Buthelezi's friendship for Israel is music to the ears of the many South African Jewish leaders, who have grown increasingly concerned over the prospects of an ultimate ANC victory and the establishment of a pro-Soviet regime.[58]

The Washington *Jewish Week* published the Buthelezi interview as part of a front page spread which delivered a clear message—straight from Israel: "Israeli officials are reluctant to criticize the ANC publicly for fear of appearing pro-apartheid. Privately, however, they freely share their growing concern over the prospect of an ANC takeover." The spread containing the Buthelezi interview appeared at the same time a wider effort was set in motion by the right wing of organized Jewry to defame the ANC.

In May 1986 the Anti-Defamation League of B'nai B'rith (ADL) had circulated its newsletter to members of Congress with a front page headline promising "A Closer Look" at the ANC. The piece was written in old-time McCarthyist style, as if for an audience not aware that most industrial democracies have communist parties which contest and win elections.

Although the ADL built its reputation on original research on racist hate groups, the article it sent to Congress was simply a collection of clippings on the ANC and "evidence" from testimony given at 1982 hearings conducted by far-right Sen. Jeremiah Denton (R-AL), arranged to "prove" that "the ANC is oriented toward the Soviet Union and its East Bloc allies, who have furnished it with arms, funding, military training and other logistic support."[59]

The ADL did not trouble to set forth the context of what it described as the 30-year alliance between the ANC and the South African Communist Party, for years the only multiracial anti-apartheid organizations in South Africa. Besides, the article was in error about the length of the association. "It's been 65 years, not 30," noted Lifford Cengue, a West Coast representative of the ANC, explaining that the alliance between the two organizations goes back to 1921, the year the SACP was founded, and has been public knowledge since that time. Cengue pointed out that the ANC was founded in 1912, "before the October Revolution."

The ADL article also delved into the ties between the ANC and the PLO, an organization with few defenders in Congress.

> As a revolutionary national liberation movement oriented toward Moscow, the ANC has long echoed Soviet attempts to undermine the legitimacy of Israel. Moreover, the ANC is a strident supporter of the Palestine Liberation Organization.

It noted that some ANC members "trained in the USSR with PLO cadres" and refers to statements critical of Israeli policy made during the 1970s by Oliver Tambo.[60] As have many governments and international organizations, the ANC has long been critical of Israel's treatment of the Palestinians under occupation; its criticism has been informed by Israel's close ties with South Africa. The ADL's assault on the ANC came at a time when Congressmembers of both parties were calling for the release of imprisoned ANC leader Nelson Mandela, and the State Department was moving toward contacts with the ANC.[61]

The ADL article had great value for friends of South Africa, as well as apologists for Israel's ties to the apartheid regime. As Smith Hempstone commented approvingly in the *Washington Times*, which is generally acknowledged to support the white minority government:

None of this [the ADL's "findings"] is particularly original stuff. The same points have been made many times by this columnist. But when B'nai B'rith gets into the game, congressmen who know on which side their political bagels are buttered are likely to sit up and take notice.[62]

In the same issue of Washington's *Jewish Week* that carried the interview with Buthelezi was a second piece of propaganda authored by Charley Levine, this one titled to play on a prevalent theme of the times: "Arab Terrorists Aid South African Groups." And it was a far more sophisticated job than the ADL's smear job, admitting, for instance, that Sweden contributed more to the ANC than the Soviet Union. Along with some of the same data employed by the ADL, Levine concocted his piece on the seemingly authoritative statements of unnamed "Israeli and South African intelligence sources." (Perhaps they were the source for a rather singular item included by Levine about black South African Muslims forming Libyan "hit teams.")

Levine wrote of instances when he says the PLO gave military training to the ANC—the one about the training of parachutists is particularly interesting given that the USSR has not provided the ANC with the kind of aeronautical assistance Israel has given South Africa—and confided that "Israeli experts on international terrorism" have concluded that the ANC's tactics are similar to those of the PLO.[63]

These journalistic efforts were made just as anti-apartheid activists were intensifying their lobbying of Congress for sanctions against South Africa.

Soon after Buthelezi's departure, Israel would host another group of South African blacks—and again use the opportunity to demonstrate its "anti-apartheid" credentials, without, of course, jarring its vital links to white Pretoria.

Political and Cultural Ties ....

Friends Hunt "Authentic" Blacks for Israel

In Los Angeles in 1984, a gathering at the home of Tom Hayden, former Chicago Seven radical, currently a member of the California State Assembly, and his wife, actress Jane Fonda, left a bitter taste. Guest of honor Bishop Desmond Tutu had lambasted Israel that night for its support of South Africa and Jewish guests took issue with his remarks.

Afterwards, a "deeply disturbed" Tom Hayden consulted Prof. Steven Spiegel, a Middle East specialist at UCLA about a remedy for "an ever deepening antagonism of South African blacks towards Israel."

Four years earlier Speigel had started a think tank, the Center for Foreign Policy Options (CFPO),[1] but in 1986 it was virtually unknown to the foreign affairs community in Los Angeles.[2] After talking to Hayden, Spiegel went to Israel, spoke with a variety of leaders, and developed a plan. He selected Shimshon Zelniker, a professor at Beit Berl, the Labor Party's college, to be "field director."

After strenuous attempts, Tom Hayden persuaded then-Bishop Tutu to meet with Zelniker, whose way the CFPO then paid to South Africa. There, in June 1985, Zelniker met with Tutu and a number of his associates. They were harshly critical of Israel.[3] The Nobel laureate who would later be appointed Archbishop of Cape Town accused the Israelis of having a "monopoly on the Holocaust"[4]—that is, ignoring or downplaying the sufferings of other peoples. Ultimately Zelniker was able to sell the group on CFPO's idea of bringing groups of black South Africans to Israel for what might loosely be called leadership training. Bishop Tutu refused to become involved.[5]

In January Shimshon Zelniker went back to South Africa to select trainees. It proved difficult to recruit black leaders whose authenticity was widely recognized in their communities. Not one of the nine men and eleven women Zelniker signed up would admit to membership with the—legal and mainstream—United Democratic Front. Yehuda Paz, Director of the Histadrut's Afro-Asian Institute which ran the program, called them "leaders in the struggle against apartheid."[6] Paz and Zelniker, it should be noted, had also met with Chief Buthelezi when he was in Israel.

In April 1986, the trainees arrived in Israel to take part in a workshop, which, given by Histadrut, was entitled "The Role of People's Organizations in Community Building and National Development." According to Israeli officials it was designed to provide the students with skills they would need in the event of a transition to black rule in South Africa. Oblivious—or antagonistic—to the rapidly developing South African trade union movement, the training program Histadrut devised for the visitors "focus[ed] on unionizing the country's 12 million black laborers."[7]

Meanwhile, Tom Hayden and CFPO's fundraiser had been promoting the project in Israel.[8] They gained the endorsement of the Israeli government[9] and the Israeli foreign ministry defrayed part of the expenses of one of Shimshon Zelniker's trips to South Africa.[10] CFPO also brought Zelniker to the U.S. to describe his work to Jewish organizations.[11]

While the CPFO planned to spend $1 million over a period of two years on the transportation, living expenses and training programs in Israel for 6 to 12 additional groups of South African trainees, many questions remain unanswered about the project's relationship to the South African government—especially since part of its function appears to be to propagandize for South Africa in the U.S.

In addition to Prof. Spiegel, CFPO's members include Edward Sanders, an adviser on Middle East and Jewish affairs to President Carter, Osias S. Goren (CFPO's chairman and chief fundraiser), who headed Jewish efforts for President Reagan's 1980 and 1984 campaigns, and Maxwell F. Greenberg, honorary chairman of the ADL, which has so reviled the ANC.[12]

Tom Hayden's role is also puzzling. Hayden, whose first foray into California electoral politics was a losing primary race against Sen. John Tunney (ironically, a leading foe of South Africa, whose defeat in the general election was partly attributed to South African contributions to his Republican opponent S.I. Hayakawa), revealed in 1986 that during his anti-war activities in the 1960s, he had cooperated with U.S. intelligence agents and had had intensive talks with CIA agents.[13]

During his three terms in the California state legislature, Hayden has gradually eased away from his left-liberal identification. In 1986, he dissolved his Campaign for Economic Democracy (funded by the profits from Fonda's fitness video royalties, it had, charged many critics, become simply an electoral vehicle for "Tom") and set up a new personal organization called Campaign California.

Well ahead of his metamorphosis, Hayden had established himself as a leading promoter of Israel. During the 1982 invasion of Lebanon, he and his wife visited Israeli troops on the front lines. This maneuver, during Hayden's first assembly campaign, was intended to appeal to the great numbers of Jews in his district.[14]

Hayden's involvement with the recruitment of black South African trainees for Israel is not, however, the kind of activity designed for mass voter appeal. It seems more in the nature of a quiet favor.

There is no question that the Israeli government would be pleased with CFPO's project; it was a propaganda success, with all the major North American newspapers covering it extensively and favorably. Through their Histadrut instructors, Israel could establish and maintain contact with the trainees—useful in the event that the minority government is over-thrown, and also useful for sharing intelligence with the minority government.

Was Pretoria well served by the Histadrut endeavor? That the white regime did not lift the passports of the attendees prior to their departure[15] suggests that the project enjoys at least benign indifference, if not Pretoria's actual support.

It was obvious that Israel had to tread carefully. During the mid-June 1986 state of emergency in South Africa, when Israel was casting about for ways to portray itself as opposed to apartheid, some of the Israelis involved with the project:

> were wary of recommending that Israel adopt any "crisis approach" or abrupt break with Pretoria; the white govern-ment's retaliation might mean an end to the new ties with Black organizations before they were properly off the ground.[16]

As the interactions with Buthelezi and the "leaders in the struggle against apartheid" who came to Israel for training indicate, the exact nature of the political linkage between Israel and South Africa, the ties that bind over and above the military and economic *quid pro quos,* is concealed, left to be deduced by the observer. That those ties are close and rich can be gauged by the sports, cultural and diplomatic exchanges countenanced by Israel.

Breaking the Sports and Cultural Blockade

Israel has made a practice of ignoring international boycotts against South Africa. Since the late 1960s a steady stream of athletes and performers have gone from Israel to South Africa. According to a report issued by the United Nations Special Committee Against Apartheid in 1979, the continuing sports contacts had "strong encouragement by the Government of Israel."[17] In fact, this report chronicled a revealing episode of Israeli policymaking concerning sports and apartheid.

On January 21, 1979, amidst rumors that the Soviet Union might try to block Israel's participation in the 1980 Moscow Summer Olympics, the presidium of the Israeli Olympics Committee voted unanimously to cut off sports exchanges with South Africa "at least until after the Olympics." The committee told the Israeli gymnastics team to cancel an upcoming visit.

Two days later at a plenary session—with the director of the government's sports authority in attendance—that decision was overturned and it was further decided that any Israeli sports boycott of South Africa would be limited to compliance with the rules of international sports organizations,[18] which have always lagged behind the efforts to isolate South Africa undertaken by many athletes and anti-apartheid organizations. Several days later a representative of the Foreign Ministry told the Knesset that the decision to boycott had hurt Israel's relations with South Africa.[19]

Disagreement on policy on sports exchanges with South Africa has continued to the present, with Israel displaying a considerable degree of ambivalence—or, alternatively, making a show of opposition to sports contacts for the benefit of its anti-apartheid supporters.

On the one hand, in its own struggle to gain access to international sports, Israel has made a great effort to conceal its sports exchanges with the apartheid regime. Israel itself has been barred from participation in, among others, the European soccer confederation and the Olympic Council of Asia, an exclusion made all the more bitter by the admission to that body of the Palestine Olympic Committee.[20]

On the other hand, Israel must apparently continue to cater to South Africa. In one 1985 instance, the Maccabiah Games (the quadrennial "Jewish Olympics," which brings national Jewish teams to Israel), these two exigencies clashed, then merged in a clever piece of duplicity. South African teams had been among the largest contingents in the 1973, 1977 and 1981 Maccabiah Games.

In 1985, however, Canada and some other countries objected to participating along with a South African team. After the South African Zionist Federation and the director of the Israeli Maccabiah Committee mounted a vigorous protest of this instance of mixing politics and sports,[21] the South Africans abruptly withdrew "so as to avoid serious problems for athletes from a number of participating countries." In announcing the South Africans' withdrawal, the Israeli Maccabiah director hinted that something would "happen" so that they could attend the games after all.[22] That something transpired in the form of 200 "potential immigrant" visas issued by the Israeli consul in Pretoria to the South African athletes. On the strength of these documents, usually issued to people who want to try out life in Israel, the quasi-governmental Jewish Agency registered the South Africans as "temporary residents."[23] They were then, with 20 legitimate immigrants, formed as a special team of newcomers to Israel.

It was not until the games were almost at an end that one of the phony immigrants blurted out the truth. By the time the ruse had hit the press, the games were over. Only later did it become known that the organizers of the games had plotted the whole subterfuge during a meeting in 1984.[24]

Yet another sports encounter had all the earmarks of a well-rehearsed "good cop/bad cop" routine. In November 1986, Israel's top three male tennis stars—its national Davis Cup team—went to compete in the South African Open. It was their second trip there in 1986, and their names had been on international boycott lists long before that.[25] One of the three, the young and rising Amos Mansdorf, won the tournament.[26]

Almost immediately the Foreign Ministry sent a "reprimand" to the Israel Tennis Authority.[27] The head of that body retorted that the International Tennis Federation's rules concerning South Africa only apply to to teams, not individuals, and that the Israeli players had gone as individuals.

The ministry hit back with phone calls from the political director general, reminding the heads of sports organizations about Israel's "opposition to 'all participation' by Israelis in South Africa."[28] and suggested that private trips in the future should be "coordinated" with the foreign ministry. In an editorial called "The hypocrisy syndrome" the *Jerusalem Post* wondered why the foreign ministry had professed surprise to discover the tennis players had been to South Africa.

> The true surprise is to learn that it is now national policy to keep contracts with South Africa down to a minimum.

If the government, of which the foreign ministry and its officials are presumably a part, wants to shift Israel's policy on South Africa, let it say so. If not, then the foreign ministry has ample other targets in that increasingly queer contrivance called Israel's foreign policy, on which to direct its self-righteousness.[29]

It is more likely that, with all the bases covered—to metaphorically mix sports—there was satisfaction all around.

Meanwhile, the flow of Israeli entertainers to South Africa has continued unabated, suggesting that Israel really *can't* say no. A list of 24 of these cultural emissaries covering the period between August 1981 and April 1985 tops by one a similar list of performers from West Germany,[30] one of South Africa's major trading partners and a nation with a population of 61 million, compared to Israel's 4 million.

After 1984, when the international cultural boycott against South Africa became highly effective, Israel continued to supply diversions to the apartheid state. In April 1985 Yardene Arazi, a popular Israeli singer, went to South Africa to organize a celebration of Israel's independence day.[31]

Most tellingly, in July 1986—one month after South Africa had clamped down a brutal state of emergency—Israeli Foreign Minister and Alternate Prime Minister Yitzhak Shamir cleared the Israel Chamber Orchestra for a tour of South Africa. Shamir also recommended that two South African choirs be allowed take part in a song festival in Israel. One of the South African choirs was a white boys' ensemble; the other was a black group from Bophuthatswana. The festival organizers had urged the decision on the government in advance of the South Africans' request to come to Israel. According to the festival manager, the decision was based on a variation of the old South African standby: "no room to mix music and politics."[32]

The following month South Africans also participated in a puppet festival in Jerusalem.[33]

More intimate than players on the field or stars on stage, Israeli-South African relations also proceed along that corridor established by governments for people-to-people contacts by their citizens. In late 1984, a Ben Gurion University organization called the Associates of South Africa drew attention for its active promotion of cultural and scientific exchanges.[34]

Haifa and Cape Town are sister cities, and there are frequent exchanges of various sorts between the two cities and their universities.[35]

Tourism

Israeli tourism in South Africa has defied international trends, growing 50 percent between 1981 and the end of 1985,[36] and rising by 12.5 percent during the first six months of 1985 alone.[37] This was undoubtedly providential, as tourism to South Africa had just about dried up, with 1985 hotel occupancy reaching an eleven-year low.[38] South Africa was the first government to establish a tourism office in Israel, but it is quite likely that the tone established by the government in Tel Aviv is equally responsible for the high rate of Israeli travel to the apartheid state. (Pretoria is fond of nabbing tourists for interviews on its external radio service; all these visitors swear that they've had a fine time and weren't even aware that there was anything unpleasant going on.)

The 1986 tourism event of the year had to have been "Malchi's dream holiday on board the luxurious cruise ship Achille Lauro to South Africa," which sailed November 26 from the Israeli port of Ashdod. A year earlier the Italian liner had been hijacked on the way to Ashdod, an event resulting in the murder of a disabled American, Leon Klinghoffer; the U.S. hijacking of the plane on which the ship's hijackers were traveling to their negotiated freedom; and the fall of the government of Italy, where the plane was forced down. (Another casualty of that week was Alex Odeh, Southern Regional Director of the American-Arab Anti-Discrimination Committee, killed by a bomb the morning after a television appearance during which he had stressed the desire for peace of PLO Chairman Yasir Arafat.) Malchi Shipping Tours and Travel Ltd. of Haifa promised stops in the Seychelles and Durban and a tour through Kruger Park, Cape Town, Johannesburg and Sun City, the notorious entertainment complex in the bantustan called Bophuthatwana. "World known Italian cuisine," enticed Malchi's advertisement, "more surprises every day!" The advertisement bore the logos of SATOUR, and SAA, the South African government's tourism agency and its airline.[39]

There was also a 30 percent increase of South Africans traveling to Israel between July and September 1986. In October 1986 (when detentions under the state of emergency were being estimated in the thousands), the Director-General of Israel's Ministry of Tourism made a secret trip to South Africa. Rafi Farber "met important South African travel agents and discussed with them the possibility of increasing bilateral tourism through a public relations and marketing campaign." Farber also wanted South Africa to increase its investment in Israel's tourist sector.[40]

It is possible that a series of articles, "South Africa Without Prejudice," extolling South Africa—with all the usual phrases about the rapid pace of "reform" underway in South Africa and the "complexities" of the situation there—that appaeared in the *Jerusalem Post's* weekend magazine in November and early December 1986 were one result of those talks.[41]

How exactly do the citizens in question regard their governments' moves to bring them together? Strongly enough—on both sides—to come out and demonstrate. The Mapam Party has picketed a performance by visiting South African entertainers.[42]

Israeli supporters of South Africa—among them many immigrants from the Soviet Union—have also come out to wave their banners proclaiming that "South Africa Has Been Israel's Ally."[43] In late 1985 after Israeli leftists had mounted several attention-getting demonstrations protesting the assignment of a new ambassador to South Africa,[44] 60 supporters of the white government met in the presence of the South African ambassador to Israel and formed an Israeli-South African Friendship League.[45]

What exactly does Israel get out of its alliance with South Africa that it is willing to spit in the face of the very international community it is trying to beguile? This question is likely to provoke the snap response that Israel and South Africa have so much in common, from their militarism to their racism to their intransigence and thus their consequent isolation from the main current of the human family. Or, it might be offered, Israel is eager to have its cake and eat it too—a feat which it can accomplish as long as its appetite and its tenacity do not impede its relations with its main protector, the United States.

Something else should be considered, however: blackmail. Several observers believe that it would more damaging for Tel Aviv to attempt to extricate itself from its involvement than to continue pandering to South Africa. "They say to Israel 'Look, if you don't continue with this relationship on every level, we're going to blow the guff on you,'" Michael Wade, a professor of African Studies at Hebrew University in Jerusalem said to National Public Radio. Himself of South African birth, Wade said the South Africans were quite capable of embarassing Israel before the world by revealing details of the relationship.[46] Others believe that South Africa might be able to make trouble for Israel with Washington by revealing intelligence or technology thefts. Another possibility is that Israel's involvement in Muldergate went much father than has yet been revealed and includes various manipulations of the U.S. media and the electoral process.

A hint of such a South African hold on Israel came in October 1984 when an Israeli paper, *Ma'ariv*, noted that Pretoria had requested the Israeli Foreign Ministry to "provide the exact wording" of a statement about apartheid Prime Minister Peres had made during a visit to the U.S. Press accounts of the remarks credited Peres with calling apartheid "a stupid system."[47]

The Link Feeds on U.S. Tolerance

There was really no "South Africa problem" for Israel as long as Washington was willing to declare in the face of damning evidence that the white regime was reforming itself, just as there was absolutely no problem for Israel as long as an avowedly anti-apartheid Congress continued simply to mumble its self-imposed collective ignorance of Israel's dealings with the apartheid government, and was willing to accept without challenge the Carter Administration's short-circuited investigation of the 1979 Israeli-South African nuclear weapons test.

In late 1986, however, its indissoluble bonds with Pretoria began to give Israel moments of profound discomfort. Ronald Reagan's supportive policy of "constructive engagement" was wearing thin, as South Africa declared its cataclysmic June state of emergency and jailed thousands of its critics, while escalating its attacks on neighboring countries. Before the year was over, Congress, motivated by an almost unanimous citizenry, would pass its first real anti-apartheid legislation—and then pass it again over the President's veto.

A little noticed Section 508 of the Comprehensive Anti-Apartheid Act of 1986 contained language that demanded a White House report to the House and Senate within 180 days of the legislation's passage "containing a detailed assessment of the economic and other relationships of other industrialized democracies with South Africa."

This amendment—authored by retiring Republican Senate Foreign Relations Committee member Charles McC. Mathias—was "clearly a threat to Israel," according to the *Jerusalem Post*,[48] raising the possibility of a cutoff of Israel's U.S. military aid.[49] It came on the heels of another jolt, a decision by the European Community (EC) to impose an array of limited sanctions on South Africa.

Previously, Israel had temporized on the possibility of sanctions, but the government had frequently alluded to Israel's conformity to the (dastardly) positions of the Western powers: "keeping in line with what the

Western countries are doing, no more and no less," was how a senior Israeli diplomat phrased it in July 1986.[50] The West African nation of Cameroon had just been persuaded to establish formal diplomacy with Tel Aviv, and Israel, making urgent efforts to engineer a domino effect, was working hard to convince African countries of the sincerity of its opposition to apartheid.[51]

Taking all these factors into account, it apparently became expedient to order a "reassessment" of Israel's South Africa policy. In late August "a special internal discussion" on Israeli ties to South Africa was convened by the Director-General of the Foreign Ministry David Kimche. Kimche, who had always been a public critic of ostentatious contacts with South Africa and the bantustans, warned that Israel must prepare for the possibility that the West would impose stringent sanctions on South Africa.[52] Out of these discussions came a reaffirmation of the policy of "stay[ing] in line with the Western democracies." A large loophole was left, however, because of Israel's "special" concern for the South African Jewish community.[53]

This concern has frequently been debunked as "patent nonsense" and "inexcusably shortsighted"[54]—during one heated round of discussion on the validity of using South African Jews as an excuse, a former director of Israel's foreign ministry noted that the South African Jewish community itself was "compromised...by passive collaboration with the evil of apartheid"[55]—but it remains Israel's second line of defense after its ritual denunciations of apartheid.

Another Israeli concern about sanctions is that once a precedent is established, Israel will also be subject to an international attempt at behavior modification. "We have no reason to highlight our relations with South Africa, but we have no wish to join sanctions either, the likes of which have often been employed against Israel," said Prime Minister Shamir.[56]

Rita E. Hauser, an influential figure in the U.S. Jewish community, embedded the identical point in a more sophisticated rationale for a hands-off policy toward Israel and South Africa:

> The sense of embattlement and isolation felt by these two Western-oriented nations comes in no small part from the policies of the Western Alliance. The United States and its NATO allies, in recent years, have not been able to separate clearly the pressures put upon them by black Africa and the Arab states with respect to the internal policies of South Africa and Israel from the external, geopolitical situation now operative in the Middle East and southern Africa. Even if they are correct in the conviction that Israel must yield control over the West

- Bank to some form of Palestinian nationalism and that South Africa must devise a method of sharing power with the blacks, there is no justification for policies which isolate and weaken these two countries to the detriment of vital Western interests.[57]

After a time that reassessment was forgotten, only to emerge again with a spurious offer to phase out military contracts with South Africa over the coming years[58] several weeks before the April 1 date set for the submission of the report stipulated by the 1986 anti-apartheid act. The U.S. followed the EC with the imposition of even stiffer sanctions and the world learned that Israel had supplied South Africa with refueling aircraft.

Some day, maybe not until the next century, someone will talk about what it was that kept Israel dancing to the apartheid government's tune. At present it is very clear that Israel will not have to exert itself very hard to convince Congress that it has stopped dealing with Pretoria (a poignant task, since Israel has never officially admitted its military and economic sanctions busting). Should the moment come, Israel will have to employ all its wiles to buttress what will predictably be Congress' easy credulity against an outcry from activists.

Part II ....
Israel and Central America

El Salvador ....

Introduction: Central America

A world away from South Africa, Israel's activities in Central America come more clearly under the aegis of the U.S., the seigneurial power in the region, which sets up dictators in some nations and targets the governments of others for destruction—and then, under pressure by Congress and the U.S. public, sometimes abandons its allies. Yet, even when Israel picks up the slack for Washington, its role in Central America is seldom if ever that of an out-and-out proxy or surrogate.

In the 1970s, Israel was attracted to the troubled region by the opportunity to sell weapons and military advice, and perhaps to pick up some diplomatic chits. At the present, however, aside from supplying arms and training to the contra mercenary forces the Reagan Administration has flung against Nicaragua, the imposition of "pacification" regimes—some of this work is financed with U.S. funds—on the rural populations of El Salvador and Guatemala appears to be replacing arms sales as Israel's most significant function in the region.

Rural "pacification," as it was used in Vietnam and as it is now being applied in Central America, is an attempt to suppress forever a people's ability to organize against an oppressive order. Israel's involvement with pacification is carried out in the guise of the innovative technical assistance programs it brought to African, Asian, and Latin American countries in the 1960s. Even those U.S. officials opposed in principle to intervention in Central America don't seem to care about it.

95

In fact, in 1985 and 1986 one prominent Democratic liberal actually helped Israel set up some agricultural projects right on the perimeter of the war against Nicaragua, which, after four years of Reaganite subversion, had spread out over a great part of Honduras and Costa Rica.

The Democrat was Howard Berman of Los Angeles, a congressman with a sterling record of votes against aid to the contras and aid to the U.S.-backed government in El Salvador. In 1984, Berman drafted legislation mandating the United States-Israel Cooperative Development Research, or CDR, a made-for-Israel program whose stated purpose was "to help meet a growing demand for Israel's unique technical assistance," and to "build ties between Israel and developing countries."[1]

In testimony given during a hearing on Berman's legislation, which sought $20 million of U.S. Agency for International Development (AID) funds, it was pointed out that such a project would help "strengthen Israel's relations with the Third World."[2] Ultimately CDR was funded at $2 million for 1985. Congress gave it $5 million for fiscal 1986.

In late 1985, the Jewish Telegraphic Agency (JTA) wrote a glowing article about Israel's CDR activities, mentioning cashews being improved in Thailand, forest fungi research in Ghana, and similar projects in Portugal, the Philippines, and Malawi. The article mentioned that funding for each project was limited to $150,000.[3]

Not mentioned by the JTA, and, while not classified, informally shielded from public view, were three other Israeli "research" projects—in Honduras, Costa Rica, and El Salvador— all funded under CDR by U.S. AID, at a total of $850,000.

At $393,000 the Costa Rican project was more than double the $150,000 cap. Papers relating to the project described it as a two year assignment for two Israeli technicians to help a newly-established private growers association to find the most suitable export crops for irrigated growing (an Israeli specialty). The site of this scientific activity was Guanacaste, at the time an area of heavy contra activity near the border with Nicaragua. Another part of the project was to study tomato-growing techniques in other Central American countries.

In Honduras $360,000 was budgeted for two Israeli irrigation experts to set up demonstration sprinkler and drip irrigation system in Choluteca, a city close to the border with Nicaragua, in an area of significant contra activity.

A more modest program in El Salvador was focused on labor intensive export fruit and vegetable production. (Labor intensive nontraditional export produce is a key element of Israeli "pacification" doctrine in Central

America.) This project was to be coordinated through FUSADES, which a Central America specialist identified as a Salvadoran "think tank."

In all three projects, the Israeli experts were government employees, assigned by Mashav, the Israeli equivalent of U.S. AID. Certainly the three projects were ideal opportunities for Israeli civil servants to work among the local population, and should Washington and Tel Aviv agree, to gather intelligence that might be inaccessible to an identifiable "gringo." In the Honduran project, the local government was to provide the Israeli experts with, among other services, contact with farmers and laborers.[4]

In their time frame of the heyday of the activity that became known as the Iran-contra scandal (in which Israel was a major player) and "low intensity conflict"[5] and in terms of the sordid history of Israel's involvement in Central America, the three CDR projects appear relatively innocuous. It is Rep. Berman's role that is surprising—or maybe just instructive.

When questioned in May 1986, Berman's office acknowledged a continuing connection with CDR. When asked whether the Congressman would endorse his legislation funding projects in Central America, Lise Hartman, Berman's legislative assistant for foreign policy, said the question was an "interesting" one to have raised.

However, said Hartman, it was raised at "a bad time" and no one in the office "not even the person working on it, would have details" on the program for the next few weeks. At that time, she continued, Rep. Berman would begin meetings with representatives from AID and from the Israeli government to determine the details of the program for fiscal 1987. All three parties, Hartman said, would have a say in setting the direction of CDR.[6]

This story raises some profound questions for those constitutents who endorsed Berman, voted for him, perhaps even campaigned to elect him, and who also support Salvadorans and Guatemalans struggling for liberation and the sovereignty of the Nicaraguan government. Does Rep. Berman—and dozens of others like him—think he has done right by his anti-intervention constituents by voting as they wish a few times and then attempting to please other sectors with a claim on his allegiance, letting the contradictions fall where they may?

What Congressperson—for that matter, what movement leader—has ever said, above a mumble or a whisper, that passing U.S. victims on to Washington's close ally Israel for further target practice was morally and politically unacceptable? There have been vast stretches of silent space in the Central America policy of the United States; the Carter Administration's human rights policy of aid cutoffs to especially gory U.S. clients opened further tracts. Israel has often filled these gaps, serving its own interests and, on occasion, the interests of far right sectors of the U.S. establishment.

El Salvador

From its earliest attempts to establish itself as an arms exporter, Israel had enjoyed the patronage of the military of El Salvador, which ruled that small, densely-populated country on the Pacific side of the Central American isthmus on behalf of a powerful plantation oligarchy.

In 1973 Israel took orders from El Salvador for 18 Dassault Ouragan jet fighter aircraft. Israel had obtained these planes from France for its own use. Refurbished and delivered to El Salvador in 1975, they were the first jet fighters in Central America, representing a significant jump in the level of military sophistication in a region where war had flared between Honduras and El Salvador in 1969.

Other aircraft ordered from Israel by El Salvador in 1973 included six French-made Fouga Magister trainers and 25 Arava short-take-off-and-landing aircraft. The Arava is produced by Israeli Aircraft Industries (IAI) and is advertised for a variety of uses—from hauling cargo, to medical evacuation, to transporting troops in counterinsurgency warfare. The Salvadorans also bought a quantity of small arms, ammunition and rocket launchers.[7]

Military links with El Salvador actually began around 1972, when the Israeli Defense Ministry carried out a youth movement development program there.[8] Alongside their arms sales, the Israelis also sent advisers to El Salvador. Former Salvadoran Army Col. and Undersecretary of the Interior Rene Francisco Guerra y Guerra recalled that during the 1970s ANSESAL, the Salvadoran secret police, had security advisers from Israel. According to Guerra, as a low-ranking ANSESAL officer, Roberto D'Aubuisson, who would later rise to prominence as leader of a far-right faction linked to death squads, was a student of the Israeli instructors.[9]

At least one Salvadoran officer, Col. Sigifredo Ochoa was taught by Israeli trainers in El Salvador and also went to Israel for training in the mid-1970s. Ochoa, who was credited with a massacre of civilians in 1981[10] made no secret of his preference for his Israeli mentors over the U.S. advisers who came to El Salvador after 1981. The Americans, he noted scornfully, "lost the war in Vietnam." During the Israeli siege of Beirut in 1982, Ochoa proffered an "Israeli solution" for Central America: a combined assault by El Salvador, Honduras, Guatemala and the anti-Nicaragua contras against Nicaragua.[11]

When the Carter Administration took office in 1977 it wasted little time putting into practice a principle enunciated during the presidential campaign and by Congress in 1976: U.S. aid would be cut off to recipients who were gross and persistent abusers of human rights.[12] The idea was to encourage dictatorial regimes to modify their behavior and reinstate themselves in Washington's good graces.

It was a fairly reasonable assumption; after all, many of these tyrants had been through U.S. military programs[13] and had adopted the anti-communist line that a succession of U.S. governments had encouraged. Washington had sired both the Nicaraguan and Guatemalan regimes, and was not without profound influence in El Salvador.[14]

In the 1960s, the U.S. had presided over the foundation of CONDECA, a regional military council intended "to coordinate and centralize military command of the region under U.S. military supervision."[15] In El Salvador, the Kennedy Administration set in motion a series of meetings among Central American leaders that led to the establishment of the feared ANSESAL secret police and its "parallel domestic security agencies in Guatemala, Nicaragua, Panama, Honduras, and Costa Rica." Years later the CIA connections of ANSESAL would come to light in close connection with the death squads which have terrorized El Salvador since the 1970s.[16] Also in the 1960's AIFLD, (the American Institute for Free Labor Development, the AFL-CIO's foreign operation dedicated to foiling the formation of left wing unions) tried to organize a "tame" network of rural cooperatives in El Salvador. According to one report the project was budgeted at $1.6 million and had the assistance of the Israeli Histadrut labor federation.[17]

Even the prideful way that El Salvador and Guatemala responded when their aid was terminated—both preempted the U.S. move by cutting military ties with the U.S.[18]—might have been expected to blow over. That was without reckoning on Israel, which was quick to fill the gap. Indeed, one analyst believes the "surprisingly defiant position" of the Central American clients was based on their advance knowledge that they could maintain their military capacity by dealing with Israel.[19]

El Salvador simply began to buy its weapons from Israel. Between the 1977 U.S. cutoff and the resumption of U.S. aid in 1981, El Salvador obtained over 80 percent of its weapons from Israel. The balance came from France and Brazil.[20] The earlier aircraft orders still in the pipeline were delivered and small arms and ammunition from Israel undercut the intent of the Carter policy.[21] By 1979 came the first report that Israeli advisers had been giving the Salvadoran military counterinsurgency training both in Israel and El Salvador.[22]

During this period as well, Israeli technicians began installing a computer system able to monitor utilities usage, thus giving the military the ability to pinpoint houses where the telephone is heavily used, presumably signifying that political organizing is going on. (A similar system provided by Israel to Guatemala does the same with water and electricity use; see below.) According to former Col. Guerra, the Israelis began work on the system in 1978. As an electronic engineer familiar with El Salvador's telecommunications installations, he did not believe that another company would be brought in to finish the work, despite two changes of government and the reentry of the U.S., following the installation of the Reagan Administration.[23]

It is quite certain that installation was completed. A CIA source described a telephone-monitoring computer system to a journalist in El Salvador, and Arnaldo Ramos of the FDR (the Democratic Revolutionary Front, the political grouping fighting against the U.S.-backed government) has spoken of another use to which the Salvadoran regime puts the computer equipment:

> They periodically block several downtown areas and take the ID's of people, just to check who they are. If they find the person happens to be downtown in an area where he's not supposed to be too often during the week, that right away makes him a suspect.[24]

Once the new human rights policy was implemented, little attention was paid in the U.S. to what was going on in El Salvador. The Carter policy had the virtue of slackening the long embrace between Washington and Central American dictatorships; it had the obvious fault of not offering redress for the century of manipulation of Central American governments by the U.S. government and corporations. And it had the predictable ground-level threshhold for tolerating a strengthening of the left—which in El Salvador would bring Washington running to the assistance of the old order in 1980.[25] But in the early years of the Carter Administration there was little fretting over El Salvador and even less over the fact that Israel had so quickly filled the traditional U.S. shoes.

Not surprisingly, however, there was great awareness of Israel's role among Salvadorans. In 1979, FMLN (Farabundo Marti National Liberation Front, the armed wing of the Salvadoran revolution) forces kidnapped Ernesto Liebes, Israel's honorary consul, but unlike many of the other people kidnapped by the FMLN for ransom, Liebes was executed "as a war criminal because of the role he played in the sale of Israeli aircraft to the Salvadoran armed forces."[26] On December 11, 1979, the Israeli embassy in San Salvador was bombed, although it was never determined who was responsible.[27] Soon after, Israel closed its embassy.[28]

By 1979, a series of successful actions by a quickly-unifying Salvadoran left drew U.S. attention back to El Salvador. The triumph over Somoza in July 1979 inspired stepped up political and military action by the Salvadoran left and an intensified campaign of murder, disappearances, and brutality by the military and paramilitary death squads. Well before young officers seized power late that year, the Carter State Department had begun to involve itself in the search for a viable centrist leadership for El Salvador.[29] During the tenure of the first junta, limited military aid ($5 million, largely "nonlethal") was promised—it was briefly held up in an attempt to pressure the Salvadoran authorities to investigate the murder of four U.S. religious workers[30]—and the first U.S. advisers were sent to El Salvador in January 1981, two months before Ronald Reagan took office.[31]

During this period, the newly installed Reagan Administration, inevitably attracted to ostentatiously grisly tyrannies, sought fast money for what was at that point an essentially military government. Israel agreed to loan—in actuality to defer receiving—$21 million of its U.S. assistance.[32]

Even after the Reagan Administration committed itself fully to the Salvadoran government in 1981—its civilian figurehead in those days was Jose Napoleon Duarte—Israel received an order from El Salvador for three Arava aircraft in 1982.[33] There was an unconfirmed report that Israel had sold El Salvador three Super Mystere aircraft.[34]

As late as 1984, the Salvadoran military was using napalm it had purchased from Israel. The use of napalm on the civilian population was verified by a number of U.S. medical workers, including Harvard University burn specialist Dr. John Constable. The Israeli origin of the napalm was disclosed by the U.S. Ambassador to El Salvador after persistent questioning by members of Congress and journalists.[35]

In May 1982, Joaquin Aguilar, the representative in Italy of the FDR, was brought to Israel by a local solidarity committee to lobby against continued Israeli arms sales to the Salvadoran regime. The leaders of most of Israel's leftist factions met with Aguilar and, at the FDR representative's request, Shimon Peres, at the time leader of the Labor opposition, also agreed to meet with him.

The Salvadoran ambassador to Israel bitterly denounced the meetings with Aguilar as dealing with a "terrorist," and issued pointed warnings about the Salvadoran opposition's connection to the PLO. Aguilar acknowledged that the FDR had relations with the PLO, "which represents the Palestinian people." But he also stressed the FDR's awareness of Jewish suffering.

> I want to deliver a message of peace to the Israeli people—a people who have suffered so much. That is why I think the people of Israel can understand the suffering of the people in El Salvador, who are under fascist repression by a dictatorship that uses Nazi means and mass murder to defeat the people.[36]

According to one report, Aguilar "left empty-handed after talks with Peres..."[37] Yet it is still not altogether clear whether Israel has continued to sell weapons to the Salvadoran military, which continues to get most of what it needs for such tasks as its daily bombing runs on the civilian population from the U.S.

In any event, after the advent of the Reagan Administration, Israel did maintain advisers in El Salvador.[38] "I never heard that those advisers left El Salvador," noted Col. Guerra y Guerra, who went into exile after the fall of the first junta in 1980, but in 1983 was still informed about events in El Salvador. In numbers estimated at 100-200[39] in 1982, they undoubtedly filled in the holes left by Congressional restrictions limiting the U.S. to 55 advisers. In 1984, its Salvadoran proteges having been slow to benefit from U.S. training, the Pentagon asked Israel to supply more advisers.[40]

The proliferating Israeli "security" firms made up of retired Israeli military and intelligence officers have sent personnel to the Salvadoran armed forces. The connection of these firms and the Israeli government is direct: "One source said the Defense Ministry in fact often passes less-desirable clients to private consulting firms when 'the government is reluctant to have [active military] personnel directly involved.'"[41]

The Embassy and the Strings Attached

Israel continued to pursue its own relationship with El Salvador. On April 13, 1984, El Salvador's Ambassador to Israel had nailed a large seal on a doorpost in Jerusalem: "Republic of El Salvador in Central America— Embassy." He ran a Salvadoran flag up next to the Israeli flag. An Israeli foreign ministry official said Israel hoped to increase its cultural and developmental ties with El Salvador.[42] It was a radical move. In 1980, all 14 nations which had maintained embassies in Jerusalem relocated them to Tel Aviv, in compliance with UN Security Council Resolution 478 dis-avowing the annexation of East Jerusalem by the Israeli Knesset earlier that year. Israel captured East Jerusalem from Jordan in 1967, and under international law it is regarded as occupied and disputed territory; the significance of Jerusalem to three major religions—Christianity, Islam and Judaism—only increases the sensitivity of the issue. Prior to the Salvadoran decision, only Costa Rica had defied prevailing sentiment and in 1982 relocated its embassy to Jerusalem.

Radio Venceremos, the voice of the Salvadoran insurgency, condemned the embassy transfer as "a shameless violation of UN resolutions" and condemned interim President Alvaro Magana—installed in 1982 after Roberto D'Aubuisson's far right ARENA (Nationalist Republican Alliance) party captured the National Assembly in a dog and pony show election and dismissed Duarte—for aligning El Salvador with Israel.[43]

In El Salvador, the Israeli ambassador presented his credentials, and interim President Magana voiced hopes for a security agreement and aid from Israel. The following week, the Washington media was rife with stories (which later turned out to be part of an administration pressure campaign to get Israeli support for the contras; see below) that a meeting between Israeli Foreign Ministry Director-General David Kimche and State Department officals would discuss setting up a special fund, independent of the U.S. budget, for Israeli "technological and agricultural projects in Central America and Africa" and, in exchange, using Israel as a conduit for aid to the Salvadoran government and the contras. Israel, noted all the accounts, should be in a generous mood toward El Salvador because of that country's recent recognition of Jerusalem.[44]

According to an official at the Salvadoran foreign ministry, the ministry had also assumed "that something concrete had been offered in exchange for the transfer since it contradicted the Foreign Ministry's policy."[45]

Foreign Minister Fidel Chavez Mena had supported the 1980 UN resolution that asked members to withdraw their embassies from Jerusalem. Chavez Mena had been working to develop El Salvador's ties with Middle Eastern countries; he was a friend of the Egyptian Ambassador. Now, some Salvadoran officials began to worry that Arab governments might recognize an insurgent government[46]—a justifiable worry as the FMLN-FDR controlled a significant part of northern El Salvador.

This did not occur, but on April 20 Egypt and other members of the Islamic Conference Organization broke relations with El Salvador and Costa Rica.[47] The rupture was intended as a warning to the U.S., where a bizarre election year roller coaster was gathering steam as Democratic candidates competed in the strength of their commitment to a bill mandating the move of the U.S. embassy in Israel from Tel Aviv to Jerusalem.[48] Congress passed the bill, which was non-binding, so President

Reagan simply ignored it. But that spring Egypt and other Arab nations suspected—erroneously—that El Salvador had been encouraged to make the move to Jerusalem by Washington, as a kind of trial balloon.[49]

In fact, the Salvadoran move had almost nothing to do with U.S. politics and a great deal to do with the machinations of the Salvadoran far-right, casting bitter irony on the words of an anonymous Salvadoran official: "If Israel would help us fight our terrorism, we wouldn't have this problem with the death squads."[50] Moreover, it had all been set in motion eight months earlier, in August 1983, when a Salvadoran delegation arrived in Israel.

They were "not exactly" looking for military aid, said Ernesto Magana, although "we are quite interested in the help of Israeli 'counter-terrorist' specialists." The leader of the delegation, Presidential Secretary Jose Francisco Guerrero, also spoke of "eradicating" the worldwide blight of terror and of strengthening Israeli-Salvadoran relations.[51]

At a meeting with Prime Minister Menachem Begin, the delegation informed him that El Salvador was willing to relocate its embassy to Jerusalem. Begin was so delighted he embraced Ernesto Magana.[52]

It is still not certain exactly what—or who—propelled the Salvadorans to Israel, although in retrospect it appears as though the initial move was a not very well thought out fishing expedition. The Salvadorans were taken on a tour of Israeli military installations and IAI plants,[53] but when the embassy relocation was announced, aside from a pledge to support each other at the UN,[54] the terms of the agreement seemed somewhat vague.

> In exchange for a gesture from El Salvador, Israel plans to reopen its embassy here and begin a cooperation program that could lead to Israeli military and internal security aid...The arrangement also includes hopes in the Salvadoran government [sic] that the influential pro-Israel lobby in the United States will lend a discreet hand in congressional debates over the wisdom of administration policy on Central America and the level of military aid for the U.S.-supported government of provisional President Alvaro Magana.[55]

At any rate, despite El Salvador's stated intention to set up shop in Jerusalem in September, through late 1983 and early 1984 nothing happened, a sign perhaps of opposition to the move in El Salvador from either the foreign ministry, where the well-educated staff was generally opposed to Israeli policies,[56] or even the U.S. embassy. It certainly was an indication that Israel had not put enough on the table to match the Salvadoran gesture. If the visit of top Salvadoran military officers to Israel which Guerrero had said would occur later in 1983[57] took place, it was under the strictest secrecy.

The move finally occurred in April 1984, only weeks before an election that was critical to the continuation of U.S. aid to El Salvador. The situation was a classic: an administration in Washington trying to present to Congress and the U.S. public a credible image of a working democracy[58] and the emergence of a centrist government. In this case the Christian Democratic Party of Jose Napoleon Duarte—or what remained of it after the more principled elements joined the FDR—was pitted against the far right ARENA Party. Led by cashiered army major Roberto D'Aubuisson, ARENA was a carefully constructed above-ground political arm of the death squads which had plagued El Salvador, causing the greater part of 40,000 civilian deaths between 1979 and 1983, although at the time the degree of overlap was not known.[58] The party of Francisco Jose Guerrero, the top aid in the caretaker Magana government who had led the August 1983 delegation to Israel, had been eliminated in the initial round of the presidential elections on March 25 and its support was regarded as a wild card; but, with its ties to the growers and military, not much of one.

In the U.S., Congress had made itself quite clear: if D'Aubuisson won the election the Administration's requests for military aid for El Salvador would almost certainly be rejected. (With the 1984 elections approaching the Democrats in Congress had briefly entered the zone of principle and were vociferously blocking the Administration's war plans for Central America. The mood soon passed.)

Likewise, led by Dale Bumpers (D-AR) the Senate had put itself on record as willing to stop all military aid to El Salvador should its elected government be deposed by a coup d'etat. That resolution was passed unanimously in the midst of coup rumors.[60]

It is significant that the embassy-moving ceremony took place between the elmination of Guerrero from presidential contention and the May 6, 1984 election of Duarte. Guerrero, according to one foreign journalist who spoke with him extensively, had been fixed on the idea of moving the embassy ever since he had returned from Israel. He greatly admired the Israeli agricultural arrangements of "civil defense systems on farms in endangered areas," and he believed that El Salvador should have a fallback international backer.

The Salvadoran far right had also thought about an alternative to the U.S., with its annoying lectures about human rights abuses and its history of abandoning its client/allies. Georgetown University Center for Strategic and International Studies fellow Robert Leiken had pointed out that, in pursuit of their own agendas, the Salvadorans and other Central American "anti-Communist (sic) military cliques" would disregard U.S. interests. He also noted that Taiwan, Israel, Chile and South Africa "are countries that...are frequently invoked by D'Aubuisson's supporters, increasingly bitter and outspoken about U.S. 'meddling,' as substitutes should American aid be cut off."[61] It was also evident that, if elected, Duarte would hold to the Christian Democrat position on Jerusalem, that the status of the city is still to be negotiated, and would never move the embassy. The timing of the move, less than a month before the election, clearly suggests an attempt by the Salvadoran right to establish links and curry favor with Israel.

Just as clearly, it suggests that when its own interests are involved—in this case a sop to the legitimacy of Jerusalem as its "eternal" and "undivided" capital—Israel has little interest in coordinating its activities with Washington. Apparently it does not have to. Nor did it seem to require the kind of distance from Roberto D'Aubuisson upon which even the Reagan right (minus Sen. Jesse Helms) insisted.

Ultimately, with the benefit of money the CIA pumped into the election, Duarte defeated D'Aubuisson.[62] Soon after assuming office Duarte was asked about the embassy. He answered

> Regarding Jerusalem, that is a problem that concerns the Foreign Ministry. I still do not know why this decision was adopted. I hope to receive the official report from the foreign minister...however, it is quite logical to think that at this moment he is not completely aware of the details but will give us a report regarding the situation, what has happened...[63]

Nonetheless, when in July 1984 Duarte came to the U.S., he won the hearts of Congress, which approved $70 million emergency military aid in August.[64] Could those "hopes in the Salvadoran government" that Israel would put its powerful lobby to work have come true for Duarte?

Much later, Salvadoran officials would reveal that there had been disappointment when, following the embassy relocation, Israel had not provided the hoped-for economic and military aid.[65] Therefore, they explained, President Duarte delayed naming an ambassador to the new embassy in Jerusalem.[66] In any event, Duarte—and even the negative Fidel Chavez Mena—would later reap the benefits of Magana's move to Jerusalem and the never quite defined "cooperation program."

"Pacification"

In March 1985, El Salvador's Deputy Minister of Defense and Public Security Col. Reynaldo Lopez Nuila visited Israel.[67] Lopez was the strongest advocate in the Duarte cabinet of "citizens defense committees" to guard plantations and businesses against insurgent attacks. By July 1984, the Salvadoran Assembly had passed a law approving the creation of such units. In 1985 an enthusiastic Col. Sigifredo Ochoa began establishing "self-defense" committees in Chalatenango province, in towns which the military had succeeded in occupying. In May, Ochoa boasted that his troops had organized 30 such committees.[68] These forces, argued Lopez Nuila, "have worked in many other countries."[69] Later Lopez Nuila and the director of the Salvadoran police academy visited Guatemala for advice on counterinsurgency; while there they set up permanent links with their counterparts.[70] Israel has long advised the Guatemalan military and police (see below). It is more likely, however, that Nuila's mission was related to the "self-defense" forces which the Salvadoran government was trying to set up.

These attempts came in the context of efforts the U.S. had been making to establish the same kind of rural "pacification" program that it had employed in Vietnam, the well-remembered Phoenix Program of winning hearts and minds with a combination of civic amenities and murder. In El Salvador it was called the National Plan. Begun in 1983, the program in San Vicente province was a monumental failure. "Guerrillas stole medicines from National Plan hospitals and held night classes at National Plan schools."[71] Corruption in the ranks of Salvadoran officials accomplished what the insurgents could not.[72]

The military then began an intensified bombing campaign to depopulate areas whose residents were thought to support the rebels.[73] It developed its own pacification plan, and it was probably inevitable that Israel would become involved.

Actually, Israeli aid to Salvadoran attempts at "pacification" might have predated the embassy-moving agreement. At the April 1984 ceremony in Jerusalem, the Salvadoran ambassador had noted that, "We have all the time a representation of Israel, mainly in the field of agricultural cooperation, organization of communities."[74] In early 1985 the Salvadoran military instituted a program called the Patriotic Youth Movement—"to restore civic and moral values and seek rapprochement with the nation's teachers and students"[75]—the same name as that run by Israel many years before.

At the end of 1984 the Salvadoran government introduced something called Project 1,000, designed to settle 500,000 war refugees in 1,000 "fortified communities." Total cost of the project (not counting the cost of creating refugees, which is covered by U.S. military aid) was estimated at $70 to $100 million.[76]

At first Salvadoran officians thought that U.S. AID and the UN Development Program would provide funding.[77] Perhaps because at one point the Salvadoran government suggested restricting the distribution of U.S. food aid to those who moved to the new communities—the government offered as an excuse for this gambit that there was a new marginal class of parasites resulting in "dependency, vagrancy, crime, prostitution [and] frustration,"—U.S. AID was emphatic in denying it had any connection with Project 1,000.[78] The International Commitee for the Red Cross and other established aid organizations said that they would not participate in the program. AID officials said they were working on resettlement plans with the Catholic Church, and an official of a major relief organization charged that Project 1,000 was a plan for population control: "People are displaced from conflicted or rebel-held zones in an effort to drain away support from the guerrillas, then these people are herded into camps where they are monitored and controlled."[79]

By early 1985, the promoters of Project 1,000 were speaking of obtaining the financial wherewithal from European and Latin American nations.[80]

In late 1985 the West German government granted El Salvador $17.9 million for use in "agrarian reform and social projects in fields of health and education, and to promote cooperatives."[81] Agrarian reform has not been implemented in El Salvador for several years. The word "cooperative" has been used at least once to describe the fortified villages established by the Salvadoran military.[82]

On New Years Day in 1986, El Salvador's ambassador to Jerusalem presented his credentials to the Israelis. (Ambassador Enrique Guttfreund Hanchel was a former president of the Jewish community in El Salvador and also of the Central American Confederation of Jewish Communities.[83]) The following month Israel's ambassador in El Salvador said, "We will be reinforcing our technical cooperation in the agricultural and community development fields, in which we are considered specialists."[84] By that mouthful of euphemisms the ambassador meant that Israel would help El Salvador strip the last shreds of dignity and hope from thousands of civilian victims.

Harking back to the scorched earth military pacification plan which Israel had helped Guatemala implement (see below), a nongovernmental community development worker spelled out the nature of Israel's specialization: "Once you have Israeli technicians coming into the country, you can have military trainers coming in under the guise of agricultural technicians. That is what they did in Guatemala." An adviser to President Duarte said the government hoped that Israel's agricultural assistance would prop up the agrarian reform program and "keep thousands of peasants from joining rebel ranks out of frustration." The Israeli ambassador said that his country's aid would be channeled through the government agency supporting the military's relocation projects, Dideco.[85]

In July 1986, Fidel Chavez Mena, now El Salvador's Planning Minister, arrived in Israel and signed an agreement covering both agricultural and industrial assistance. The financing to support the Israeli technicians was reported to be coming from the World Bank, West Germany and the U.S. According to the Israeli daily *Davar*, Chavez and his counterpart Gad Yacobi discussed the possibilities of "technical assistance for agricultural cooperation among the nations of Central America."[86]

A week before the signing of that agreement James LeMoyne, the *New York Times* correspondent in El Salvador, wrote about the likely recipients of Israeli aid.

> The peasants captured for supporting the guerrillas represent an especially difficult challenge for the Government. Winning their sympathy will be extremely hard.
> The villagers have been rounded up in army counter-insurgency campaigns that are intended to separate guerrilla sympathizers from armed rebel units. It is an unpleasant business. The army enters selected guerrilla areas and burns the peasants' fields, wrecks their homes and seizes anyone it can catch.[87]

If the Israelis' work is going to be done in conjunction with the latest comprehensive counterinsurgency plan announced by the Salvadoran government, "United to Rebuild," there will be at least $18 million of U.S. funds involved.[88]

Should the U.S. be forced to pull back from all or part of its misguided commitments to El Salvador, Israel is ideally positioned to carry on the work. In 1932 the Salvadoran military massacred 30,000 in quelling a revolution.[89] Col. Guerra y Guerra recalls hearing hardline Salvadoran officers say that they were prepared to kill 300,000 of their countrymen to extinguish the current insurgency.[90]

Should the Salvadoran far right win political control from the Duarte Christian Democrats, thanks to its decisive action in relocating the Salvadoran embassy in 1984, the Salvadoran right has an account with excellent credit waiting in Jerusalem.

Major Israeli Weapons Sales to El Salvador

Item	Comments	Reference Source
25 IAI–201 Arava planes	Ordered September 1973; delivered 1974–1979. Unit cost $0.7 million	Stockholm International Peace Research Institute (SIPRI), *World Armament and Disarmament Yearbook 1979*, pp. 212–213.
6 Fouga Magister trainers	Licensed production in Israel. Ordered 1973; delivered 1975	SIPRI, *Yearbook 1976*, p. 274.
18 refurbished Dassault Ouragan fighters	Ordered 1973; delivered 1975. From Israeli air force stock	*Ibid.*, p. 275.
200 80-mm rocket launchers	Delivered 1974–77	U.S. Congress, House, Committee on Foreign Affairs, *Economic and Military Aid Programs*, p. 84.
200 9-mm Uzi submachine guns	Delivered 1974–77	*Ibid.*
Ammunition Spare parts		*Ibid.*
"Security" equipment		"Armas Israelis Contra America Latina," *OLP Informa* (Mexico City), February 1982, p. 8.
Galil assault rifles		Penny Lernoux, "'Who's Who of Dictators Obtain Arms from Israel," *National Catholic Reporter*, 25 December 1981.
4 Mystere B–2 bombers	Ordered and delivered 1981; unconfirmed	SIPRI, *Yearbook 1982*, p. 213.
Armored vehicles		Interview with "Miguel," nom de guerre, International Relations Department of the Salvadoran FMLN, Managua, Nicaragua, 17 August 1982; interview with "Santiago," International Relations Department of the Salvadoran Communist Party, Managua, Nicaragua, 17 August 1982.
3 Arava STOL planes	Sold in 1982	*Latin America Weekly Report*, 17 December 1982, p. 6.
Napalm bombs		*Hadashot*, 2 October 1984, p. 13.

Chart from *Israel and Latin America: The Military Connection*, Bishara Bahbah, New York: St. Martin's, 1986.

Guatemala...

Salvadoran rightists are aware of how well their counterparts in Guatemala have done over the last decade—without the United States and with the help of Israel. The history of Israel's relations with Guatemala roughly parallels that of its ties with El Salvador—except the Guatemalan military was so unswervingly bloody that Congress never permitted the (all-too-eager) Reagan Administration to undo the military aid cutoff implemented during the Carter years.[1]

Weaponry for the Guatemalan military is the very least of what Israel has delivered. Israel not only provided the technology necessary for a reign of terror, it helped in the organization and commission of the horrors perpetrated by the Guatemalan military and police. And even beyond that: to ensure that the profitable relationship would continue, Israel and its agents worked actively to maintain Israeli influence in Guatemala.

Throughout the years of untrammeled slaughter that left at least 45,000 dead,[2] and, by early 1983, one million in internal exile[3]—mostly indigenous Mayan Indians, who comprise a majority of Guatemala's eight million people—and thousands more in exile abroad, Israel stood by the Guatemalan military. Three successive military governments and three brutal and sweeping campaigns against the Mayan population, described by a U.S. diplomat as Guatemala's "genocide against the Indians,"[4] had the benefit of Israeli techniques and experience, as well as hardware.

111

As with El Salvador, the popular response to Israeli aid to the military government was expressed with a bombing attack on its Guatemala City embassy on the night of January 12, 1982. Guards fired at the fleeing attackers, whose bomb did slight damage to the building.[5] A few months later another bombing blew out windows in the embassy, and a simultaneous bomb throwing attack on Guatemala City's only synagogue resulted in no damage.[6]

Israel and Guatemala had more of a history than did Israel with El Salvador. In 1947, Guatemala's representative at the UN was appointed to the UN Special Committee on Palestine (UNSCOP), charged with drafting a plan for Jewish and Palestinian nations in what was the British Mandate of Palestine. After a trip to Palestine, where he met the pre-state terrorist Menachem Begin, Jorge Garcia Granados was well disposed toward the Jewish settlers; he is considered to have been instrumental in drafting the plan of partition that created the state of Israel.[7]

History, however, has not run a straight course, and Israel's occasional claims that it is somehow obligated to Guatemala are dubious. As Milton Jamail and Margo Gutierrez note,

> Although Israel points to its early special relationship with Guatemala, it is important to note that that relationship began between a progressive government in Guatemala and what was perceived by the Guatemalans as an anti-colonial struggle in Palestine. The situation has changed considerably in the ensuing forty years. Guatemala's military dictatorship of today is the direct descendant of a right-wing government that took power in 1954 by overthrowing the government that had forged such good relations with Israel.[8]

In the 1960s and 1970s, Israel conducted quite an extensive technical assistance program in Guatemala with the emphasis on agriculture. By 1970, 16 Israeli advisers had worked on projects in Guatemala. In 1971 the two countries signed a cooperation agreement, following which Israel taught a "youth leadership" course and established a "workers' bank" in Guatemala.[9]

As it did to El Salvador, the Carter Administration wrote Guatemala off of the U.S. military assistance ledgers in 1977.[10] Guatemala had actually been confronted with a U.S. aid cutoff two years earlier, when the Ford Administration had held back arms shipments at the request of the British government after Guatemala threatened to invade neighboring Belize, then a British colony, on which Guatemala had long held territorial designs.[11]

Israel began selling Guatemala weapons in 1974 and since then is known to have delivered 17 Arava aircraft.[12] In 1977 at the annual industrial fair, Interfer, Israel's main attraction was the Arava. "An operative Arava is to be parked outside the IAI pavillion for public inspection, although its silhouette in flight is a common sight over the capital and countryside."[13]

Referring to the Aravas, Benedicto Lucas Garcia, chief of staff during the rule of his brother Romeo Lucas Garcia (1978-1982) said, "Israel helped us in regard to planes and transportation—which we desperately needed because we had problems in transferring ground forces from one place to another."[14] By 1982, at least nine of the Aravas had been mounted with gun pods.[15]

Among the other weapons sold by Israel were 10 RBY armored personnel carriers, three Dabur class patrol boats armed with Gabriel missiles, light cannons, machine guns and at least 15,000 Galil assault rifles.[16] The Galil became Guatemala's standard rifle[17] and Uzis were widely seen as well.

According to Victor Perera, "Uzis and the larger Galil assault rifles used by Guatemala's special counterinsurgency forces accounted for at least half of the estimated 45,000 Guatemalan Indians killed by the military since 1978."[18]

In 1977, authorities in the Caribbean nation of Barbados seized two separate shipments of Israeli arms and ammunition bound for Guatemala.[19] Barbados, a Commonwealth member, had supported an OAS resolution favoring Belize's independence and territorial integrity.[20] That year it was reported that Guatemala's feared Kaibiles (special forces) were based in Peten near the Belize border "with new Israeli automatic rifles."[21]

From the beginning, both sides took the arms buying and selling seriously. In 1971, Guatemalan armed forces Chief of Staff Kjell Laugerud Garcia visited Israel. Soon after, Laugerud was (fraudulently) elected president. In 1974 he paid another visit "to widen cooperation with Israel."[22] Three years later, Israel's President Ephraim Katzir reciprocated with a visit to Guatemala. According to Laugerud, his purpose was mainly to discuss arms and military aid.[23]

After Guatemala was cut off from U.S. military equipment, Israel continued to fill in the gaps. Chief of Staff Lucas Garcia said he maintained contact "with Israelis who advised us on matters of military purchases." Lucas said that while Israel did not provide "large amounts" of weapons, "it was the only country that gave us support in our battle against the guerrillas."[24] It is particularly difficult to know exactly what was supplied and how much it cost. Young officers complaining of corruption on the part of their superiors charged that between 1975 and 1981 some Guatemalan generals had claimed $425 million in weapons purchases from

Israel, Italy, Belgium and Yugoslavia; however, according to the young officers, only $175 million had really been spent on arms—the difference was deposited in the Cayman Islands bank accounts of the generals.[25]

Some of the payment for Israeli arms is thought to have been made in quetzals, Guatemala's currency, which Israel would then use in its other dealings with Guatemala.[26] Although there were reports of a big sale of Israeli Kfir fighter planes to Guatemala,[27] these were never seen and would have required a U.S. re-export license, which the Carter Administration was not willing to give Israel for resale to Ecuador.[28] It is possible the reports of Kfirs were born out of earlier reports (during the flare up of tensions over Belize) that Israel (or France) had provided Guatemala with 24 "earlier type" Mirage combat aircraft.[29]

Likewise, there are reports of helicopter sales, although the number of aircraft involved have not been determined. The transaction is said to have been a barter arrangement, with Israel accepting Guatemalan currency to be used for buying Guatemalan goods or financing Israeli operations in Guatemala.[30]

In 1985, the army's chief of staff said that several of the air force's helicopters were at the time in Israel undergoing repairs and recon-ditioning.[31] In March 1986, Greek officials impounded the West Lion, sailing from Israel and carrying a dismantled Augusta Bell 212 helicopter. The first of several destinations given for the ship was Guatemala. It was also carrying 209 tons of reinforced TNT, bazookas, machine guns and ammunition (although some of this could well have been intended for the contras; see below).[32]

It is certain that over the years Israel has delivered quantities of smaller items to Guatemala: flak jackets, helmets,[33] until "[a]rmy outposts in the jungle have become near replicas of Israeli army field camps."[34] "When I see the quantity of arms involved in some of these transactions, such as Guatemala at the height of the internal terror!" commented former Foreign Minister Abba Eban, now head of the Knesset's defense and foreign affairs committee.[35]

Under an agreement with Guatemala's air force, Israel trained pilots.[36] A 1983 report said that Israel had built an air base in Guatemala.[37]

Israel also installed a radar array at Guatemala City's La Aurora International Airport; in 1983 the radar was reportedly run by Israeli technicians.[38]

When the Reagan Administration took office it was determined to do everything it could for Guatemala. It had promised as much during the election campaign. Never had Ronald Reagan seen a rightist dictatorship he didn't like; during his 1980 campaign he met with a representative of the right-wing business lobby *Los Amigos del Pais,* and, referring to the Carter Administration's aid cutoff, told him, "Don't give up. Stay there and fight. I'll help you as soon as I get in."

The Guatemalan far-right apparently helped Reagan *get in.*

> Guatemalan business leaders reportedly pumped large illegal contributions into the Reagan campaign coffers. Their tentacles reached right into the core of the new administration through the lobbying activities of the Hannaford-Deaver law firm of White House troika member Michael Deaver. Within three days of the Republican victory on 7 November 1980, Hannaford-Deaver were busy arranging a Capitol Hill briefing for *Amigos del Pais.*[39]

Congress, however, did not change its attitude about Guatemala, and as late as 1985 remained adamant about denying it military aid. In 1981, Reagan's Secretary of State Alexander Haig "urged Israel to help Guatemala."[40] In July 1985 Israel helped the administration move a shipment of 40 assault rifles with advanced night sights and 1,000 grenade launchers from Israel to Guatemala on a KLM (Royal Dutch Airlines) flight.[41]

In late 1983, the Guerrilla Army of the Poor (EGP) issued a communique saying that the previous May a munitions factory producing bullets for Galil rifles and Uzi submachine guns had begun operation in Alta Verapaz.[42] Subsequently the director of Army Public Relations confirmed that the military was producing Galil rifle parts, had begun armor plating its vehicles at the factory, and that the facility would soon be capable of building grenade launchers.[43] The following year the factory began manufacturing entire Galil rifles under license from Israel.[44]

Israeli advisers set up the factory and then trained the Guatemalans to run it, said Gen. Benedicto Lucas Garcia, who had headed the army at the time. "The factory is now being run by Guatemalans," he added.[45] There are hopes in Guatemala that 30 percent of the plant's output can be sold to Honduras and El Salvador.[46]

The EGP said in 1983 that there were 300 Israeli advisers in Guatemala, working "in the security structures and in the army."[47] Other reports were less specific as to numbers, but suggested that these Israeli advisers, "some official, others private," performed a variety of functions. Israelis "helped Guatemalan internal security agents hunt underground rebel groups."[48]

Gen. Lucas said Israeli advisers had come to teach the use of Israeli equipment purchased by Guatemala.[49] Throughout the 1960s and 1970s the Guatemalan police agencies had had extensive U.S. training in "riot control training and related phases of coping with civil disturbances in a humane and effective manner," a euphemism for the terror campaigns in which these forces participated that in 1967-1968 took 7,000 lives while ostensibly fighting a guerrilla force that never numbered more than 450.[50] When Congress forbade U.S. forces to train the internal police forces of other countries—passed in 1974, this law was supplanted in 1985 by legislation that put the U.S. back in the police-guidance business[51]—the Israelis stepped in and "set up their intelligence network, tried and tested on the West Bank and Gaza."[52]

Israeli noncommissioned officers were also said to have been hired by big landowners to train their private security details. (Under Marcos, Israel did the same in the Philippines.[53]) These private squads, together with "off-duty military officers formed the fearsome 'death squads' which later spread to neighboring El Salvador, where they have been responsible for an estimated 20,000-30,000 murders of left-wing dissidents."[54]

Not only did the Israelis share their experiences and their tactics, they bestowed upon Guatemala the technology needed by a modern police state. During the period Guatemala was under U.S. tutelage, the insurgency spread from the urban bourgeoisie to the indigenous population in the rural highlands; with Israeli guidance the military succeeded in suppressing (for now) the drive for land and political liberation. The Guatemalan military is very conscious of that achievement, even proud of it. Some officers argue that with the help of the U.S. they could not have quelled the insurgency, as Congress would not have tolerated their ruthless tactics.[55]

In 1979, the Guatemalan interior minister paid a "secret and confidential" visit to Israel, where he met with the manufacturers of "sophisticated police equipment."[56] In March of the following year Interior Minister Donaldo Alvarez Ruiz was in Israel to conclude an agreement for police training. Following the overthrow of Lucas Garcia, the home of Interior Minister Alvarez was raided, "uncovering underground jail cells, 50 stolen vehicles...[and] scores of gold graduation rings, wrenched from the fingers of police torture victims."[57]

Israeli advisers have worked with the feared G-2 police intelligence unit.[58] Overseen by the army general staff, the G-2 is the intelligence agency—sections charged with "the elimination of individuals" are stationed at every army base—which has been largely responsible for the death squad killings over the last decade. The present civilian government has dissolved the DIT, a civilian organization subordinate to G-2, but not G-2 itself.[59]

In 1981, the Army's School of Transmissions and Electronics, a school designed and financed by the Israeli company Tadiran to teach such subjects as encoding, radio jamming and monitoring, and the use of Israeli equipment was opened in Guatemala City.[60] According to the colonel directing the school, everything in it came from Israel: the "teaching methods, the teaching teams, the technical instruments, books, and even the custom furniture...designed and built by the Israeli company DEGEM Systems."[61]

At the opening ceremony the Israeli ambassador was thanked by Chief of Staff Gen. Benedicto Lucas Garcia for "the advice and transfer of electronic technology" which, Lucas said, had brought Guatemala up to date.[62] Calling Guatemala "one of our best friends" the ambassador promised that further technology transfers were in the works.[63]

Perhaps the most sinister of all the equipment supplied by Israel to Guatemala were two computers. One was in an old military academy and became, as Benedicto Lucas called it, "the nerve center of the armed forces, which deals with the movements of units in the field and so on."[64] The other computer was located in an annex of the National Palace. The G-2 have a control center there, and, since the days of Romeo Lucas Garcia, meetings have been held in that annex to select assassination victims. According to a senior Guatemalan army official, the complex contains "an archive and computer file on journalists, students, leaders, people of the left, politicians, and so on." This material is combined with current intelligence reports and mulled over during weekly sessions that have included, in their respective times, both Romeo Lucas and Oscar Mejia Victores.

> The bureaucratic procedures for approving the killing of a dissident are well-established. "A local military commander has someone they think is a problem," the officer explains. "So they speak with G-2, and G-2 consults its own archives and information from its agents and the police and, if all coincide, it passes along a direct proposition to the minister of defense. They say, 'We have analyzed the case of such and such a person in depth and this person is responsible for the following acts and we recommend that we execute them.'"[65]

The computer, installed by Tadiran, and operational in late 1979 or early 1980,[66] was used to sort through dossiers and to distribute lists of those marked for death. Said a U.S. priest who fled the country after appearing on a death list, "They had printout lists at the border crossings and at the airport. Once you get on that—then it's like bounty hunters."[67]

The computer was also capable of monitoring utilities usage and identifying surges in consumption that might indicate a meeting underway, a mimeograph producing leaflets, bombs being made. In 1981, relying on information generated by the computer system, the Guatemalan military raided 30 safe houses of the Revolutionary Organization of People in Arms (ORPA).[68]

Along with the computer system came public registration. In May 1983, the government announced that Col. Jaime Rabanales, a specialist in counterinsurgency propaganda, had been put in charge of a program to register the entire population,[69] a task that would be undertaken "with the help of Israeli intelligence."[70] Soon after he wrested power from Rios Montt, Gen. Oscar Mejia Victores called a halt to the census-taking, which he said was a burden to the military and a public relations disaster.[71]

Something resembling that plan cropped up again in August 1984, according to a report by the Mexico City *El Dia* about a "sectoral" (sectorization) plan to contain urban political activity. The paper said the plan was modeled after "Israel's experiences in Palestinian areas," and called for eight police for each four blocks, a census of the residents and reinforcement of neighborhood organizations—"a form of the civil self-defense patrols." The paper also said that this plan would contribute to accomplishing the computerization of the population already under way, "the work of Israeli experts."[72]

By 1985, 80 percent of the adult population was said to have been entered in the computer.[73]

Israeli technicians also work training Guatemalan bureaucrats how to use computerized information and management systems.[74]

Control of the Rural Population

The aspect of Israeli cooperation with Guatemala with the most serious implications is the role played by Israeli personnel in the universally condemned rural "pacification" program. Extreme maldistribution of land—exacerbated by encroachment on indigenous land—was a major cause of the present rebellion. After trying several different approaches, the military, under Rios Montt, embarked on a resolution of the problem, substituting forced relocation and suppression for equitable land distribution.

In 1982 Israeli military advisers helped develop and carry out Plan Victoria, the devastating scorched earth campaign which Rios Montt unleashed on the highland population. In June 1983, the Guatemalan embassy in Washington confirmed that "personnel sent by the Israeli government were participating in the repopulation and readjustment programs for those displaced." Rios Montt himself told the *Washington*

Times that the Israeli government was giving his administration help with the counterinsurgency plan called *"Techo, tortilla y trabajo"* (shelter, food and work).[75] The "three T's" followed an earlier Rios program called *Fusiles y Frijoles,* or beans and bullets, where wholesale slaughter was combined with the provision of life's necessities to those willing to cooperate with the military.[76]

> The success of the government's initially savage but sophis-
> ticated campaign against the rebels has come without significant
> U.S. military assistance, and top field commanders say that none
> is necessary now to finish the guerrillas.

"We declared a state of siege so we could kill legally," Rios Montt told a group of politicians. The Roman Catholic Conference of Bishops called what Rios was doing "genocide."[77] Following Rios' overthrow, his successor Mejia Victores continued the program, proclaiming that model villages would be extended throughout the country.[78]

As the army bombed, strafed and burned village after village, an estimated 100,000 peasants escaped across the border to Mexico[79] or to the mountainous territory controlled by the guerrillas. Others were captured by the military. Many of those who went to the guerrillas were later forced by hunger to surrender themselves to the military. Their fate was confinement in model villages, what were called strategic hamlets during the U.S. assault on Vietnam. In Guatemala there was a plan drawn up grouping these in four "poles of development." The scheme piggybacked on a series of older plans involving the corruption of cooperatives.

There was a short-lived cooperative movement in Guatemala in the early 1970s, spearheaded by Roman Catholic priests. It was meant to provide credit and agricultural support that would obviate the need for indigenous people to migrate to coastal regions for ill-paid and unhealthy seasonal employment picking coffee and other export crops. At one time it involved 750,000 Mayan peasants. U.S. AID provided funds for credit unions, and briefly, the movement was sponsored by the Laugurud government. Although the cooperatives did not begin to address the basic tragedy of the Indian highlands—landlessness—the government's support of the program was attacked by the Guatemalan right as "communist." The army took over at least one large cooperative and later, when the government moved to open up land for settlement by landless Indians, large tracts were immediately grabbed up by the military and the wealthy.[80]

In 1977, two Laugurud officials, Col. Fernando Castillo Ramirez, director of the National Cooperative Institute, and Leonel Giron, head of colonization programs in the northern area (the Franja Transversal del

Norte) that was to be opened for development, visited Israel. Following that visit

> Israeli advisers arrived in Guatemala to plan civil action programs in the conflictive Ixcan area, heartland of support for the...EGP and scene of constant military repression of local cooperative members.[81]

In 1978, Israel began a two-year scholarship program under which numerous Guatemalan officers and government officials studied "cooperativization and rural development," courses provided by the Israeli Foreign Ministry's International Cooperation Division. Lucas Garcia adopted some aspects of Israel's kibbutz and moshav (collective and non-collective agricultural settlements, respectively) into his 1979 "Integral Plan of Rural Communities" aimed at zones of conflict.

Israeli techniques—surpassing inspiration that also came from Taiwan and South Korea—were also the main guiding principles for the far more sweeping "pacification" program designed and implemented in 1982 under Rios Montt. [82]

The model villages turned the cooperative philosophy of user- or owner-control on its head. In the model villages of the Program of Assistance to Areas in Conflict (PAAC), food—often donated by international relief organizations—was doled out in exchange for compliance with the military's orders.

> In model villages the military or military-appointed commissioners control everything from latrine installation to food distribution and have created a structure parallel to civilian administration, which is left essentially powerless.[83]

Another twist to the model village scheme is the emphasis on the growth of non-traditional specialty crops for export. Air Force Col. Eduardo Wohlers, who in 1982 assumed charge of the civic action aspect of PAAC, visited Israel and studied "the elements of agricultural production on the kibbutz." Wohlers designed an agricultural collective based on the kibbutz[84]—a "distorted replica of rural Israel" commented one observer[85]—and construction was begun on a prototype in July 1983 at Yalihux in Alta Verapaz.[86]

Col. Wohlers described how the cooperatives would be turned into profitable operations:

> We foresee huge plantations of fruit and vegetables, with storage and processing facilities and refrigeration plants. We aim to put in the entire infrastructure for exporting frozen broccoli, Chinese cabbage, watermelons—a total of 15 new crops.[87]

Members of the Guatemalan military—many have grown wealthy over the last two decades—have invested in warehouses and refrigeration facilities in order to realize the economic opportunities of these new specialty exports.[88] One colonel said that the pacification plan called for the incorporation of one million people into the poles of development—"the entire hinterland."[89]

In addition to training Col. Wohlers and his colleagues, the Israelis have provided technical assistance for the model villages.[90]

It is a devilish plan, turning to the world a face of peaceful existence and productivity—the perfect model of a "backward" people in the process of development. Daily existence in the model villages is a matter of complete subjugation. The military assigns inmates to various projects such as road building—the roads are to provide the military with access it did not have when early in the decade it attacked the highlands—and tells them what crops they will plant. Two representatives from each project sit on a central decision making board which also includes representatives of the Guatemalan military and the civil patrols which they dominate.[91] This "monolithic structure...guards against the risk that the community will develop objectives contrary to government or military policy."[92]

The military has also encouraged the formation of producer associations, which give the impression of voluntary organizations.[93]

The domination also has its exploitative angle, as the military controls not only each individual's daily life, but is also the sole source of seeds, fertilizer and credit. Naturally, the military is also the sole marketing agent for the villages' produce.[94]

The comprehensive manner in which villages are governed has disrupted traditional of lines of authority. "Previous systems of settling disputes and selecting leaders have no meaning in this context."[95]

The forced relocation has wrenched the indigenous people from their land, from which they drew much of their identity, where they buried their dead and the umbilical cords of their children.[96] Being forced to grow alien crops in the place of the corn which occupies a central place in Mayan culture is, as the military is no doubt aware, a "deliberate act of cultural destruction."[97]

Confinement in a model village is sometimes preceded by a term in a political "reeducation" camp,[98] lasting from two to six months.[99]

One of the most oppressive features of Guatemala's pacification program is the "civilian self-defense patrols,"[100] whose ranks are filled by coercion, with most joining out of fear of being called subversive,[101] and thus marked for torture or execution.[102]

Those who do serve in the patrols must "turn in their quota of 'subversives.'" Otherwise, "they will be forced to denounce their own neighbors and to execute them with clubs and fists in the village plaza."[103]

The patrols are believed by most analysts to have been suggested by Israelis.[104] They have had a profound effect on Mayan society, both psychologically, "a permanent violation of our values or a new negative vision," as the country's Catholic bishops charged,[105] and practically, as long shifts on patrol prevent fulfillment of family and economic obligations.[106]

In 1983 the Guatemalan government estimated that 850 villages in the highlands had "self defense" units.[107] The following year the U.S. embassy in Guatemala estimated that 700,000 men had been enrolled in the units,[108] armed with Israeli assistance. Currently 900,000 men are organized into the civil patrols.[109]

In late 1983, U.S. customs agents in Miami held up an Israeli freighter carrying 12,000 rifles—reports varied as to whether they were World War I bolt-action Remingtons or Mausers—headed for Guatemala, which chief of state Mejia Victores confirmed Guatemala had bought from Israel.[110] Mejia said they were for "troops in training."[111] It appears as if these totally antiquated arms were purchased after the U.S. turned down an appeal by Mejia's predecessor for a donation of "old rifles for use by civil defense patrols."[112]

In May 1984, SIAG (*Servicio de Informacion y Analisis de Guatemala*) released details of a meeting between U.S. and Israeli representatives and members of the Guatemalan government in Guatemala on December 10 and 12, 1983.

According to SIAG, plans were formulated at that meeting for industrial development in a number of regions, among them the Indian-dominated highlands and a stepped-up effort to quell the insurgency, which by that time had unified in an umbrella organization URNG (*Unidad Revolucionaria Nacional Guatemalteca*). The report said that the cheap labor to run the planned industries would be drawn from the development poles.[113]

Whether or not this plan is ever fully implemented, the implications of the labor conditions already established in the model villages are enormous. In 1983, labor leaders charged that work was performed in the model villages "without remuneration."[114]

In 1985 inmates of three model villages in Quiche said that they were often formed up into press gangs by the army to repair roads, work on fortifications, "clear fields of fire," and build new model villages, all without pay. Moreover, the residents told a reporter that the work for the army did not leave time to work the insufficient plots of land they had been assigned and that they were not allowed to leave.[115]

Food was obtainable, in at least some instances, only from military stores (a version of the company store in so many North American mining towns) giving the military yet another means of control over the village inmates.[116]

In 1986, opposition sources within Guatemala also knew of instances in which work in the model villages was not performed for wages, but only in exchange for staple foods—the very corn and beans the inmates are no longer allowed to grow for themselves. In a word, slave labor.[117]

> The Guatemalan government, in facing a broad based popular movement, has come to resemble the Israelis on the West Bank and Gaza: they are an occupying army. They must use force to stop dissent, but also need to plan for the more long-range effort of social control. Thus the Israeli plans at home provide a prototype for solving Guatemalan problems.[118]

It is no accident that the Guatemalans looked to the Israelis for assistance in organizing their campaign against the Indians, and having followed their mentors' advice, wound up with something that looks quite a bit like the Israeli occupation of the Palestinian territories of the West Bank and the Gaza strip. As the Israelis wrecked the local economy and turned the occupied territories into a captive market and a cheap labor pool, the Guatemalan military has made economic activity in the occupied highlands all but impossible.[119]

As it is openly acknowledged in the Israeli media that the Palestinian population must not be allowed to exceed the Jewish population,[120] it is common knowledge that the Guatemalan military would like to reduce the Mayan population to a minority.[121]

But most of all there is the unyielding violence of the suppression. The occupation regime Israel has maintained since 1967 over the Palestinians (and its occupation of the Syrian Golan Heights, the Egyptian Sinai and Southern Lebanon) has trained "an entire generation of Israelis...to impose Israeli rule over subject peoples."[122] "The Israeli soldier is a model and an example to us," Gen. Benedicto Lucas said in 1981.[123]

It was in the coercive resettlement program that Israel's activities in Guatemala intersected most directly with those of the Christian right surrounding the Reagan Administration. This was particularly true during the reign of Rios Montt. Montt was a so-called "born-again Christian," a member ("elder") of the Arcata, California based Church of the Word, a branch of Evangelical Gospel Outreach.

In Guatemala, the Christian right was interested in converts—by the end of 1982 reactionary Protestants had succeeded in recruiting 22 percent of the population to their theology of blind obedience and anti-communism.[124] They were particularly hostile to Catholicism, especially "Liberation Theology," which many of the Guatemalan military deemed responsible for the insurgency.

Right-wing Christian organizations seemed to be especially drawn to the harsh social control being exerted on the highland Mayans. During the Rios Montt period, foreign fundamentalists were permitted access to military operational zones, while Catholics were turned away—or attacked. During this period "many Catholic rectories and churches in Quiche [a highland province] [were] turned into Army barracks."[125] In late 1983, the Vatican itself protested the murder of a Franciscan priest in Guatemala and the (exiled) Guatemalan Human Rights Commission (CDHG) charged that in the space of several months 500 catechists had been disappeared. In October the police caught and tortured some religious workers.[126]

Meanwhile, Rios Montt surrounded himself with advisers, both North American and Guatemalan, from his Verbo church, and what appeared to be a loose coalition of right-wing fundamentalist organizations, most notably Pat Robertson's Christian Broadcasting Network, began an extensive fundraising drive and also started sending volunteers to Ixil Triangle villages under military control. Rios Montt chose Love Lift International, the "relief arm" of Gospel Outreach, Verbo's parent church, to carry the food and supplies purchased with the money raised. Verbo representatives, along with an older evangelical outfit, the Wycliffe Bible Translators (WBT/SIL, the latter initials for the Summer Institute of Linguistics, an organization whose CIA connections are long and impeccable and which has often been charged with involvement in massacres of indigenous peoples throughout the Americas), arranged with the government "to take charge of all medical work in the Ixil Triangle, and for all education in Indian areas up to the third grade to be taught in Indian languages with WBT/SIL assistance," through the Behrhorst Clinic. WBT/SIL and the Clinic's parent, the Behrhorst Foundation, incorporated with Verbo Church into the Foundation for Aid to the Indian People (FUNDAPI), whose stated purpose was to channel international Christian donations to refugees and which coordinated volunteers from U.S. right-wing religious organizations.[127]

Although nothing has yet emerged which definitively ties Israeli activities in Guatemala to those of the religious right, it is reasonable to assume there is contact. Since the late 1970s the government of Israel has devoted considerable energy to befriending such political luminaries of rightist evangelism as Jerry Falwell and Pat Robertson, having turned to these groups after the National Council of Churches passed some mildly reproving resolutions about the Middle East. The Christian extremists tell Israel what it wants to hear. Jerry Falwell found justification in the Bible for an Israel encompassing parts of "Iraq, Syria, Turkey, Saudi Arabia, Egypt, Sudan and all of Lebanon, Jordan, and Kuwait."[128] Pat Robertson praised the Reagan Administration's veto of a UN Security Council resolution condemning Israel's invasion of Lebanon with some gobbledygook tying the invasion to the fundamentalist superstition that Israel will be the site of the last battle, Armageddon: "Israel has lit the fuse, and it is a fast burning fuse, and I don't think that the fuse is going to be quenched until that region explodes in flames. That is my personal feeling from the Bible."[129] Robertson urged his viewers to call the White House and voice their support for the Israeli invasion.

Untroubled by the scene in Armageddon when all the Jews will be converted (or damned), Israel welcomed the "Christian Voice of Hope" radio station and its companion "Star of Hope" television to Southern Lebanon, and, even though proseletyzing is illegal in Israel, provided the stations with Israeli government newscasts. Supported by donations from U.S. right-wing evangelicals, and in particular by Pat Robertson's Christian Broadcasting Network, the stations were "used as a military tool" by the Israeli proxy South Lebanon Army.[130]

Aside from the religious right and their secular allies, the Guatemalan model villages have been universally condemned. Until 1985 a bipartisan majority opposed the granting of any U.S. aid that would strengthen the development poles.[131] This, of course, stopped short of undercutting support for the "pacification" program, as funds received from U.S. AID and other foreign sources freed up government funds for use on the model villages. In 1984, U.S. AID granted Guatemala $1 million which was used for constructing infrastructure for the model villages.[132] Americas Watch Vice Chairman Aryeh Neier pointed out that humanitarian assistance from the U.S. has "played an essential role in the Guatemalan Army's counterinsurgency programs," enabling the army to distribute (or with-hold) food to exact compliance with its resettlement program.[133]

Even with the transition to an elected government in 1986, the model villages continued under military control. The military made sure of that: before it turned power over to its civilian successors, the Mejia Victores regime promulgated a series of decrees defining the programs relating to the poles of development as part of the "counterinsurgency," and thus its purview.[134]

The model villages also received the economic backing of the elected government of President Vinicio Cerezo, which exempted vegetable exports from a proposed tax on exports.[135] In the first few months of Cerezo's administration, new villages were begun in Alta Verapaz and El Quiche departments.[136]

This is not so surprising when it is recalled that the Guatemalan military decided to step aside (formally speaking) because during the final six years of its rule the nation's once-robust economy had withered. The quetzal had declined from its half-century of parity with the dollar to 3.80 in late 1985.[137] Most foreign funders had conditioned aid to Guatemala on the election of a civilian government. Wishing to avoid responsibility for the sinking economy, the Guatemalan military ceded some of the trappings of power to obtain foreign aid for its pacification program .[138]

In 1984, elections were held to seat a Constituent Assembly, charged with writing a constitution. Two rounds of presidential elections followed in late 1985. While the 1985 election campaign was in progress Col. Byron Disrael Lima, the commander of Quiche department and head of the local "Interinstitutional Coordinator," a body set up by the army to extend its direct control to every locality, noted that even after the transfer to civilian government, military influence on the local body would continue. Lima believed that was the natural order of things. He noted that,

> there's a civilian wave in Latin America now, but that doesn't mean military men will lose their ultimate power. Latins take commands from men in uniform...The civilians don't work until we tell them to work. They need our protection, control and direction.

Lima went on to express his admiration for Napoleon and Hitler and his respect for conquerers and "warriors" like the Israelis.[139]

Also in Quiche, a model village resident said "here we don't know about political parties. I don't know what party I would vote for. The lieutenant says that political parties are not good for us."[140]

In June 1986 Guatemalan refugees, Mayans living under the protection of sanctuary workers in the U.S., told a reporter for National Public Radio that if they return the Cerezo government says they must go first to an indoctrination camp and then be assigned to a model village.[141]

The real tragedy is the number of foreign officials willing to be fooled. In January 1985, Rep. Stephen Solarz visited Guatemala City and promised a resumption of U.S. aid as soon as power was turned over to a civilian government.[142]

In the Autumn of 1986 President Cerezo toured Europe and assured less-than-skeptical heads of state that human rights abuses in Guatemala had ceased. Beyond the massive assault on the rights of those confined to model villages, the kidnappings, disappearances and broad-daylight executions had continued since Cerezo's January 14, 1986 inauguration and were still going on as he spoke. The European media carried the allegations about the ongoing official violence in Guatemala by representatives of GAM, the Mutual Support Group, made up of relatives of the disappeared,[143] but Germany, France, and Belgium did not flinch from commitments made that summer to provide aid to Guatemala.[144]

Inroads into Economic and Political Life

As with its links to South Africa, Israel's military relations with Guatemala have led to a number of economic and political bonds. The Guatemalan ambassador to Israel summed up the present state of bilateral relations:

> From Israel, we buy electronics, radar and communications equipment and we send it civilian machinery for repairs. Likewise, dozens of young Guatemalan professionals attend international cooperation centers to acquire Israeli know-how, especially in agronomic industry. Israel imports from Guatemala coffee, cardamom, precious wood, Guatemalan crafts, sesame and nickel amongst others, and provides technical assistance for the exploitation of Guatemala's many natural resources. This forms the basis for the excellent relations that fortunately exist between the peoples and governments of Guatemala and Israel.[145]

For Guatemala, it was easy: "We're isolated internationally," said a prominent Guatemalan. "The only friend we have left in the world is Israel."[146] Toward the end of his rule, Gen. Mejia Victores was scheduled to visit Israel but had to cancel the trip when a political and economic crisis erupted.[147] As with the leaders of the apartheid government, the Guatemalan head of state would not have received a warm welcome in many other countries.

The bonds have been building for several years. On June 15, 1982, just nine days after Israel invaded Lebanon, Guatemala's Minister of Economy Julio Matheu Duchez visited Israel to sign a trade agreement under which each nation granted the other "most-favored nation" status and pledged to cooperate in the fields of industry, agriculture, development, and tourism. Signing for Israel was Trade and Industry Minister Gideon Pat, who disclosed that a joint commission of representatives from each country would meet "from time to time" to monitor the agreement's implementation.[148]

According to George Black, the tourism component of the agreement involved a special pitch to Jewish communities in New York, Miami and Los Angeles about the wonders of Guatemala. Discussions were held between Israel's El Al airlines, Guatemala's AVIATECA and Air Florida about joint promotion campaigns involving the Sheraton Hotel in Guatemala City. The hotel is owned by the Kong family, "which has extensive links to the far-right Movement of National Liberation (MLN)."[149]

American Jews might be targeted because apparently it is not safe for Israelis to tour Guatemala. The Israeli consul in Guatemala said he could not guarantee one of his countrymen's safety.[150] The threat might not come only from the insurgents: by 1985 there were complaints among Guatemalan noncombatants about Israel's extensive involvement in Guatemala's internal affairs.[151]

On November 17, 1983, according to the Guatemala-based *Central America Report,* the two signed another trade and economic cooperation agreement, its purpose "to strengthen friendly and commercial relations and to facilitate as far as possible economic cooperation on a basis of equality and mutual advantages."[152]

Israel also promised help with Guatemala's telephone system,[153] and an Israeli arms dealer set up a school for training telephone company personnel.[154]

Israeli firms are now said to have extensive agribusiness investments, held through intermediaries, in Guatemala.[155]

Israeli "security" firms have also found employment in Guatemala, sending rent-a-Rambo commandos to implement security for wealthy planters. These portable goon squads, which have proliferated in Israel as the large officer corps reaches retirement age in a soured economy, are by no means strictly private operations. All must pass a government test and all the techniques and equipment they take abroad must be approved by the defense ministry.[156]

Israel's Tadiran and South Africa's Consolidated Power have established a joint undertaking in Guatemala to assemble and sell electronic equipment.[157] Always eager for international contact, South Africa followed Israel to Guatemala where it too is involved in advising the "pacification" program.[158] In the early 1980s, the white government also offered to send counterinsurgency troops to Guatemala.[159] The relationship clicked with the Guatemalan military. In August 1986, the army overrode the national assembly's motion to break diplomatic relations with the apartheid regime.[160]

Israel began dealing arms out of Guatemala. Eagle Military Gear Overseas set up shop on a secure floor of the *Cortijo Reforma* Hotel in Guatemala City, opposite army headquarters. In 1982 Ignacio Klich wrote that Eagle's Tel Aviv headquarters was referring Central American buyers to its regional sales office in Guatemala.[161] Also known as Eagle Israeli Armaments and Desert Eagle, the company is owned by Pesakh Ben-Or, an Israeli paratrooper who got his start in arms dealing as chauffeur for another Israeli arms dealer.[162] By one account Ben-Or drove for David Marcus Katz, an Israeli who has lived for many years in Mexico and is known as one of Israel's major arms dealers.[163]

Under the military regime, Ben-Or's links to the Guatemalans were said to be so good that

> almost all the representatives of the Israeli arms factories, security apparatus and electronics firms who want to establish connections in Guatemala arrive at the conclusion that it is better to do it through him.[164]

That includes the giants Israeli Military Industries and Tadiran—Ben-Or claims to have had a hand in the army communications school—although these behemoths are said not to have a high opinion of him.[165]

According to a contra leader, the contras' chief link to Israel is through the Israeli embassy in Guatemala City. Pesakh Ben-Or also sold arms to the contras through the armed forces of Honduras, although it is not clear whether he made the sale through Eagle in Guatemala or from his residence in Miami.[166]

Israel got close enough to Guatemala to exercise more than a bit of leverage in internal Guatemalan affairs. There was the overthrow of Chief of State Romeo Lucas Garcia and his replacement with Rios Montt. There was also Israel's more than active interest in the 1985 Guatemalan presidential elections.

Although it was very evident to journalists that Israel did not enjoy wide popularity among the population as a whole,[167] Israel had clout where it mattered, as was demonstrated early on in the campaign, when all the major candidates met with Latin American B'nai B'rith representatives and pledged to work on the continued improvement of relations with Israel. The candidate of the ultra-right MLN party, Mario Sandoval Alarcon, pledged to move Guatemala's embassy to Jerusalem.[168]

Israel was trying very hard in 1985 to persuade Guatemala—and Haiti, Honduras, Panama and Uruguay—to follow in the footsteps of El Salvador and move to Jerusalem.[169] Already very close to Israel in 1980, when the UN asked all governments to relocate their embassies to Tel Aviv, Guatemala resisted the move. However, threatened by Arab buyers of its important cardamom crop, Guatemala reluctantly transferred its embassy. At the same time its foreign ministry said the move to Tel Aviv "would not alter Guatemala's traditional political stance toward Israel."[170]

Pesakh Ben-Or promised a $10,000 campaign contribution to one of the candidates, Jorge Carpio Nicolle, "and at a certain stage an additional $50,000 was spoken of."[171] This is only one of many reports of Israeli contributions, which are often made to defense ministries in hopes of gaining arms contracts.[172] Ben-Or also hired Israelis to train a team of bodyguards for candidate Carpio.[173]

Initially favored by the U.S., Carpio was openly antagonistic to Nicaragua[174] while Christian Democrat Vinicio Cerezo made it clear that he would follow the military's policy of neutrality in the region and steer clear of cooperating with the Reagan Administration's activities against Nicaragua. Cerezo won.

Although candidate Cerezo said he would look into Israel's relations with the military,[175] when he worked out a deal with the military (pledging no Argentine-style trials and no interference with such "security" matters as the development poles) and promised the landed aristocracy that there would be no agrarian reform,[176] he might have included maintenance of the Israeli connection as part of the package. Attending Cerezo's inauguration, Israel's labor minister somewhat embarrasedly explained to the new president that Israel was not involved in Ben-Or's campaign activities.[177]

When Foreign Minister Yitzhak Shamir visited Central America the following May, Guatemala was one of the stops on his itinerary. It was expected that Shamir would receive a chilly reception,[178] but from what could be observed, he had a full measure of official attention, meeting with President Cerezo and addressing the national legislature.[179]

Whether or not Israel was disappointed with the outcome of the elections, Hebrew-speaking security operatives stood guard at the election night press center.[180] A few weeks after the inauguration of President Cerezo, Defense Minister Gen. Jaime Hernandez Mendez said that the Israeli ambassador to Guatemala had recently offered military cooperation to the new government[181] and, despite expectations that the U.S. would displace Israel as Guatemala's prime military supplier, an Israeli source said that Israel might indeed increase its military links with Guatemala.[182] It is notable, however, that in restructuring the police, the Cerezo government looked to Spain, Mexico and Venezuela for training and equipment.[183]

Relations with civilian-run Guatemala remained cordial enough for Israel to take on a bit of international diplomacy. During a July 1986 visit to

Israel, Manuel Esquivel, the prime minister of Belize, asked the Israeli government to "use its influence" and act as a restraining force on Guatemala. Esquivel said that Israel's arms sales to Guatemala gave the Jewish state the "right to speak about, to influence the use of those arms."[184]

In September 1984, Belize, formerly British Honduras, had established diplomatic relations with Israel for that very reason. Belize was in constant fear of its neighbor, whose military rulers frequently trumpeted their irredentist claims (usually when the Guatemalan economy merited having popular attention deflected elsewhere).[185]

During Esquivel's 1986 visit, Israel was able to score a minor diplomatic coup by bringing the Guatemalan ambassador to Israel to a state dinner in his honor. The two sat at the same table.[186] It was the first time that representatives of the two countries had such a meeting. Shortly after the dinner encounter, Guatemala's President Vinicio Cerezo said if a delegation from Belize came to Guatemala and requested a meeting he would be happy to meet with them.[187]

Considering that the election that brought Cerezo to power was geared toward obtaining aid from European nations, Guatemala was not lacking in motivation to attend the dinner: better relations with Britain, a member of the European Community would certainly help that process along.[188] Guatemala was at the same time moving toward the reestablishment of diplomatic relations with London, broken in 1981 over the issue of Belize.[189] Although given independence in 1981, Belize has been protected against Guatemala by a garrison of British soldiers. Nonetheless, it is not often that Israel, in its international isolation, has had an opportunity to play such a role.

Israeli advisers continue to work in Guatemala. During his 1986 visit, Shamir said he had offered to increase the technical and scientific links that bring many Guatemalans on scholarship to Israel each year.[190] Exactly how many are involved in the development poles is not known. An Israeli foreign ministry spokesperson admitted to three Israelis, teaching "irrigation and techniques for organizing youth movements and community centers."[191] The numbers are also probably euphemistic.

Certainly the advisers are not a democratizing force. Mercedes Sotz Cate, the financial secretary of the Guatemalan Municipal Workers Union, was seized and tortured for five hours on February 12, 1986. His abduction came at the beginning of a violent union-busting campaign by the mayor of Guatemala City, Alvaro Arzu Irigoyen. Sotz said that his torturers were Israeli agents in the employ of the mayor. When questioned, Arzu "admit[ted] only to people of different nationality who work for the city without a salary." At least one Israeli was identified as part of a group "advising" the municipality and Arzu confirmed this.[192]

As to Israel's influence over Guatemala: whatever else it was, it made the military government impervious to U.S. wishes. In 1979 the Carter Administration proposed restoring a $250,000 military training grant to Guatemala out of concern "that U.S. relations with the Guatemalan military were deteriorating to the point of endangering all of Washington's influence in the largest and most populous Central American country."

The Carter State Department wanted to have Guatemalan officers and military technicians back for training in the U.S. "as a wedge to get back on better terms with the military leaders."[193] Congress didn't buy this, just as it did not yield to the Reagan Administration's far more passionate representations for a reestablishment of ties with Guatemala.

The extent of Guatemala's independence from U.S. pressure was clearly evident in 1983 and 1984, when the Reagan Administration was trying to organize Central America against Nicaragua. Guatemala refused to participate in the reactivation of CONDECA, a regional military pact established in 1964, and, irrespective of the shrill anti-communism of its domestic politics, continued to adhere to a neutral—sometimes an even vaguely supportive—position toward Nicaragua. A National Security Council document classed this position "a continuing problem" and proposed increasing pressure on Guatemala.[194]

Indeed, while ignorning Reagan entreaties for cooperation, the Guatemalan government under Mejia Victores sought to approach Washington through Israel, lobbying the 11th convention of the Federation of Jewish Communities of Central America and Panama, held in Guatemala City, to help Guatemala improve its relations with the U.S. Addressing the convention, Guatemala's foreign minister "denounced U.S. policy toward Guatemala as not equitable and praised Israel's friendship and cooperation."[195]

Abdication of Responsibility

It is a mistake to conclude that U.S. complicity in the genocidal war of the Guatemalan generals ended when the Carter Administration pulled the plug on military aid in 1977. When the U.S. intervened in Guatemala and overthrew its liberal, democratically elected government in 1954,[196] it effectively transferred rule to the country's military, which has held power ever since. Even the civilian presidency of Julio Cesar Mendez Montenegro was (with U.S. acquiescence) immediately subjugated by the military.[197] To cite only one example of the continuity that makes the last three tragic decades of Guatemala a U.S. responsibility: the dossiers that formed the basis of the intelligence unit G-2's death squad selection process also date back to 1954. After the fall of the government of Jacobo Arbenz, the army confiscated the membership lists of the many organizations which had blossomed during the all-too-short hiatus between repressive regimes— Guatemala was ruled by the oppressive dictator Jorge Ubico until 1945, when he was bloodlessly replaced by a popular government under Dr. Juan Jose Arevalo—and from these lists culled 70,000 "communists." These files were updated during the 1960s and used for assassinations during a U.S.-supported counterinsurgency.[198] In the 1970s Israel stepped in and helped with the computerization of the whole bloody system.

It does not take convoluted reasoning to conclude that "both the U.S. and Israel bear rather serious moral responsibility" for Guatemala.[199] Since 1978, however, Congress has done little more than beat down the most outrageous of President Reagan's requests for aid for the military regime. Nor did large numbers of peace and solidarity activists mount an active campaign, even when the slaughter reached a peak.

Major Israeli Weapons Sales to Guatemala

Item	Comments	Reference Source
7 201–IAI Arava planes	Ordered and delivered 1976	SIPRI, *Yearbook 1977*, p. 316.
10 201–IAI Arava planes	Ordered 1977; delivered 1977–78	SIPRI, *Yearbook 1978*, p. 262; SIPRI, *Yearbook, 1979*, pp. 214–215.
5 troop-carrying Asimo helicopters		"Growing Arms Race in Central America May Heat up Region," *Christian Science Monitor,* 28 October 1981.
10 RBY MK armored cars	Delivered 1974–77	U.S. Congress, House, Committee on Foreign Affairs, *Economic and Military Aid Programs,* p. 84.
5 field kitchens	4 delivered 1974–77	*Ibid.;* Klieman, *Israel's Global Reach,* p. 135.

(continues)

(continued)

Item	Comments	Reference Source
50,000 Galil assault rifles	15,000 delivered 1974–77	*Christian Science Monitor*, 28 October 1981.
1,000 machine guns		*Ibid*.
3 naval coast guard ships (Dabur boats)	Talks started in 1978	Mauricio Goldstein, "Con Armas Israelis Asesinan al Pueblo Guatemalteco," *Punto Final Internacional*, August 1981, p. 14; interview with "Emilcar," nom de guerre, high ranking official in the Political Wing of the Guatemalan EGP, Managua, Nicaragua, 18 August 1982.
Grenade launchers 81-mm mortars 120 tons of ammunition	Arrived in Guatemala's Santo Tomas de Castilla port 3 months after suspension of U.S. military aid	Goldstein, *Punto Final Internacional*, August 1981, p. 14; *Nuevo Diario*, 28 September 1981.
Bulletproof vests Military tents		*Ha'aretz*, April 1979, quoted in Ignacio Klich, "Guatemala's Back-Door Arms Deals," *8 Days*, 13 March 1982.
Shields Tear gas Gas masks	Bought by Interior Minister Donaldo Alvarez in 1980 visit to Israel	Interview with Emilcar.
Fire ejectors	Used to burn bushes and people. Captured by EGP from government troops	*Ibid*.
Tactical transmission system	Cover the whole country. Bought 1977 or 1978	*Ibid*.; "Israel Aliado de la Dictadura Guatemalteca," *OLP Informa* (Mexico City), April 1982, p. 8.
Radar system	Has 5 receivers. Bought end 1980. Israeli controlled and directed	*Ibid*.; *News from Guatemala* 3 (October 1981): 1.
High-tech products: • Radar • Intelligence information computing		*Latin America Weekly Report*, 5 September 1980, p. 8; *El Dia*, 8 May 1982: interview with Emilcar; John Rettie,

(continued)

Item	Comments	Reference Source
and communications equipment • Radar circuits to detect guerrillas smuggling arms		*Manchester Guardian Weekly,* 10 January 1982.
Helmets		*Le Monde,* 25 January 1979.
5 million rifle bullets	Bought in 1977 for $1.8 million through David Marcus Katz	*Excelsior,* 18 July 1977, p. 2A; interview with Emilcar.
Shipload light arms	65 tons delivered 1977	SIPRI, *Yearbook 1980,* p. 144.
10,000 105-mm HEAT (high-explosive anti-tank) ammunition	Supplied 1981–82 to the army for $6 million	SIPRI, *Yearbook 1982,* p. 188.
Kfir fighters	Unspecified number	Klieman, *Israel's Global Reach,* p. 135.

Chart from Bishara Bahbah, *Israel and Latin America: The Military Connection*, New York: St. Martin's, 1986.

Nicaragua Under Somoza ....

Stretching Somoza's Lifeline

With few qualms and minimal outside criticism, Israel came to the rescue of Nicaraguan dictator Anastasio Somoza Debayle and, from September 1978 to July 1979, helped him stave off history. Later it would be thrown up to Israel that when Washington and just about every other government in the world was boycotting Somoza, Israel had been willing to provide him with weapons.

But Israel was indebted to Nicaragua, was always the rejoinder. The "debt" in actuality was not to Nicaragua, but to the father of Somoza Debayle, Anastasio Somoza Garcia, who had been installed as head of the National Guard by the U.S. marines in 1933 and had muscled his way into what he called the "presidency"—it was definitely the top spot in the government—the following year.

Somoza Garcia was assassinated in 1956. For the next eleven years a son Luis and a chorus line of Somoza relatives filled his position, which was finally assumed by his son Anastasio Somoza Debayle. The debt of which the Israelis speak was incurred in the late 1930s when Somoza Garcia acted as a front for arms purchases the pre-state Zionist military forces, the Haganah, made in Europe. He was well paid for the trouble he took to sign his name to the required documents.

After World War II, Somoza gave Haganah buyers Nicaraguan diplomatic passports and again signed the receipts for the weapons they purchased. He took cash up front for his services, over $200,000 deposited in his *personal* New York bank account and a large diamond and some other gifts on the side. He never complained about a balance due.[1]

Some Israeli leaders might have cherished feelings of gratitude for Anastasio Somoza Garcia. They might have wanted to do his son, who visited Israel in 1961[2] a good turn. That there was a distinction between the national entity, Nicaragua, blurred as it was by four decades of Somozas who owned much of the country as well as ruled it, and the Somoza family dynasty might not have occurred to the Israelis. It is remarkable that it has not occurred to many in the United States.

If scales must be used, it should be taken into account that, following a technical aid agreement in 1966, Israel made Nicaragua a major beneficiary of its development programs. It also provided emergency relief after Nicaragua was devastated by an earthquake in 1972.[3]

To reckon its debt to the Somozas, Israel sometimes notes the unswerving support Nicaragua gave it at the UN, voting in favor of Israel more often than the U.S.![4] Those votes, however, did not represent the people of Nicaragua; they reflected the Somoza family's political interests, primarily staying in the good graces of U.S.-connected loan givers. Somoza Debayle was notorious for taking heavy commissions on loans to the Nicaraguan government—sometimes even pocketing the loans themselves. Part of the $1.6 billion debt left when he was driven from Nicaragua was for loans to his own and his associates' private businesses. (The new Nicaraguan government reluctantly assumed all the dictator's debts, as that was the only way to obtain credit with Western lenders.[5])

These Israeli debts were repaid in a strange coin to the people of Nicaragua, who were bombed and shot with Israeli-supplied ordnance in a carnage that went on for weeks, if not months, longer than it would have without help from Israel, which supplied 98 percent of the dictator's weaponry during the last six months of his rule.[6]

Somoza had been introduced to Israeli weapons in 1974 at a special showing arranged for him in Managua.[7] He had bought Dabur class patrol boats and Arava STOL aircraft; by the time he fought his final battle he would have 14 Aravas to rush his troops from place to place.[8]

Soon after Somoza's U.S. aid was blocked, insurrection flared against him. In September 1978, there was fighting in most of Nicaragua's cities and a massive general strike in Managua that was supported by virtually the entire business community. Somoza shot his way out of it. His National Guard used 1,000 Uzi submachine guns and Galil rifles from Israel, and

Somoza was expecting "thousands more" Galils.[9] Although most Latin American leaders were hoping for his downfall, Somoza survived the September challenge. "Israeli-made weapons helped to save the Somoza dynasty," read one headline.[10]

That autumn, Israeli rifles and ammunition arrived in large quantities. Some of the Galil rifles were "sent directly to a special terror unit commanded by Somoza's son, which carried out the murder of political opponents, among them women and children."[11] The Guard also used the new Israeli weapons in its "clean-up" operations, which went on during October 1978 in half a dozen cities. The majority of the victims—many of them were shot by the Guard at their own front doors—were between 14 and 21 years of age and were marked for execution simply because they lived in neighborhoods where the Sandinista National Liberation Front (FSLN) had been active.[12]

An Israeli adviser "who presented himself as an Israeli army officer" was also present in Nicaragua and worked in Somoza's bunker in Managua. The adviser allegedly represented David Marcus Katz, the Mexico-based Israeli arms dealer with close ties to the right wing Israeli settlers movement, Gush Emunim.[13]

Israeli arms shipments continued to arrive. Several shipments came by air and were delivered at night during a curfew. Among the weapons delivered this way were surface-to-air missiles (although the Sandinistas did not have an air force). Israel had at one point given its word that it would not ship arms to Somoza. Now it denied doing so, but U.S. officials said that Israeli arms were still arriving in Nicaragua. "Our people in Managua tell us that the streets are starting to look like Jerusalem because the National Guard is wearing Israeli berets," said one U.S. official.[14]

By the following spring Israel was sending Somoza really big stuff: nine combat-armed Cessna aircraft and two Sikorsky helicopters. The FSLN shot down seven of the Cessnas.[15] Somoza got better use out of the helicopters, which he called "skyraiders."[16] He had his Guards use them as platforms for machine gun strafing; and from 3,000 feet above ground, soldiers rolled bombs out of the helicopter doors.[17]

"The Government is dropping 500-pound bombs from helicopters on rebel-held shantytowns, reportedly killing as many as 600 people in one day. Soldiers routinely kill suspected rebels they capture," wrote the *New York Times* correspondent in Managua of the final weeks of the war.[18] After having all but five cities and a great part of Nicaragua's industrial infrastructure destroyed,[19] on July 17, 1979, Somoza cleaned out the national treasury and fled the country.

Less than three weeks earlier, Israel had at last agreed to honor a request from the U.S. Embassy in Tel Aviv to halt its weapons shipments to Nicaragua. Israel ordered a freighter carrying two patrol boats to divert its course from Nicaragua, and "agreed to call off other planned shipments of ammunition and weaponry to Somoza for the time being."[20] Somoza claimed that another ship carrying Israeli weapons was turned back only miles from Nicaragua's coast and he could not get that shipment out of his mind. The arms it carried, he said,

> had been paid for before the ship ever left Israel... That ship carried, among other military items, ten thousand anti-tank and anti-personnel grenade rifles with ammunition... That precious cargo could have won the war for the anti-Communist forces of Nicaragua... Somewhere in Israel there is a large consignment of arms and ammunition which could have saved Nicaragua.[21]

Certainly there had been some criticism of Israel's role in the bloody war against the Nicaraguan population. The opposition newspaper *La Prensa* had said that the Nobel Peace Prize given to Israeli Prime Minister Menachem Begin was "tainted" by Israel's arms sales to Somoza.[22] And the Costa Rican paper *La Republica* wrote that "the whole world should join in asking Israel to stop sending weapons of aggression, oppression and death..."[23]

But in the United States, where the Carter human rights doctrine had supposedly constituted a decisive step in the right direction, there were blank stares—in the other direction. Somoza's henchmen are said to have killed one member of every family in Nicaragua. It seems fairly obvious in retrospect that many Nicaraguan lives might have been saved had peace and solidarity activists in this country made loud and persistent demands that Israeli arms shipments be stopped.

There had been so little public interest in what Israel was doing for Somoza, however, that the State Department felt secure in dishing out nonsense on the subject. A representative from Nicaragua's Broad Opposition Front visited Washington in November 1978 to ask the Carter Administration to stop the Israeli arms shipments. A State Department source said the appeal had been rejected and that the administration had decided not to prevent Israel from supplying "light weapons" to Somoza: "If Somoza goes, we would prefer to see him go peacefully. We would not like to see him toppled in an armed revolt." The thinking was that, given time, a "moderate element" might emerge to succeed the dictator.

Forcing Israel to stop supplying Somoza with arms "remained a U.S. option that might be used in the future," continued the source, who expressed confidence that although there was no legal mechanism by which the U.S. could stop Israel, U.S. influence could certainly force a halt to Israeli gunrunning.[24]

When the administration finally did compel a halt to the Israeli arms shipments the reason it gave was strikingly similar: "additional arms would undercut efforts to replace Somoza with a moderate government."[25]

In the aftermath of the war, leaders of the victorious FSLN presented Cuban leader Fidel Castro with a Galil rifle captured from the National Guard.[26] Nicaragua repudiated the small debt remaining on the books for Somoza's arms purchases from Israel.[27] Relations between Israel and the new Nicaraguan government were frosty; according to one account the nonresident Israeli ambassador to Nicaragua did not receive accreditation from the new government.[28] Nicaragua invited the PLO, with which some of the Sandinistas had long had close ties, to establish an embassy in Managua and in 1981 warmly welcomed the organization's leader, Yasir Arafat. On August 6, 1982, citing the "annihilation" of Lebanese and Palestinians during Israel's siege of Beirut, Nicaragua announced that it was breaking diplomatic relations with Israel.[29]

There is a certain symmetry to all the indebtedness: Somoza I giving his friendship for cash in advance; Somoza II giving his support at the UN, and then paying cash up front for weapons. And then, years later, the wretched remnants of the National Guard turning up in Israel, claiming that last boatload of weapons. By then they were called contras.

There is another dire symmetry to this story: while Israel's relatively autonomous aid to Somoza delighted the forces of the far-right who were blocked by the Carter Administration from aiding him themselves, when the contras were created and thrown against Nicaragua by the Reagan Administration, Israel was a reluctant participant, but nonetheless a key one, demanding a heavy price for its help.

Major Israeli Weapons Sales to Nicaragua

Item	Comments	Reference Source
14 201–IAI Arava planes	Ordered 1973. 5 delivered 1974, the rest 1975–77. Unit cost $650,000	SIPRI, *Yearbook 1974*, p. 282, *Yearbook, 1975*, p. 240, *Yearbook, 1977*, p. 330.
4 armed patrol boats	Only one or two are left. Somoza loyalists used the rest to flee	*Newsweek*, 20 November 1978, p. 68; Interview with Marwan Tahbub, PLO Ambassador, Managua, Nicaragua, 15 August 1982.

(continues)

(continued)

Item	Comments	Reference Source
1 light military transport plane	Most likely Westwind	*Le Monde*, 4 July 1979.
67 tactical radios	Delivered 1974–77. Valued at $0.3 million	U.S. Congress, House, Committee on Foreign Affairs, *Economic and Military Aid Programs*, p. 84.
Helicopters Small patrol boat Heavy mortars Machine guns	Delivered 1978	*Latin America Weekly Report*, 16 May 1980, p. 10.
Heavy combat tanks Light artillery Missile launchers Patrol vehicles Helicopters	Old Sherman tanks delivered May 1975. Other cargo ships were in route	*Ha'aretz*, 10 May 1978; interview with Ambassador Tahbub.
2–3 radars	Delivered to Somoza but no time to set them up	Interview with Ambassador Tahbub.
Trucks Flack jackets Mortars		*Newsweek*, 20 November 1978, p. 68.
Missiles	Anti-aircraft, surface-to-surface missiles and ground-to-ground missiles. Delivered secretly by two Israeli planes	*Ibid.; New York Times*, 19 November 1978; *Excelsior*, 8 June 1979, p. 20A.
500 Uzi submachine guns 500 Galil assault rifles		*Newsweek*, 20 November 1978, p. 68; *Haolam Haze*, 4 October 1978.
5 plane loads of arms	Delivered November 1978. Planes landed at a private track in Montelimar, east of Managua	*El Sol*, 18 November 1978.
2 plane loads of arms	Delivered at Las Mercedes Airport November 1978. Other sources indicated there were 3 planes	*Jerusalem Post*, 15 November 1978; *Newsweek*, 20 November 1978, p. 68.

(continued)

Item	Comments	Reference Source
Sea-to-sea missiles		*World Business*, 6 October 1980.
T–54 and T–55 tanks		Klieman, *Israel's Global Reach*, p. 135.

Chart from Bishara Bahbah, *Israel and Latin America: The Military Connection,* New York: St. Martin's, 1986.

Israel and the Contras ....

Some accounts set the commencement of Israeli aid to the contras as far back as their launching in 1979.[1] It is even possible that Israel made a seamless transition from Somoza to the contras through its contacts with some of the figures in the private network that was exposed when the Iran-contra scandal broke in November 1986 (see below). A part of this network "began funneling aid to Somoza via Israel and EATSCO," a shipping company created by other members of the network to take advantage of the U.S. weapons Egypt would be receiving as a result of the Camp David accords, after the Carter Administration cut off aid to Nicaragua.[2] When the dictator was ousted, network associates of former CIA agent Edwin Wilson—now serving time in federal prison for selling explosives to Libya, among other deeds—and former CIA agent Thomas Clines transferred a "security assistance program" they had put together for Somoza to the contras.[3] This would have involved outfitting the dregs of Somoza's secret police in Honduras, a cynical holding operation that continued until January 1981, when the Reagan Administration took office.[4]

One of the administration's first moves was to arrange with Argentina for trainers for the contras. Veterans of the Argentine "dirty war" were enthusiastic about exporting their skills and their politics. They trained the contras until Washington and Buenos Aires came to a parting of the ways, after the Reagan Administration sided with Britain during the Malvinas/Falklands War.[5] During the Argentine period, the Israeli ambassador to Costa Rica supplied the contras with passports and aliases so that they could travel through Central America.[6] Besides traveling for their own "business," at least one contra has been implicated in a Central American assassination: that of the revered Archbishop of San Salvador, Oscar Arnulfo Romero.[7]

At the same time, the administration approached Israel to become involved in the assault on Nicaragua: in a pattern that was later to become apparent as the *raison d'etre* of the Iran-contra scandal, sometime before June 1981 Israel was provided with satellite pictures of Iraq's nuclear reactor at Osirak "within the framework of an appeal to Israel for help to the contras." Israel used the pictures to destroy the reactor.[8] It is not known to what extent, if any, Tel Aviv responded to the administration's appeal.

By late 1982, however, Nicaragua was accusing Israel of arming and aiding the rag-tag bands of National Guardsmen in Honduras.[9]

The best-substantiated knowledge of Israel's entry into the war against Nicaragua is its agreement with the CIA in either 1981 or 1982 to supply East bloc weapons to the then-covert mercenary operation. After having been "restrained" a bit by Congress during the 1970s, the CIA was experiencing difficulty procuring "untraceable" weapons for the contras and was embarrassed when some of the mercenaries appeared on U.S. television in early 1982 brandishing U.S. weapons. In a display of caution that would mark all their dealings with the contras, the Israeli government made a pretense of refusing U.S. requests for such weapons "through normal diplomatic channels," while some former Israeli intelligence officials approached the CIA with an offer to supply East bloc arms, which Israel has in abundance. The Agency assumed that the offer had the backing, awareness or sponsorship of the Israeli government. There is some question as to whether the CIA accepted this particular offer,[10] but an arrangement was indeed made in the early 1980s to supply the contras with East bloc light arms and shoulder-fired missiles, selling the weapons through the CIA, which in turn passed them on to the contras and the Afghan rebels. This particular arrangement apparently continued until 1986, "[w]hen the Israelis presented their bill for $50 million...[and] the CIA pleaded poverty, paying $30 million in arms, not cash."[11]

Former FDN Director Edgar Chamorro said the contras were speaking of Israel as an international supporter in 1982.[12] In December of that year, the FDN leadership met with Ariel Sharon, Israel's defense minister, while he was on a visit to Honduras. An arrangement was made at that time to funnel Israeli-held East bloc arms to the contras through Honduras.[13]

Sharon's activities during and after that visit suggest that he and Gen. Gustavo Alvarez Martinez, the head of Honduras' armed forces, made the Reagan Administration an offer to take over the contra program. In Israel recriminations were being directed at Sharon over the debacle of Israel's invasion of Lebanon, which Sharon had muscled through the government. Sharon arrived unannounced in Honduras, because, it was said, no one in Washington had been willing to receive him.[14] He would shortly be relieved of his defense portfolio following an investigation that established his responsibility in the massacres of Palestinians in the Sabra and Chatila refugee camps.

Accompanying Sharon were the director of the Israeli defense ministry and David Marcus Katz, Israel's Mexico-based arms agent.[15]

Although Sharon denied having come to deal arms, news immediately spread that he and Alvarez were trying to close a deal for Israel's Kfir C-2 jet fighter planes.[16]

As the Kfir contains a U.S.-made engine, Israel needed U.S. permission to sell the aircraft to Honduras. Washington had been refusing to sell Honduras the comparable F-5 because it did not want to introduce a new level of sophistication in the region's armaments. It was feared that acquisition by Honduras of such an advanced plane would justify Nicaragua's obtaining the equivalent MiG; and that, the administration had made excruciatingly clear, would be regarded as a "provocation"[17] likely to be met with an airstrike—or worse.

Even though there could be no deal for the Kfir without the blessing of the U.S., Alvarez and Sharon agreed to the sale of 12 of the aircraft,[18] at a price of $100 million. Honduras had no money for the deal (and lots of starving, illiterate people, but that didn't bother either buyer or seller), so Sharon asked the Reagan Administration to finance it.[19] An agreement Israel signed with the U.S. in 1979 included such a funding mechanism, which is most unusual, as it flies in the face of the rationale for U.S. military assistance—the recipient must "buy American."[20] However, until late 1986 there was no evidence that Washington had ever contemplated bankrolling an Israeli arms sale.

The only thing that could possibly have tempted the Reagan White House into such a deal would have been a Sharon-Alvarez proposal to take over the contras, which were then in the process of being abandoned by their Argentine trainers.

There is no question that Sharon and Alvarez would have enjoyed leading the mercenaries into Nicaragua. Alvarez was an obsessive anti-communist and an advocate of the Argentine-style security state. Whether against Nicaragua or his domestic oponents, he advocated "preventive" war without frontiers.[21] Ariel Sharon once said Israel's own "strategic and security concerns" stretched from Central Africa to "beyond the Arab countries in the Middle East."[22] Going in the other direction, he said that Israel had strength enough to "reach the gates of Odessa." Sharon would have played to the administration's obsession with the "Soviet threat" in Central America.[23]

Even though it would soon be pressing Israel to do exactly what Sharon put forward, the Reagan Administration did not accept Sharon's proposition, most likely because Sharon was roundly disliked in Washington[24] and other Israeli officials might have nixed any dealings with him.

Four years later, when U.S.-Israeli dealings over the contras had become firmly established, Israeli Defense Minister Yitzhak Rabin offered NSC staffer Oliver North 20-50 Spanish-speaking advisers for the contras in exchange for approval of the sale of Kfirs to Honduras.[25] In 1982, however it would have been difficult for the administration to finance the sale of Kfirs to Honduras without exposing to the public, especially to the Congress, a great deal more of its thinking about Nicaragua (i.e., that its real plans had nothing to do with interdicting arms to the Salvadoran rebels, its excuse at that time, but were really aimed at overthrowing the government in Managua). The then-burgeoning CIA might have been planning to make a big splash with Nicaragua; it would be several months before the full glare of congressional scrutiny withered the agency's grasping tentacles and sent the administration begging to Israel.

In 1983 reports of Israeli weapons shipments to the contras surfaced. ARDE, the Costa Rica-based Revolutionary Democratic Alliance contra group led by Eden Pastora had received 500 AK rifles from Israel.[26] In October 1983, FDN—the Nicaraugan Democratic Front—Director Edgar Chamorro said that the Honduran-based main mercenary force had received 2,000 AK-47s from Israel.[27] At the time, that was one-quarter of the FDN's armed membership.

It is interesting that while the FDN mercenaries were most closely identified with the Somoza regime which Israel had aided so loyally, it was with ARDE in Costa Rica that Israel seemed to be the most involved in 1983 and 1984. Pastora had fought with distinction (and flamboyance) in the revolution and had been in the Sandinista government. It is widely understood that Pastora quit the Directorate, the government that held power in Nicaragua prior to the November 1984 elections, when he realized that he would not be top dog. That he then chose to actively oppose Managua might also be attributed to his suspected links to the CIA, dating back to before the fall of Somoza.[28]

Pastora always distinguished himself from the FDN leaders, who were close associates of Somoza. It is not clear that his men were so ideologically discriminating. Many deserted him for the paymasters of the FDN when the CIA, after sustained attempts including a May 1984 bombing that claimed the lives of eight bystanders, finally succeeded in shutting ARDE down.[29] But in 1983-84 Pastora made it a point of pride to claim that he received no money from the CIA. The agency went along with this contention, as Pastora was an attractive exhibit for members of Congress who got a little queasy about the *Somocistas* in Honduras. It was also hoped that he could win over some elements of the Socialist International.

However, it was generally assumed that Pastora was receiving laundered CIA support.[30] Certainly the CIA was active in Costa Rica, bribing officials to tolerate the presence of the contras[31] and running its own mercenaries, a motley bunch of Europeans (some with service for the South African minority regime) and right-wing Vietnam veterans.[32]

Israel was apparently one of a number of channels through which arms and funds came to Pastora, and the date when the pipeline was turned on can be set rather precisely to July or August 1983. In June of that year, ARDE had been on the verge of folding, its coffers down to $3,000. In September Pastora was able to increase his guerrilla force from 300 to between 2,000 and 3,000 and was planning to arm an additional 2,000 to 3,000. He boasted of "increased donations from individuals in Venezuela, Colombia, Mexico, Peru and some European countries," as well as "private American organizations and some Jewish groups." [33] But later, pointing to the armaments he had received, Pastora said, "only the CIA or the Israelis could give us these."[34] Pastora also told one reporter that the Israeli ambassador had offered to sell him weapons.[35]

The mention of assistance from Jewish groups was a repetitive theme with ARDE. It is not clear whether ARDE leaders used "Jews" as a euphemism for Israel, or if one or more U.S. Jewish organizations had actually been funding the contras.

Alfonso Robelo, then political leader of ARDE, said the mercenary grouping received "financial aid from German and Venezuelan citizens, Mexican organizations, U.S. Jewish organizations, as well as from Germans and Cubans in exile." He said he did not care where these donors got the funds they gave ARDE.[36] Another time Robelo reeled off a list of ARDE backers that included "the democrats of Venezuela and Mexico, the Nicaraguan exile community [*colonias nicaraguenses*] and the Jewish communities of the United States."[37] Yet another time Robelo said "we are receiving help from many democrats and private companies in France, Spain, Venezuela, Mexico, Colombia, and even Jews."[38]

Israeli arms also reached ARDE through Panama. In the autumn of 1985, Alvin Weeden, a Panamanian attorney and former secretary general of the Popular Action Party (PAPO), said that Gen. Manuel Antonio Noriega, commander-in-chief of the Panama Defense Forces, had been obtaining the "materiel needed by the Southern Front to continue its struggle" from Israel. Noriega then distributed the supplies to ARDE, and, according to Weeden, reaped profits for himself.

Weeden said his information came from Dr. Hugo Spadafora. Spadafora, a Panamanian physician, had fought with other guerrilla movements before volunteering with ARDE. Weeden, who said the physician had left ARDE because of Pastora's close connection with Noriega, had been engaged by Spadafora to represent him in making declarations about Noriega's malfeasance and links with narcotraffickers. Spadafora was gruesomely murdered soon after.[39]

Israel had very close links with Noriega, who had met with "high-ranking" Mossad agents in Canada and Europe as well as Panama. At one point, U.S. intelligence agencies suspected that a campaign "contribution" of many millions of dollars from Israel to Panamanian President Eric Arturo Delvalle had been an indirect payoff to Noriega "who is well placed to intercept and relay coded U.S. data on Latin America—a lucrative arms market for Israel."[40]

In early 1984, as Congress took steps to curtail and then cut off funds to the contras, Israeli support for the mercenaries "became crucial to the war's continuation."[41] Several contra leaders said that they had made arrangements to get Israeli assistance.[42]

When their U.S. aid was all spent, Israeli aid to the mercenaries began to escalate. In early 1985, both Reagan Administration officials and members of Congress said that Israel had stepped up shipments of rifles, grenades and ammunition and sent more advisers.[43]

At a March 31 press conference in Managua, government spokesperson Rosa Passos announced that Nicaragua had intercepted a ship delivering a large cargo of weapons to the contras in Honduras. The ship had come from Asia, Passos said, and the shipment had been arranged by the Israeli government.[44]

Nicaraguan soldiers were also finding Israeli-made weapons and uniforms on dead contras.[45] A reporter for National Public Radio saw Israeli-made artillery pieces at the FDN's Las Vegas camp in southern Honduras.[46] In a display set up by the government in Managua, there were many captured Israeli weapons.[47]

Jack Terrell, a former mercenary now at the International Center for Development Policy in Washington, said he was in Honduras when an Israeli shipment arrived for the contras. Terrell also recounts an experience that suggests that regular and frequent shipments came from Israel. In November 1984, he asked FDN chief Adolfo Calero for Uzis and 9 mm ammunition for a commando raid on Managua. Calero told him, "I'll get this as soon as I can. We're expecting two ships in from Israel in February. When they get in, you will get your stuff." Terrell said that the Uzis arrived and were given out to the contras.

The sales were made by Israeli arms dealers, he said, and the documents covering the shipment were signed by Honduran officials (who made 30 percent on the deal).

Terrell also said that Adolfo Calero's brother Mario had been to Israel to buy 10,000 AK-47s, said to have been captured in Lebanon.[48]

Contra leaders said that they normally obtained arms from Israel through the Israeli embassy in Guatemala. They explained that it was rare for the contras to deal directly with Israel and even more unusual for one of them to go to Israel. "We do not have a formal relationship with the Israelis," explained a contra leader. "We work with them quietly, usually outside Israel. There is no need for us to go directly to Israel."[49]

This circumspection was dictated by Israel's fear that congressional opponents of contra aid would be angered—a fear which later proved unwarranted—if its contra connections were exposed in the U.S. media.

Yet in addition to the visit by Mario Calero, at least one other high-ranking contra, Julio Montealegre, a Miami-based aide to Adolfo Calero, went to Israel seeking arms—specifically Somoza's last consignment, which Israel recalled just before the dictator fell. Montealegre spent two weeks in Israel in January/February 1986.[50] It is ironic that the contras, whose Washington backers tried so hard to portray as "democrats," considered themselves entitled to weapons paid for by Somoza. But they did: "We have been trying to get those arms for a long time," said a contra leader.[51] A member of the Israeli Knesset said that the government had agreed to Montealegre's request.[52]

The timing of Montealegre's trip, immediately after the U.S. and Israel started shipping arms to Iran under a secret Presidential "Finding" and an arrangement between the White House and the Israeli government that some of the (inflated) profits from those sales were to go to the contras, suggests that the contra aide was after more than Somoza's last arms order. As the diverted funds are believed to have been recycled in Israel to purchase arms for the contras,[53] it is likely that Montealegre was picking out weapons from Israel's inventory for the contras.

During the 1985-86 period, Israel sent at least six shiploads of East bloc assault rifles, grenade launchers and ammunition to Honduras for the contras. [54] Also, some of the 400 tons of weapons supplied to the contras by the "private" network coordinated by Lt. Col. Oliver North of the National Security Council staff came from Israel. These arms were delivered to Ilopango Air Base in El Salvador by Southern Air Transport,[55] a former CIA proprietary and, during the second Reagan term, one of the companies included by North in what he called Project Democracy. One planeload of arms—it included AK-47 rifles and ammunition—came directly from Israel to Honduras in November 1986.[56]

Another shipment, a "significant quantity" of East bloc arms, was offered by Israeli Defense Minister Yitzhak Rabin on September 12, 1986. They were picked up during the following week and taken on a foreign-flag vessel to Central America. But, after the Iran-contra scandal broke, this ship—like Somoza's last ship—was recalled to Israel.[57] This was the arms consignment for which President Reagan was asked to "thank" Prime Minister Peres during a September 15, 1986 meeting.[58]

Many, if not most of these sales were made through the private dealers Israel uses to establish "plausible deniability" of its politically risky dealings. With the breaking of the Iran-contra scandal, some of the activity of those dealers were exposed, revealing an interconnected web of operators. It is striking that all of the Israeli dealers involved in the Iran arms sales also made at least one sale of weapons to the contras, perhaps to oblige the Reagan Administration, which was making it possible for them to earn fat commissions on the Iran-Iraq war.

Well before the Iran-contra operation began, in late 1984 and early 1985, Al Schwimmer, one of Israel's premier arms dealers, an initiator of the Iran arms sales involving Washington, and a close friend and special assistant to Prime Minister Shimon Peres, had "made an undetermined number of sales of Israeli-owned weapons" to the contras.[59]

Ya'acov Nimrodi, who figured prominently in the arms-to-Iran dealings, also handled arms shipments financed with a donation of several million dollars, given by the Israeli government to the contras at the request of CIA Director Casey.[60] A former Nimrodi employee said the sales were made through a U.S. company owned by Nimrodi, who had done the deal as a "favor" to the contras, taking only a "small fee" for himself.[61]

Pesakh Ben-Or, an Israeli arms dealer based in Guatemala and Miami, sold three shipments to the contras through the Honduran military. He gave the Israeli defense ministry documents of sale bearing the signature of Col. Julio Perez, chief of logistics in the Honduran Army's Ordnance Corps.[62]

The consignments included such items as RPG-7 grenade launchers, which the Honduran army does not even use; the contras, however, do use them.[63]

Another company with Israeli links is Sherwood International Export Corp. Former U.S. diplomat Wayne Smith said the Reagan Administration had "used Sherwood before for weapons sales to the FDN" and that the CIA had frequently used it so that Israel wasn't directly supplying the contras. Smith said he had been told by an administration official that a shipment of weapons Sherwood sold the contras had come from Israel's East bloc stocks.[64]

As likely as not, the SA-7 surface-to-air missile which the contras used to bring down a Nicaraguan helicopter in December 1985 came from Israel. The contras bought the missiles "by the dozens" starting in mid-1985.[65] Some were purchased by Gen. John Singlaub, others came from Israel.[66] Opinions vary as to whether Ben-Or or Sherwood[67] was the source.[68] Possibly both were.[69]

Moreover, Ben-Or's operation and Sherwood are connected by a tangle of other Israeli arms dealers. At the time it was selling arms to the contras, Sherwood employed Pinhas Dagan and Amos Gil'ad, an Israeli transport officer, in senior positions.[70]

Dagan, who had once represented IAI in territory stretching between Mexico and Colombia, had lived in Ben-Or's Miami house.[71] Gil'ad was an acquaintance of Gerard Latchinian, arrested by the FBI in an assassination plot against then Honduran President Roberto Suazo Cordoba. Gil'ad introduced Latchinian to Pesakh Ben-Or.[72]

Latchinian, whose role in the assassination plot was to obtain the necessary weapons, had at one time employed Emil Sa'ada,[73] identified by Honduran military sources as one of two former Israeli military men who had "helped arrange" arms shipments to the contras in deals dating back to 1984.

The other Israeli was Yehuda Leitner, who worked for one of Sa'ada's Honduran operations. Leitner was also employed by ISDS, an Israeli "security expertise" exporter.[74]

Both Sa'ada and Leitner were former Israeli military officers.[75] Both denied having sold arms, charging they were being scapegoated in the shuffle resulting from the Iran-contra scandal and from rivalry among regional arms deals, "including Marcus Katz."[76]

David Marcus Katz "helped broker [a] deal with the contras in 1985."[77] To bring the connection around full circle, Pesakh Ben-Or began his career as Katz's chauffer.[78]

Israel or its associated arms dealers might also have participated in the diversion of U.S. arms to the contras. A former U.S. Army combat pilot and supply officer now working as an arms expert for a conservative Washington think tank said that he had quizzed "Americans who had visited rebel training and supply camps in Honduras, and their conclusion was that the U.S. Defense Department was the ultimate source, through theft, cut-out deals with Israel and other governments, of most of the rebel arms." He said that items such as batteries and aircraft parts had been officially accounted as discarded scrap and "had actually been diverted in good working order to the rebels."[79]

Former CIA analyst David MacMichael said that there had been a great deal of stolen ordnance; and much that was reported used in training at an Alabama base could have gone to the contras.[80]

The Israelis vehemently denied *any* arms shipments to the contras, or any contact with them at all. They kept on denying any contra connection even after the Senate Intelligence Committee investigating the Iran-contra affair issued its January 1987 report which implicated the Israeli defense minister in the sales.

The nearest Israel came to acknowledging its role with the contras was in a leaked government story that attempted to explain how Yitzhak Rabin had become personally involved in one particular shipment: An Israeli "senior security source" explained that after "Oliver North drove us crazy with his requests to supply arms to the contras," Rabin had agreed to send "several hundred Soviet-made rifles" to the administration to do what it wanted with them. These same sources claimed that all Israeli shipments destined for the contras were actually sent to "official U.S. Administration elements."[81] Rabin himself was more terse in his denial:

> I turned down the request of a U.S. official—a member or employee of the National Security Council at the White House—who made such a proposal to Israel. I told him we had enough problems of our own and we had no plans whatsoever to give any direct assistance, either in the form of instructors, advice, or weapons.
>
> Moreover, to the best of my knowledge, Israeli weapons did not reach the contras.[82]

Advisers

In early 1983, 50 Israeli specialists in guerrilla and psychological warfare were said to have gone to El Salvador and Honduras.[83] That summer intelligence sources said that Israel was providing "special" guerrilla training to the contras.[84]

From all appearances the only thing "special" the contras learned to do was brutalize the civilian population of Nicaragua and kidnap young men for incorporation into the mercenary ranks. Yet the Israelis drew top pay for their work: $6,500—$10,000 a month, compared with the $5,000-$7,000 for Argentine advisers. The CIA is thought to have paid their salaries.[85] Perhaps the pay was based on the fearsome international reputation of the Israeli military—Israeli "security companies" regularly charge double the going rate for bodyguards for European businessmen[86] —rather than their performance.

An Israeli mercenary who had served in Central America said that Israelis were training *and supervising* the contras. He said they were recruited by "foreigners with excellent Israeli connections." Another Israeli mercenary said that the Defense Ministry was aware of the Israelis working with the contras and that they use IDF manuals and catalogs.[87] These are clear signs of an official connection.

Although the Israeli government gets extensive mileage out of claiming that its nationals, often retired military officers, working as advisers or arms merchants, are merely private citizens, there is over-whelming evidence that those who follow both professions are under the control of Tel Aviv.

Every "security technique" must be approved by the government for export. In 1986, there were approximately 20 "security companies" licensed by the defense ministry to export their services; many of these were newcomers to a rapidly expanding field. The defense ministry "often passes less-desirable clients to private consulting firms."[88]

One such company is International Security and Defense Systems (ISDS, see above). Its offices in a kibbutz near Tel Aviv are full of mementos from the Honduran, Salvadoran, Chilean and Ecuadoran militaries. A company employee trained the Honduran president's body-guard in 1982.[89]

Even when these "experts" are not on government business their activities are regulated by the Israeli government. There is an obligatory six-month course given by the Israeli government "which trains people in special security methods." At least one of the proliferating Israeli "security companies" requires its employees to take the course.[90]

The private Israeli "security" teams work all over the world, from the gaming tables of Sun City in South Africa to the plantations of wealthy Latin Americans. The going rate for an Israeli is $5,000 per month.[91] One of the Israeli companies even gives courses for children, executives and individuals.[92] Another provides a "Tour and Secure" package, a two-week stay in Israel evenly divided between touring and learning karate and weapons handling for a cost of $2,800 including round trip airfare from New York.[93]

All of this is done in close proximity to, if not in conjunction with, another Israeli growth industry—the marketing of sophisticated "security" devices. Items such as 360-degree video cameras in car antennas, laser beams that capture conversations in rooms hundreds of feet away, and virtually undetectable infrared audio monitoring devices[94] are available in retail outlets.[95]

Major weapons systems, however, are sold to governments. The Israeli individuals who make the sales—mostly retired military officers unable to find suitable employment in the civilian economy—do so on behalf of the government, for a commission of at least ten percent.[96] Their function is to provide protective layers of "deniability" between the Israeli government and the bad publicity that often follows disclosures of arms sales to outlaw regimes and mercenary bands.

Until recently, Israeli arms dealers (700-800 by official estimates) carried letters of introduction from the defense ministry. Following a number of scandals, most notably the arrest of retired General Avraham Bar-Am in an attempted $2.5 billion sale sale to Iran,[97] the procedure was changed. Now the dealers are issued two official certificates for each sale. The first document will list the purchaser, the intermediaries in the sale, and the precise weapons involved. The second document will be a permit containing the terms of sale and specifying the payment arrangements.[98]

When he was Israel's military attache in Washington, Gen. Uri Simhoni met with contra leader Adolfo Calero to discuss working with the contras. "I heard that he might be of service to us once he retired," Calero said.[99]

Several months after U.S. military aid to the contras resumed in late 1986, the Israelis were still in demand as advisers. Speaking anonymously on the state-run television, an Israeli said "I conducted negotiations with the contras. They need light weapons, ammunition...They want advisers from Israel." He said there were more Israelis working with the contras, and that relations between the two groups were "outstanding"; in his words, "you feel after a day like you've known them for years."[100]

A report in early 1987 said that Israeli advisers were training the contras at U.S. Army bases in Honduras. There were conflicting reports as to whether the Israelis were being paid by the Honduran government or, as Israeli military sources claimed, "American sources or intelligence groups."[101]

Laundered Funds

As soon as President Reagan started to feel pinched by congressional restrictions on CIA spending for the contras, he began asking Israel to donate or launder funds for the mercenaries he was fond of calling "the moral equals of our founding fathers." In early 1984, Israel gave a "well-concealed" several million dollars which was believed to have gone through a South American intermediary. The amount was probably reimbursed in Israel's U.S. aid.[102]

By September of that year, of $15 million collected for the contras, the Israeli government gave just under $5 million.[103] Part of Israel's contribution was in East bloc and Chinese-made weapons and part was in cash to "help contras meet their $800,000 monthly payroll."[104]

In 1985 and 1986, the discreet contribution would be replaced by the wholesale kickback, as administration officials and their cronies who had recently left government posts for private life left no stone unturned in the search for funds to continue the contra war.

In July 1985, the administration legalized its solicitation by intervening in a House-Senate conference committee and insisting on the redrafting of an amendment to the $12.6 billion foreign aid bill—containing $27 million "non-lethal" aid for the contras—written by Senator Claiborne Pell (D-RI). In its original form, the Pell Amendment forbade the administration from making a formal or informal arrangement with U.S. aid recipients to aid the contras. On threat of presidential veto of the the entire bill, Sen. Pell, Foreign Relations Chairman Richard Lugar (R-IN) and White House and congressional staff sat down together and rewrote the amendment.

The State Department explained that the Pell Amendment might have prevented the president from soliciting "nonlethal" aid from Israel, Taiwan, South Korea, and other such allies, some of which had already spoken to the White House about donations.

The new language imposed by the administration read:

> The U.S. shall not enter into any arrangement conditioning expressly or impliedly the provision of assistance under this act...upon provision of assistance by a recipient to persons or groups engaging in an insurgency...against the government of Nicaragua.

Both houses of Congress passed this language without debate, just before they adjourned for the summer.[105]

CIA Director Casey and UN Ambassador Vernon Walters, himself a long time covert operator,[106] visited a number of U.S. clients and urged contributions. Both Israel and Egypt donated money in response to these pleas "when reminded of the substantial U.S. aid they receive."[107] Some of the money Israel gave is said to have been passed through Oliver North.[108]

Another round of shakedowns was carried out by retired Air Force General Richard Secord, a leading participant in the contra supply network run by the White House National Security Council (NSC) staff and also in the arms-to-Iran scam run jointly by the NSC and Israel. Saudi Arabia was the biggest giver to this campaign, and the leverage Secord had over the Saudis had quite a bit to do with Israel.

He reminded them that the administration had stuck its neck out and "defied the powerful pro-Israeli lobby" in a bruising fight to win Congressional approval of the the sale of AWACs surveillance planes to the Kingdom. As a deputy assistant secretary of defense, Secord had led the campaign for the sale. (NSC staffer Oliver North had assisted him.) He told the Saudis that he had later been forced to resign because he had angered powerful people. (Another reason Secord resigned was an investigation into his business dealings with Edwin Wilson, the former CIA operator now in prison for his dealings with Libya.)

Secord spent the Saudi money on East bloc arms from Egypt, from Israel and from international arms dealers.[109]

Recycling the money given by Israel in the Israeli economy would become a pattern. For all that Israel, with its very well known economic problems, gave the contras, it made money every step of the way. Much of what Israel put into the pot was returned to the Israeli government in the form of arms sales. The contras were a closed market to which Israel had privileged access. Former contra leader Edgar Chamorro has pointed out that arms dealers do not seek out the contras, nor do the mercenaries often make purchases on the open market. He explained that "a very few people, close to the White House, tell the FDN how to get weapons. Calero is told by the people in charge where to go to buy weapons. They even make the connections."[110]

When the Iran-contragate investigators went looking for the money that Oliver North said had been skimmed from the profits made on U.S.-Israeli arms sales to Iran and diverted to the contras, there was no hidden heap of cash to be found. Many observers are certain that the cash went to Israel, which then shipped weapons to the contras.

The Covert Alliance

Beneath the apparent symmetry of these deals were three years of anguished bargaining between Israel and the Reagan Administration. What occurred across tables and desks in the United States and Israel was at least as significant and potentially as deadly as the weapons that went to the contras. Indeed, the money, the arms, and the advisers were all offered by Israel as substitutes for what the Reagan Administration was really asking for. All the dickering began and ended with a stalemate: the administration was "delighted" with Israeli arms sales in Central America,[111] but frustrated beyond belief that Israel declined to take a splashy public role with the contras, both in Central America and in the U.S. body politic. Wishing not to antagonize its liberal supporters, Israel insisted on a covert role in both arenas. At the same time, it twisted and turned to see if it could not reconcile the two opposing claims on its loyalty. Ultimately, tensions with the White House over the level of Israel's support for the contras contributed to the Iran-contra scandal.

However, the investigative broom that sweeps out the debris of the Iran-contra mess is unlikely to disturb the murky corner in which Israel's role was generated. Behind protective shadows is a structure developed during the Reagan years that makes Israel an *ex officio*—perforce an uncontrollable—arm of U.S. foreign policy. This function was but one element of the bilateral relations, which during the Reagan years were cemented to such an extent, that, as Secretary of State George Shultz put it, no subsequent, possibly less friendly, administration would be able to dismantle them.[112]

At the heart of that structure is a "strategic alliance," committed several times to paper, but actually developed in the hothouse atmosphere of the privateering Reagan Administration.

In March 1979, after the Camp David Accords between Israel and Egypt, the U.S. and Israel had signed a Memorandum of Agreement entailing U.S. commitments to help Israel boost its weapons exports. On November 30, 1981 the Reagan Administration signed a Memorandum of

Understanding (MOU) on Strategic Cooperation with Israel, incorporating some elements of the 1979 pact and adding some mild language about mutual defense.

The term strategic—a word very popular in the Reagan years with men who wished to clothe their base idiocies with a smug semblance of considered policy—referred to cooperation the two countries planned to undertake in the developing world. This was the heart of the agreement. Of prime interest to Israel was Africa, where it hoped to use U.S.-funded programs to tempt the continent's governments back into its diplomatic embrace.[113]

Signed by Secretary of Defense Alexander Haig and Defense Minister Ariel Sharon, the MOU was suspended almost immediately, after Israel annexed the Syrian Golan Heights. Tel Aviv insisted that the MOU lived on in spirit, and that parts of it were covered by the 1979 memorandum.[114]

Its actual revival would come when the administration became interested in what Israel could do for it in Central America, an interest which also helped Washington overcome its "anger" at Israel's behavior during the war in Lebanon. In fact, both Israeli and administration sources said that Israel's potential as a helpmeet was the *only* bright spot in relations between the two countries during the 1982-1983 period.[115]

In 1983, the administration made a direct request to Israel to arm the contras.[116] It also wanted Israel to lend its political support to the contras, which had not, to say the least, attracted an instant following in the U.S. When Israel was not forthcoming, the administration first attempted to force the issue by making it public. The *New York Times* was the vehicle of choice.

On its front page one July morning was news that the administration had encouraged Israel to increase its presence in Central America "as a way of supplementing American military aid to friendly governments and supporting insurgent operations against the Nicaraguan Government," especially if Congress moved to forbid the CIA from continuing its support. Israel had begun sending artillery pieces, mortar rounds, mines, hand grenades and ammunition captured in Lebanon to Honduras "for eventual use by the contras," and was behaving more like a U.S. surrogate than the private arms dealer it used to be. Israel heatedly denied the part about being a surrogate.[117]

The administration then attempted to coax Israel into a more favorable mood. Israel was, at the same time, trying to nail down some concessions from the U.S. Alexander Haig, who had been very partial to Israel, had resigned, and over the course of 1983 there had been considerable sparring within the administration over the nature of U.S.-Israeli relations. Haig's successor, George Shultz, had begun his tenure determined to maintain the friendship of Arab nations with an "even-handed" policy in the Middle East. However, after intensive lobbying by pro-Israel forces in the State Department and by the Israeli ambassador to Washington, Shultz was persuaded to a policy skewed toward Israel: complete favoritism expressed in an open alliance. The Israelis had argued against the traditional "even-handedness" of U.S. policy (in reality the "balance" had been little more than rhetoric), pushing instead the notion that an overt U.S. alignment with Israel would "show the Arabs" that their cause was hopeless and that close relations with Washington must be achieved via deference to Israel.[118]

Shultz, joined by former Haig aide Robert McFarlane, at the time deputy national security adviser, presented a position paper to the President recommending "strategic cooperation" with Israel. Their main selling point was that such a pact would help contain the Soviet Union. In October 1983, President Reagan signed National Security Decision Directive 111 establishing strategic cooperation with Israel.[119]

In Washington on November 29 of that year, Israel's Prime Minister Yitzhak Shamir and President Reagan announced that their two governments had agreed on closer cooperation, which Shamir said included "a dialogue on coordinating activity in the third world."[120] (It was perhaps coincidental that the agreement was sealed on the day set aside by the UN for the Palestinian people, but given the Israeli attention to detail, perhaps not.) A formal agreement was signed the following March,[121] by which Israel agreed to become an unreachable arm of covert U.S. policy. No public debate. No outcry from the Congress. Liberal members were then battening on wine and cheese provided by anti-intervention activists and giving assurances of their commitment to opposing the Reagan foreign policy.

During his Washington session Shamir was also promised increased U.S. aid, short term economic credits, concessions on the sales of Israeli weapons systems to the U.S., and a Free Trade Agreement.[122] There was, as Secretary of State Shultz admitted, "no visible *quid pro quo* in the pact with Israel."[123] There was only the Boland Amendment, forbidding U.S. agencies from aiding the contras, passed several weeks earlier, and the beginnings of a concerted search by the White House and CIA Director Casey to find alternate sources of support for the obsessive campaign against Nicaragua.[124]

That semi-formal discussions about Central America had been going on between the U.S. and Israel for some time before the administration moved to offer Israel the strategic agreement, strongly suggests that Israel was being offered incrementally greater rewards to persuade it to play a leading part in the war against Nicaragua. These discussions began in the framework of a bilateral political-military committee put together by Robert McFarlane. In 1982, as an aide to Secretary of State Haig, McFarlane had come to know (and deeply admire) David Kimche, director-general of the Israeli foreign ministry, the nation's top civil service post. Kimche had been the number two man in Israel's secret service, Mossad, and during the prime ministership of Yitzhak Shamir (late 1982 to late 1984) he served as *de facto* foreign minister. When McFarlane transferred to the White House, he established links between Kimche and senior State Department officials which resulted in a committee, whose charge was to meet every spring and fall (alternately in Washington and Jerusalem) and "look at the big picture," meaning everything outside the Middle East.[125] The committee would eventually be subsumed under the November 1983 strategic agreement.

In June 1983 the group had discussed Central America—specifically "the intention of the U.S. Administration to get Israel to supply the armies of the pro-American regimes there" with the funds "the U.S. cannot directly transfer to its allies in the region...paid to Israel directly from the United States."[126] At other meetings they discussed ways of countering Nicaragua's growing international political support; once they conspired on ways to block Nicaragua from becoming the chair of the Nonaligned Movement.[127]

However, the strategic agreement, signed eleven days after contra aid ran out, failed to move Israel into the proper frame of mind for declaring war on Nicaragua. A former U.S. official "who routinely reviewed intelligence reports" said that the administration made "at least two attempts in 1984 to use Israel to circumvent a Congressional ban on military aid to the contras."[128] The requests included "bridging financing" (funds to tide the mercenaries over until congressional or other means of support could be found), weapons and training. Israel later refused a request to launder and pass along U.S. funds to the contras.[129]

After the last covert contra money was spent on March 8, 1984,[130] with Congress still howling about the CIA's mining of Nicaragua's ports, the administration went several steps beyond polite requests.

With David Kimche due in Washington in April for the regularly scheduled meeting of the political-military committee, the administration tried to drag Israel over the threshhold separating overt and covert with an unparalleled series of news leaks.

A story popped up in Israel that the committee would be discussing a U.S. proposal for making Israel a conduit for U.S. aid to anti-communist forces in Central America and that the U.S. would establish a fund "independent of the government budget to finance projects suggested by Israeli experts"[131] in Central America and Africa.[132]

In addition to passing money, said another Israeli report, the administration would seek "a higher Israeli political profile in support of U.S. policy in Central America" in exchange for funding Israeli foreign projects. Additionally, "the administration would like to see Israel encourage its own supporters in the Congress, the Jewish community and elsewhere to become more assertive in backing the contras."[133]

It is almost certain that the leaks were generated in Washington, where "some Administration officials in recent weeks ha[d] talked privately about the possibility of persuading friendly governments, such as Israel to help."[134]

CIA Director Casey let it be known he was thinking about asking another country, "such as Saudi Arabia," for money for the contras.[135] Later the CIA admitted having "unofficially" asked Israel and Saudi Arabia to support the contras.[136] When the Iran-contra scandal broke, Israel and Saudi Arabia would appear as major supporters of the contras.

Perhaps the most unifying moment in the history of the venal and fractious contra movement came when the administration lined up mercenary spokesmen to make public statements about the possibility of Israeli aid. The Somocist FDN said that as Congress had not voted the $21 million sought by the White House, it was going to ask Israel for aid. On April 15, FDN officials said they were meeting with U.S. intelligence officials "to discuss their options for finding new funds." FDN chief Adolfo Calero said, "We have looked for private money, but there isn't enough. We need a government. We think the Israelis would be the best, because they have the technical experience."

Another contra leader suggested that Israel might help the contras "as a favor to the Reagan administration," and out of consideration for the $2.6 billion in U.S. aid it received from the U.S. that year.[137]

That same week, ARDE leader Eden Pastora lamented that non-U.S. aid came to ARDE on condition of anonymity.[138]

The FDN's Washington representative also implored Israel to come to the aid of the contras. Arguing that Israel and the contras had overlapping interests because the PLO was aiding Nicaragua, Bosco Matamoros also warned that there was an "increase in anti-Semitism and anti-Israeli feeling in other countries in Central America, where rebels are being helped by the Sandinistas and the PLO."[139]

The most spectacular blast in the administration's campaign came from Honduras, courtesy of network television. Pentagon reporter Fred Francis said that NBC had "learned" that Israel, "at Washington's urging, has armed a quarter of the rebel army."

Enrique Bermudez, the FDN's military chief, appeared on camera to say: "We received some weapons from the, the, that Israeli government took from PLO in Lebanon [sic]." While the camera followed a contra air drop "into Nicaragua," Francis' voice-over was more to the point: Washington has kept the contras on a short leash, won't let them win, and instead might be about to completely abandon them; at which point, said Francis, the contras will be "forced to turn again to Israel and others to save themselves from becoming refugees of a war lost in a divided Washington."[140]

There is no doubt that the contra appeal was stage-managed. Israeli radio pointed out that the CIA "keeps a tight reign" on the contras and that Bermudez would never have spoken "without CIA approval or encouragement."[141]

It is likely that Israel protested the publicity. The State Department issued a statement saying that the U.S. had "no intention of providing funds to third countries for the purpose of supporting covert activities in Central America."[142]

By the time David Kimche actually met with Lawrence Eagleburger of the State Department on April 26, there was intense media interest in what Israel might be about to do with the contras. The Israeli Embassy in Washington relayed a message "that the growing controversy over the Administration's policy in Central America could damage Israel's standing with Congress."[143] Israel had also been warned by congressional Democrats that it should stay far away from the administration's operations in Central America.[144]

The real sticking point, however, was Israel's objection to the role the administration had envisioned for itself. Israel was perfectly willing to participate in a joint attack on Nicaragua, but not, in the words of a former diplomat, "to get the onus for assisting the contras while the U.S. is standing aside and keeping their hands clean."[145]

After his meeting, Kimche had breakfast with reporters and "acknowledged that the talks had included discussion of how Israel might increase its technical assistance programs in Third World areas, including Central America." But, he insisted, he hadn't "come to arrange how Israel is going to take over the contras," and said the aid under discussion would be limited to "peaceful projects."[146]

Nevertheless, in reporting that breakfast meeting, National Public Radio noted speculation about a new fund that the U.S. would create "ostensibly for non-military aid projects which reportedly would allow the

U.S. to funnel extra money for covert aid which could then be channeled by Israel when needed."

Kimche ran through the gamut of Israeli denials: Israel had no contacts with or arms sales to the contras; Israeli policy is to only sell arms to "constitutionally organized countries and not to unofficial organizations"; Israel might have been mentioned in connection with East bloc arms supplied to the contras, but those shipments were "without our consent and without our knowledge"; stories of Israeli arms going to the contras might have come from the contras "in the hopes that members of Congress sympathetic to Israel would then look more favorably on U.S. covert activity."[147] All of these were lies, yet even after the breaking of the Iran-contra scandal they continue to be blithely issued in the face of overwhelming evidence. No matter, they were always accepted at face value by Congress and, to a lesser extent, the media.

Disappointed, the administration lined up behind Israel with a statement that no agreement had been reached on funding Israeli aid programs and that the U.S. had not asked Israel to become involved in the contra program.[148] As a consolation prize, Israel increased its aid to the contras. It would soon begin supplying money for the contras as well as arms.

There is no question that this tension ultimately led to the proposal to transfer funds from the secret (and massive) sales of arms to Iran in which Israel involved the administration beginning in August 1985. There may have been other factors and other covert operations involved,[149] but the Israeli desire to keep the U.S. involved with the Iran program set against the administration's constant pleas for Israeli help with the contras is the transparently logical genesis of the scam whereby Iran was overcharged and the excess funds were applied to the war against Nicaragua.

This lends credence to evidence given to the Senate Intelligence Committee by Attorney General Edwin Meese, that Oliver North had described the idea in detail as having originated with the Israelis. Uncertainty stemming from the informal circumstances in which Meese interviewed NSC staffer Oliver North over which Israeli—David Kimche or terror adviser Amiram Nir—was the intellectual author of the scheme has been used to discredit the notion of the idea's Israeli origin.[150] Conveniently forgotten is a report that the Senate Intelligence Committee had been given "secret evidence strongly suggesting that the plan to divert money from the Iran arms operation to the Nicaraguan Contras was first put forward by Mr. Shimon Peres, then the Israeli Prime Minister."[151]

The decision was an official Israeli government one, at the highest level. The other Israelis had simply been the messengers, bringing the suggestion to Washington during crucial January 1986 meetings on whether the U.S. would continue with the Iran arms sales. Israel had already been using some of the Iran arms sales profits to pay off Iranian "moderates" at the suggestion of arms dealer Ya'acov Nimrodi. Israel hadn't wanted to tell its American partners about this nifty trick, according to Adnan Khashoggi, the Saudi arms dealer involved in the U.S.-Israeli dealings with Iran,[152] but apparently did so to save the Iran program and forestall another barage of administration publicity about how Israel should take up the cudgels against Nicaragua.

Soon after Israel refused an overt role with the contras, Undersecretary of Defense Fred Ikle asked Israel to send advisers to El Salvador "openly, as a demonstration of Israeli participation in the load the United States bears in Central America."[153] The request underscored one of Israel's two main attractions to the administration—the extensive and longstanding ties Israel had developed throughout Central America. (The other was Israel's domestic political clout, discussed below.)

In 1983 Israel probably knew its way around Costa Rica and Honduras better than the CIA did.

Honduras

Honduras was one of Israel's first arms customers in Central America. Between 1975 and 1977, this second poorest of all countries in the Western Hemisphere bought 20 French super-Mystere fighter planes from Israel. Delivered at a time when it was U.S. policy to discourage the acquisition of sophisticated weaponry in Central America, these were the first supersonic aircraft in the region; some were equipped with Israeli-made Shafrir heat-seeking missiles.[154]

The Hondurans bought a range of other Israeli arms: Arava STOL aircraft,[155] a fleet of armored vehicles mounted with recoilless rifles,[156] and Galil rifles and Uzi submachine guns.[157] For all its poverty, when Ariel Sharon visited Honduras, he was calling on one of Israel's three biggest clients.[158] In the wake of Sharon's visit came more arms and training—both in Israel and Honduras—for officers, pilots and troops.[159]

In 1981, Israeli radar operators were at work at a Honduran airbase.[160] Honduran officials never chafed at the Israeli presence—on the contrary, on one occasion, exasperated with the on-again off-again contra war, Honduran military leaders suggested that Israel, Chile, Colombia or Brazil take over the contra program for the U.S.[161] Gen. Julio Perez, the Honduran army logistics chief, signed false end user certificates for Israeli weapons shipments to the contras.[162]

Israel also benefited from the fits and starts with which Honduras assented to serve as a U.S. "aircraft carrier." In October 1986, in an effort to get Honduras to agree to tolerate U.S. training of contras on its soil, the U.S. revived the notion of selling the Hondurans advanced aircraft. Emblematic of Israel's in-touch status in Honduras, before Washington could prepare the papers for the F-5Es it was offering, Israel had the Tegucigalpa government's signature on a preliminary agreement to buy 24 Kfir combat aircraft—a deal that could be worth as much as $200 million. To coax their quick agreement, Israel had assured the Hondurans that Washington would finance the deal. An incredulous State Department official said no such approval had been given. At the time the *Jerusalem Post* said that the National Security Council would have final say on the arrangements.[163] Later it would be revealed that the Kfir sale was one side of a *quid pro quo* which would have sent Israeli advisers to the contras. Still later, the Kfir sale fell through.

Costa Rica

Someday it may be precisely known how great a role Israel played in subverting the government of Costa Rica to accede to Washington's use of its territory as a secondary base in the war against Nicaragua. More is presently known about how the U.S. bribed Costa Rican officials to turn a blind eye to the contras; how they ran a CIA and then a "private" operation the northern part of the country, which included foreign mercenaries, drug running, a clandestine airstrip, and at least two assassination attempts and managed to exercise a progressively greater influence on the small, relatively democratic nation's media, as the contra campaign wore on.[164]

Israel, however, had the inside track. Luis Alberto Monge, elected to the Costa Rican presidency in 1982, is probably one of the strongest Zionists in Central America. Formerly Costa Rican ambassador to Israel, during his presidential campaign Monge promised to move Costa Rica's embassy to Jerusalem, while his foreign-minister-to-be said that the National Liberation Party would hold relations with Israel to be a "principal preoccupation."[165] In May 1982, Costa Rica became the first government to return its embassy to the city which all other nations had deserted when Israel annexed and declared Jerusalem its undivided capital in 1980.[166]

Costa Rica did not have an army, but it did have one of the highest foreign debts in the world, and that gave Israel somewhat of a handle. Soon after his election, Monge met in the U.S. with Israeli Prime Minister Menachem Begin, who introduced him to a number of leading bankers, thus helping him to renegotiate Costa Rica's debt to private banks.[167]

Begin pressed Monge hard to abandon the neutrality Costa Rica had maintained since 1948, in effect seconding the words of Reagan's UN Ambassador Jeane Kirkpatrick, that if Costa Rica wanted aid from Washington, it would have to create an army.[168]

Begin offered military aid[169] and in January 1983 the Costa Rican Public Security Minister visited Israel, touring defense plants and meeting with Defense Minister Sharon, Begin and Foreign Minister Yitzhak Shamir.[170] Shamir had been in Costa Rica the previous October and offered non-military cooperation.[171]

Limited amounts of Israeli military aid began to flow to Costa Rica's police forces,[172] and Israelis came to train the security police, special tactical squads[173] and intelligence agents.[174] Israelis themselves carried out various "intelligence activities" in Costa Rica.[175]

Israel's parastatal Tahal collaborated with with U.S. AID to develop a border barrier comprising roads, electronic barriers, and an agribusiness/ settlement scheme.[176] It was an open secret that this installation was part of the campaign against Nicaragua.

A Classic Case of Disinformation: "Anti-Semitism and the Sandinistas" .....

The War for the Jews

There is probably only one thing for which the Reagan Administration must be forgiven: its failure to understand why Democrats in Congress fairly swooned with approval for Israel's acts of military aggression, while remaining obdurately disapproving of similar moves made by the White House.[1] At least half of the administration's effort to make Israel a full partner in the contra war was aimed at harnessing Israel's political clout to a policy which the public consistently found utterly loathsome.

As an Israeli columnist put it, "American cooperation with Israel can, during any U.S. military activities in the Caribbean, make the difference between success and failure in the House of Representatives."[2]

When Israel's political support was restrained by its need to cater to its liberal constituency, which includes not only members of Congress, but the vast majority of Jews in the United States, the obvious task for the administration was to convert that constituency.

From mid-1983, when it began importuning Israel to get involved, until Congress passed contra aid in June 1986, the administration carried out a nonstop effort to win Jewish support for the contras. Using methods that were sometimes crude, sometimes slick, occasionally anti-Semitic and almost completely unsuccessful, the administration hammered away.

The same July day that leaked news of Israel's activities in Central America appeared on the front page of the *New York Times* marked the debut of a campaign to smear Nicaragua's government with charges of anti-Semitism. The previous day the President had used a White House briefing for Jewish groups to launch a campaign of spurious charges of anti-Semitism against the government of Nicaragua. This was part of what the White House called "public diplomacy"—appeals to various special interest groups to support its policies, especially its contra policy.[3] The Jewish appeal had been cooked up by the CIA, and it was anti-Semitic to the core.

Former FDN leader Edgar Chamorro told of how he had met with three CIA officers in Coral Gables, Florida in the spring of 1983. It was decided at that meeting to "target" American Jews with stories about Sandinista anti-Semitism. The CIA thought this would be a worthwhile propaganda exercise because, recounted Chamorro, "They said that the media was controlled by Jews, and if we could show that Jews were being persecuted, it would help a lot."

The CIA knew in advance that Isaac Stavisky and Abraham Gorn, the two men they planned to have at the White House briefing, had been persecuted for their collaboration with Somoza, not for their religion.[4]

The White House had also learned, four days earlier, from its ambassador in Managua that the charges were spurious. A cable from the embassy stated:

> [T]he evidence fails to demonstrate that the Sandinistas have followed a policy of anti-Semitism...Although most members of Nicaragua's tiny Jewish community have left the country and some have had their properties confiscated, there is no direct correlation between their Jewish religion and the treatment they received.[5]

Nevertheless, at the briefing the President, with the usual coy little catch in his voice, accused Nicaragua of anti-Semitism. Rabbi Morton Rosenthal, the director of the Anti-Defamation League's (ADL) Latin America division, explained that Stavisky and Gorn had been driven out by the Sandinistas, who had expropriated their property and seized the synagogue in Managua.[6]

Actually, as many subsequent investigations would point out, the Jewish community in Nicaragua had been miniscule, numbering around 50, down from around 150 before the massive 1972 earthquake.[7] In January 1979 Gorn, the recognized leader of the small Jewish community,[8] took delivery of a Honduran shipment addressed to the Somoza National

Guard.[9] The Nicaraguan human rights organization said Gorn received a telegram notifying him of the shipment from a "Jewish citizen of Honduras," the implication being that Gorn was not only a social intimate of Somoza, but also involved in Israeli arms deals.[10] Gorn's associate, Stavisky, "apparently has admitted running guns for Somoza."[11]

After the dictator's fall, many who had enjoyed his patronage—Jews and gentiles—fled. The assets of collaborators were seized under clearly defined laws.[12] And contrary to Washington's disinformation, investigators found several Jewish-owned businesses still in operation.[13]

The investigators included a delegation of members of New Jewish Agenda,[14] a group from *Moment* Magazine,[15] Rabbi Balfour Brickner of the Stephen Wise Free Synagogue in New York,[16] and the executive director of the Milwaukee Jewish Council.[17] Local groups also investigated the charges of anti-Semitism and reported back to their communities that they were spurious.

Latin American investigators were harsher in their refutations. Sergio Nudelstejer, who heads the American Jewish Committee's Mexico office, said that the Jews left Nicaragua because of "factors other than anti-Semitism, including their belonging to the propertied classes." A press release issued by the World Jewish Congress said Panama City Rabbi Heszel Klepfisc had been to Nicaragua in September 1983 and found that there was an "anti-Israel" tendency, but no anti-Semitism.[18] "The statements of Rabbi Rosenthal are not based on fact and do damage to the Jewish cause in Central America and, in my opinion, also to Israel," Klepfisz, a recognized leader of Latin American Jewry, wrote in a letter in April 1984.[19]

In its analysis of the situation, the Council on Hemispheric Affairs (COHA) noted that, "while anti-Zionism sometimes spills over into anti-Semitism, there is little evidence that this has transpired in contemporary Nicaragua." COHA saw Nicaragua's position as determined by

> the sort of sympathy with the Palestinian cause that is de riguer [sic] among left-leaning Third World regimes. This sentiment, coupled with the role Israel has played in arming rightist regimes throughout Latin America, has prompted the Sandinistas to adopt an avowedly anti-Zionist foreign policy.[20]

A State Department Bureau of Human Rights and Humanitarian Affairs team also carried out extensive interviews in Nicaragua and turned up no evidence of anti-Semitism.[21]

Journalists' reports corroborate what the investigators found. After having spoken with Jews still living in Nicaragua (this did tend to refute the charges of the entire community having been driven into exile) as well as the Nicaraguan government, Edward Cody of the *Washington Post* reported that all agreed that the synagogue was not confiscated, but abandoned by the Jews and later used by the Nicaraguans for a childrens' association.[22]

Although in 1982 the pro-government Managua paper *Nuevo Diario* had run a series of articles which the president of the Mexican branch of B'nai B'rith perceived as anti-Semitic,[23] several journalists determined that the editors had merely confused the terms for Jew and Israeli.[24] According to the Nicaraguan government's human rights unit, the article causing particular distress had been one of a series, reflecting the views of theologians who had spoken at the Church of the Nazarene in Managua.[25]

Clerical anti-Semitism in Nicaragua does not seem to be limited to pro-government forces. Bishop Miguel Obando y Bravo, an avid participant in the Reagan Administration's war against Nicaragua, preached an October 1984 sermon in Managua containing these lines:

> [T]he leaders of Israel...mistreated [the prophets], beat them, killed them. Finally as supreme proof of his love, God sent his divine Son, but they...also killed him, crucifying him...The Jews killed the prophets and finally the Son of God...Such idolatry calls forth the sky's vengeance."[26]

Obando, who has since been appointed Cardinal, did not deign to reply to a query by Rabbi Ronald B. Sobel, chair of the ADL Intergroup Relations Committee.[27] There is no trail of press clippings pointing to an ADL pursuit of this matter.

As had many other investigators, a North American Jewish woman who had lived in Nicaragua for three years noted that there was much ignorance, with Nicaraguans believing that Jews killed Christ. "The hardest question was from Nicaraguans who wanted to know why Jews and Israelis wanted to kill them. They know only one Hebrew word—Galil—written on all the weapons in the hands of the contras."[28]

For its part, the Nicaraguan government was quite sensitive to the issue. "We have broken our relations with Israel, but we go out of our way to show our love and respect for the Jewish people," stated Foreign Minister Miguel D'Escoto.[29]

That these charges were far fetched was underscored by the failure of the State Department to include anti-Semitism in the annual critique of Nicaragua it published in its *Country Reports on Human Rights Practices* for 1980, 1981 and 1982.[30] In 1983 it noted the ADL report.[31] Except for Assistant Secretary of State Elliott Abrams, who said that Nicaragua was anti-Semitic because it recognizes the PLO,[32] the State Department confined its energies to putting out tracts "proving" that Nicaragua was part of an international "terrorist" network.[33]

But the charges were not without some effect: the home of the Nicaraguan consul in Toronto was stoned by members of the Jewish Defense League. And Rep. Michael Barnes (D-MD) who, as chair of the subcommittee on Latin America of the House Foreign Affairs Committee, was always popping up on television opposing the administration's contra policy, released a letter to Managua accusing Nicaragua of "government-sponsored anti-Semitism" and declaring himself outraged at reports he had read about the "forced exile by your government of the entire Jewish community."[34]

Rather than uniting the U.S. Jewish community behind the Reagan policy, the controversy over the ADL's charges caused consternation and disputes among major U.S. Jewish organizations.[35] Without disputing the question of anti-Semitism, Henry Siegman, Executive Director of the American Jewish Congress noted that,

> The only significant question before the American people with respect to Nicaragua is whether the appropriate response to the dangers posed by the Sandinistas is military assistance to the contras...To invoke anti-Semitism as an expedient to gain support for controversial policies not only brings these policies further into question, but also compromises the battle against anti-Semitism.[36]

It is possible that the campaign even backfired, causing previously uncommitted Jews to take a stand against the contra war and the administration's Central America policy. The American Jewish Congress passed a resolution opposing contra aid.[37] Jews also began participating in the sanctuary movement, protecting refugees from El Salvador and Guatemala from the Reagan Administration. By early 1987, 340 Reform temples, a dozen Conservative congregations and several Jewish organizations, including New Jewish Agenda, had formally affiliated with sanctuary coalitions.[38]

One of the founders of the sanctuary movement, Rabbi Joseph Weizenbaum of Temple Emmanu-El in Tucson, remarked that he endeavors to convince the Central American refugees with whom he works that "there's more to Judaism than the foreign policy of Israel."[39]

In a crowning irony, it was later revealed that the *White House Digest* for July 20, 1983, the day that Stavisky and Gorn had made their debut as "victims" of the Sandinistas, had had the references to Sandinista "anti-Semitism" deleted, presumably after the cable from Ambassador Quainton.

But in his public remarks the President read the deleted text,[40] and both he and the ADL's Rosenthal would continue to preach what they knew to be lies as gospel.

Rabbi Rosenthal in particular would keep working the subject, with hysterical charges that the whole Jewish community had been driven out of Nicaragua. He issued a "white paper" reiterating his initial fraudulent allegations in March 1986—the same day that President Reagan read a televised speech containing the assertions that the Jewish synagogue in Managua had been "desecrated and firebombed"—it had a molotov cocktail thrown with small effect against its door during the war against Somoza,[41]—and that the "entire Jewish community" had been "forced to flee Nicaragua."[42] The ADL's "white paper" was distributed to members of Congress.[43]

And as regularly as clockwork, before a vote on contra aid, "victims" of Nicaraguan anti-Semitism would come forward to do what they could for the cause.

Relatives of the "exiled" Nicaraguan Jews surfaced in 1985 as part of a campaign launched to lobby for $14 million in contra aid. Billed as "conservative Nicaraguan Jews," Elena Gorn (the daughter-in-law of Abraham) and Sarita and Oscar Kellerman joined contra leaders in a national campaign "to convince American Jews that the Sandinista government is anti-Semitic and anti-Israel." The campaign specifically targeted Jewish members of Congress and members of Congress with large Jewish constituencies who had opposed contra aid. The three exiles joined contra leaders for Washington press conferences and then met individually with members of Congress, at synagogues and with "conservative" groups. They called fresh attention to the old charges of Nicaraguan anti-Semitism.[44]

In 1986 seven exiles appeared at a Washington press conference sponsored by the rightist National Jewish Coalition.[45]

Over the years, as the administration despaired and labored to recruit Israel to its cause, there were other approaches made to Jews, seeking their backing for contra aid, but also, given the intervention of Israeli diplomats in the 1986 contra aid battle, "discreetly encourag[ing] American Jewish bodies to lobby Congress in favor of the $100 million the President was asking for the mercenaries,"[46] almost certainly, to soften up public opinion to a possible future overt Israeli role in the contra program.

Much propaganda was made of the links between Nicaragua, Iran, Libya and the PLO. "If the Sandinistas are allowed to consolidate their hold on Nicaragua," intoned President Reagan, "we'll have a permanent staging ground for terrorism. A home away from home for Qadhafi, Arafat and the Ayatollah, just three hours by air from the U.S. border."[47] (At the time, of course, the man reading those lines was selling arms to "the Ayatollah.")

Under the masthead of *White House Digest*, the administration distributed, until at least early 1985, a propaganda piece entitled "The PLO in Central America." Derogatory cartoons indicated connections between the PLO and various "terrorist" organizations. The FSLN was of course included, but so were defunct groups such as the U.S. Black Panther Party and South American organizations that had long since become electoral formations. Of Israeli origin, the White House giveaway had been photocopied from a piece given out by the far-right Jewish Institute for National Security Affairs (JINSA).[48] One of the founders of JINSA was Michael Ledeen, who figured prominently in the Iran-contra scandal.

The point was made repeatedly that Khadafy, Arafat and Khomeini were using Nicaragua as a "terror base." In actuality Nicaragua's ties with the PLO were, in addition to the diplomatic sphere, mainly in civil aviation, agriculture and technical assistance.[49] In early 1985 the Nicaraguan embassy in Washington explained that some military training had been accepted from Libya, and that, even though Col. Khadafy had offered troops, these had been declined, as Nicaragua was bending over backwards to avoid anything which might be perceived by the administration a provocation.[50] The connection with Iran was primarily an oil-for-sugar barter arranged in early 1985.[51] Otherwise it was limited to verbal solidarity between two victims of U.S. aggression.[52] Only later would it become known that NSC staffer Lt. Col. Oliver North was overcharging Iran for U.S. arms and diverting the profits from those sales to the contras.

It is, of course, impossible to assess exactly what impact the anti-Semitism charges and the hyperbole about Iran, Libya and the PLO had on Jewish citizens. That the administration never altered the content of its campaign for Jewish support of its contra program did not necessarily connote success—instead it indicated a stubborn belief that Jews would respond as Jews, rather than members of the body politic. In other words: anti-Semitism. Nevertheless, right-wing Jewish groups worked eagerly with the administration to convert U.S. Jews to the contra cause.

At a White House meeting on March 5, 1986, President Reagan lobbied leaders of major Jewish organizations to support the $100 million contra aid bill to be considered by the House of Representatives. He reiterated the propaganda about the PLO, Iran and Libya, and suggested an additional special "Jewish" reason for supporting the contras: Jews should support contra aid because U.S. credibility to allies in Latin America and to Israel was at stake.

Kenneth Bialkin, the chairman of the Conference of Presidents of Major Jewish Organizations, and at the time leader of the ADL, endorsed the Reagan policy, but he stressed that he could not endorse it on behalf of the entire Jewish community which the conference purports to represent.[53]

Other Jewish rightists did not make the kind of prominent headlines Bialkin did. JINSA, for instance, confined its efforts to a letter to the editor of the *Wall Street Journal* repeating the spurious anti-Semitism charges and to repetitious anti-Nicaragua propaganda in its newsletter. In the *Congressional Record* of March 19, 1986, Rep. Vin Weber (R-MN) inserted a letter signed by prominent Jews such as Max Fisher and Jack Stein, a former president of the Conference of Major Jewish Organizations, stressing the connections between Nicaragua and the PLO and Libya.[54]

The administration also used individual Jews in its efforts to sway Jewish opinion. In the spring of 1986, the President entertained a group including Wall Street crook Ivan Boesky—before he was busted for insider trading, Boesky was a leading donor to Jewish causes—and ultraright Jewish Senator Chic Hecht (R-NV).[55]

The contras were at best half-way down the list of priorities of Jewish right-wingers, but the President's objectives neatly dovetailed with the aims of these groups, which have long sought to shift the Jewish community to the right. Premised upon the notion that the primary "mission" of Jews in the U.S. is to support Israel, the argument of these rightists is that alliances are best made with proponents of unbridled military spending and unreasoning hostility toward the nations of the East bloc and much of the Nonaligned Movement. The proponents of a Jewish shift to the right further argue that Jews, who have historically been involved in disproportionate numbers in struggles for social and economic justice, have become too affluent and powerful to have common interests with the left.

There have always been Jewish right-wingers, out of synch with the Jewish experience of suffering and persecution and out of step with the mainstream. Early in the century the high tone German-American Jews disdained Eastern European Jews who were fled pogroms and starvation to arrive in the U.S. in great numbers. The Russian Jews were labeled "anti-American" and the newcomers' Yiddish newspapers were decried as "socialistic" by the German-born Jews.[56] In more recent times, Jewish leaders worked with the McCarthy committees to "convict" leftist Jews.[57]

This push to the right was given new impetus under the Herut governments of Menachem Begin (1977-1983) and Yitzhak Shamir (1983-1984), who encouraged U.S. Jewish organizations to make common cause with televangelists such as Pat Robertson and Jerry Falwell, preachers who used religion to mobilize millions into the political process in support of 19th century social norms and madcap military spending. That these biblethumpers had traditionally been the reservoir of anti-Semitism troubled Begin not—nor, for that matter, ADL's Nathan Perlmutter.[58]

The tactics underlying this strange mating were expectations that far-right fans of military spending would support continued high levels of U.S. military aid to Israel (they do not appear to have done so with the regularity of the liberal Democrats) and that the televangelists would pump tourists into Israel. This has been the case, to a limited degree, with both Robertson and Falwell and their local clones. However, the friendship has been accompanied by the spread of a very bizarre, cultlike approach to the Jewish state. Called premillenialism, devotees literally believe Biblical predictions that the last battle of Armageddon (against the "Northern satanic force," i.e. the Soviet Union) will be fought in Israel—it will, of course, be nuclear—and Jesus Christ will "return" and gather up the true believers into a "rapture," while the rest of the world agonizes in war and turmoil.[59] There are shades of anti-Semitism to this school of superstition: believers say that all of the Jews must be gathered back in Israel before the commencement of the end of time, which they so eagerly await.[60]

Although the tours and paraphernalia of this cult are not selling quite as well as they used to,[61] those who subscribe to it become passionate devotees of Israel, visiting sites of the coming war, and adopting the Israeli line of dismissing with contempt all Arabs, particularly the Palestinians.[62]

It could not possibly be an accident that the Begin love affair with the right-wing evangelicals began at the very time that South Africa was beginning to establish links with, and funnel money to, the same groups. The religious right—to call it partial to South Africa is to understate the case—is given a great deal of the credit for the election of Ronald Reagan in 1980.

The years when the administration was trying to harness willing Jews to its Central America policies were years of considerable contention between Jewish liberals and the less extreme shadings of Jewish rightism. The invasion of Lebanon had been a watershed, with some Jewish liberals resentful of pressure from the Begin government to quell their criticism and support the war. Hoping to foster civil rights, Jewish-Arab contact, and to prevent the strengthening of settlements in occupied territories and of hardline religious institutions, some of these liberals began exploring methods of channeling their donations to Israel to projects not controlled by the government-linked Jewish Agency.[63] Some Jewish liberals began to argue that Jews must avoid making Israel the sole criterion of their political commitment and direct their political work toward multi-issue coalitions.[64]

This sparring has bypassed the many Jews outside the organized community. Jewish voters have not responded to the call from the right. Jewish males were the only white ethnics to vote against President Reagan in 1984. In the March 20, 1986 vote on contra aid, 21 of the 30 Jewish members of the House voted no. Prior to the vote, members of Congress had received a letter from the Union of American Hebrew Congregations, a grouping identified with Reformed Judaism, saying that 1.3 million Jews represented by UAHC opposed military aid to the contras. The letter also refuted the anti-Semitism charges against Nicaragua.[65]

Will the Lessons Be Learned? ....

If Israel is to be disengaged from the war against Nicaragua, the impetus will have to come from the U.S. In Israel there has been only the smallest voice of opposition to involvement with the contras and it has quavered. That voice has originated with the leaders of the Mapam party, a socialist Zionist party whose base is the kibbutzim and which, until 1984, had been part of the Labor Alignment, only breaking away when Labor joined Likud to form the 1984 unity government.

A high-ranking Mapam delegation visited Israel in late 1984 and on its return formed the Israeli Committee of Solidarity with Nicaragua,[1] a group which several Israelis described as "tiny" and "quiet."

Two years later a delegation from Nicaragua's Agrarian Reform Research and Study Center was said to have been set to visit Israeli distribution cooperatives and kibbutzim as guests of Mapam. It was possibly Mapam's hope that contact with Nicaraguan officials might lead to an improvement of relations between the two countries.[2] The visit, however, never materialized and soon after the eruption of the Iran-contra scandal the Israeli press said it had been canceled.[3]

Responding to an article in a British magazine about the visit, the Nicaraguan Ambassador to the UK said that Nicaragua had never contemplated sending a delegation to Israel.[4]

Instead of explaining why Nicaragua might under the circumstances have difficulty approaching Israel, Mapam showed journalists a letter it said

179

was from the Nicaraguan delegation. A Mapam leader said Nicaragua had canceled the visit because of "Arab pressure." Mapam also remained "curiously silent" about the sale of Israeli Kfir combat jets to Honduras, under discussion at that time[5] and deemed to be a major escalation of the situation in Central America.

The Israeli government itself has blown hot and cold about Nicaragua. Its most enthusiastic statements about improving relations, however, came soon after the Iran-contra scandal broke, as Israel sought by every means possible to demonstrate that it could not possibly have had any connection with the contras. The Israeli government propagated a story in the *New York Times* that between 1982 and 1986 it had tried to repair its relations with Nicaragua, offering development assistance programs and the possibility of diplomatic recognition as a means of boosting Nicaragua's image "with an important sector of American political opinion."[6]

The Nicaraguan government had quite a different perspective on what Israel had been trying to do. The government of Nicaragua would make no official comment on the Israeli claims, but a well-informed source, speaking on condition of anonymity, said that contacts between the two governments had been scant, limited to the occasional encounter at the United Nations. Moreover, according to this source, Nicaragua believes that Israel has played a generally counterproductive role in Central America, aiding the Guatemalan and Salvadoran military forces in their bloody attempts to stifle domestic opposition, as well as supporting the contras.

Where is the truth? Israeli officials, for instance, say that when they were offering Nicaragua diplomacy and assistance they also pointed out that Israel "was refraining from helping the contras," even though Nicaragua's solidarity with the PLO and its vote in the UN with the Nonaligned bloc were "viewed as provoking Israel."[7]

Israeli officials routinely profess support for the Contadora peace process led by Panama, Mexico, Venezuela and Colombia. However, in 1983 it took quite a bit of effort for the Contadora nations to get a statement from Israel supportive of their efforts to find a peaceful settlement for strife-torn Central America.[8]

In 1984 it was Nicaragua, not Israel, which offered to normalize ties. Talking to a visiting New Jewish Agenda delegation, Vice President Sergio Ramirez said that were Shimon Peres "to consolidate political power in Israel, there could be some prospect" for Nicaragua to reassess its relations with Tel Aviv.[9]

But under Peres, Israel aided the Reagan Administration's vendetta against Nicaragua. In June 1986 Foreign Minister Yitzhak Shamir made the bizarre charge that impoverished Nicaragua was aiding the Palestine

Liberation Organization.[10] He later said that Nicaragua was aiding "terror," which he called "an international monster spread over continents." Shamir "congratulated the United States on its anti-terror war in South America," saying that Israel "favors cooperation for the suppression of terror."[11] Several months later, Israeli military sources charged that Nicaragua's national airline Aeronica had sold Fatah, the principal component of the PLO, four DC-8 aircraft to transport troops and military equipment. William Ramirez, Nicaragua's transport minister, heatedly denied the charge. "We would certainly like to have DC-8s," he said, and went on to list all nine planes in Nicaragua's civil aviation fleet.[12]

At the UN, Israel was the only country to vote with the U.S. against a 1986 resolution demanding that Washington revoke its economic embargo against Nicaragua.[13] On an earlier resolution upholding a World Court judgment against the U.S. and demanding that Washington cease its aid to the contras, approved by the General Assembly on November 3, Israel joined El Salvador and the U.S. in casting the only negative votes.[14]

With the probable defeat of further contra aid in the wake of the Iran-contra scandal, there will again be a vacuum in Central America; floating in it will be thousands of untethered contra mercenaries. Opinion is divided on whether Israel will also withdraw or whether it will increase its involvement with the contras, spurred on perhaps by the same minority factions in the U.S. establishment which developed and ran the war against Nicaragua in the first place.

Given its past track record in Central America, if there is money to be made—two possible sources are narco-profits and donations from South Africa, which would have strong motivation for playing such an international role—and political leverage to be gained, Israel would very likely continue its low-profile assistance to the contras.

Passive speculation about which outcome is more likely is not worthwhile if the goal is to dissuade Israel from delving further into the Central American bloodbath. Public pressure applied as never before must block that option; it leads to nothing more complicated than murder—and our complicity in it.

Conclusion ....

Conclusion ....

What use is it to save Central Americans from death at the hands of U.S.-sponsored governments and mercenary bands if it is only to deliver them to the same clients and cutthroats courtesy of Israel? Is work on behalf of the liberation struggle in South Africa of any use if Israel is not prevented from arming and entrenching the minority regime? Yet, given the difficulty of restraining any of Israel's actions, is it not impossible to force a halt to these often clandestine activities, which are both lucrative and protected by powerful players in the U.S. establishment?

It might be argued that in this era when the word conservative is used where "fascist" would be perfectly appropriate, and when "liberal" connotes those who drift in and out of "bipartisan consensus," progressives should be satisfied with any shred of victory they can achieve. However, unless the goal is a smug self-delusion, that is a lame argument. And when the issue is preventing Israel's support of repressive forces, a good case can be made that progressives have not fought very hard. Despite Israeli leaders' insistence that many of these interventions are carried out as part of Israel's "strategic" alliance with the U.S.; despite the unparalleled amount of U.S. assistance Israel receives, which makes it a virtual ward of this country; and despite the reality that the victims of Israeli aggression have no reason to distinguish its depredations from U.S. policy—many progressives refuse to be informed about, much less take responsibility for, Israel's activities.

Responsibility is incumbent in the inextricable relationship between progressive victories on Central America, which have forced the U.S. to pull back, and the following escalation of Israeli involvement in the same area. Guatemala is an example in progress, albeit largely ignored. Meaningful sanctions against South Africa have also led to stepped-up Israeli efforts to arm Pretoria (sometimes with U.S. technology) and to peddle South African exports here.

However, there is much to suggest that sentiment exists for assuming that responsibility in a serious way. And there is even more cause for hope that a reasonably spirited fight against Israel's intervention will succeed. Conversely, failure to fight Israel's intervention in Southern Africa and Central America will greatly impair the U.S. left, already sorely wounded by its failure to include in its galaxy of concerns the Palestinian cause.

What are the objectives in this fight, and what are the obstacles which must be overcome? Simply stated, Israel must be identified as the scavenger of abandoned U.S. policy that in reality it is. Activists and progressive officials must be brought to understand that what Israel does outside the Middle East—and inside, too—has "made in U.S.A." stamped all over it. When Israel's actions are acknowledged to be our responsibility, it will be readily apparent that the solutions lie in U.S. leverage applied to Israel—leverage that exists in abundance, but has never been used.

Standing between the present situation and that goal is one main obstacle: fear—fear and its twisted reflection, cowardice. To a lesser extent, the bonds developed over several decades between the U.S. covert establishment and Israel will resist uncoupling.

The fear of confronting Israel is not misplaced. Often critics of Israeli policy have suffered damage to their reputations, have lost their jobs, and, in at least one case (that of Alex Odeh, Southern California director of the American-Arab Anti-Discrimination Committee, assassinated by a bomb in October 1985), have lost life itself. There is no single source of this threat, no nerve center directing damage control for Israel. Instead it emanates from a number of organizations, which over the years have developed hyperagressive methods of defending Israel.

At a minimum, Israel's defenders demand of those who wish to remain in their good graces uncritical, unswerving loyalty. The most commonly used method of extracting compliance is to brand critics as "anti-Semites." This is almost always a false charge, equating criticism of the policies of the government of Israel with hostility toward Jews. Nevertheless, in the wake of the Holocaust, it is a potent and disquieting sobriquet, reverberating especially harshly in the ears of those who have sincerely struggled to conquer their racism.

The purpose of these charges of anti-Semitism—and they are leveled with equal flagrance at Jews and non-Jews alike—is to place Israeli policy beyond the reach of acceptable public discourse. It is tremendously ironic that those who purvey them have rarely bothered to distance themselves from the far more prevalent racism directed against Arabs (but of course, this form of bigotry seems to work in Israel's favor).

One of the most extreme—and successful—examples of savaging all opposition is the U.S. Congress, where the slightest dissent against Israeli positions means almost certain opposition in the next election. In 1982, Israel's lobby AIPAC bragged that pro-Israel activists had defeated Illinois Republican Paul Findley by pumping $685,000 in pro-Israeli political action committee (PAC) contributions into the campaign of his opponent. Findley had represented his district for 22 years, had "voted consistently for aid to Israel," but had, as a member of the Foreign Affairs Committee, taken an active interest in U.S. Middle East policy, urged negotiations with the PLO, and had himself met with PLO Chairman Yasir Arafat.[1] In addition to the PAC contributions (from every state in the country), AIPAC and its allies had discouraged politicians and performers from appearing on Findley's behalf, and had organized pickets and precinct walkers to insure his defeat. Findley wondered whether he had been "chosen for a trip to the political gallows to discourage other Congressmen from speaking out." When he asked an AIPAC staffer he was told, "You were the most visible critic of Israeli policy. That's the best answer I can give." Findley wondered, "could Israel's supporters not tolerate even one lonely voice of dissent?"[2]

Curiosity and dissent are a constant threat, urgently requiring suppression. When Sen. Abraham Ribicoff (D-CT), a Jew and a strong supporter of Israel, developed a practice of freely criticizing Israeli policies at private meetings between influential senators and visiting Israeli officials in the mid-1970s, Israeli officials said "[b]y asking obviously hostile questions...he was encouraging his colleagues to take critical views of the Israeli position."[3] When Ribicoff agreed to have lunch with a representative of the PLO and another senator, Thomas Eagleton (D-MO), happened on the luncheon and joined the party, that was proof that "when a Jewish senator takes a position that undermines polices of the Israeli government ...it makes it a lot easier for the non-Jews in the Senate to abandon pro-Israeli positions."[4]

AIPAC does not wait until elections to make its influence felt. It coordinates the response of thousands of members throughout the country, who, on a moment's notice, will deluge their representatives in Washington with phone calls, letters, or even telegrams;[5] AIPAC has on file signed proxies for the latter, so there will be no delay.[6] Although it is Israel's registered foreign agent, AIPAC is also a networking mechanism for national and regional Jewish leaders, many of whom sit on its governing bodies.[7]

To the power of AIPAC must be added

the network of congressional aides strongly sympathetic to Israel who meet frequently to coordinate efforts to pass critical legislation and also write bills and speeches on Israel for the members of Congress for whom they work.[8]

In practice this works to stifle any serious consideration by Congress of issues relating to Israel. Action in Congress is limited to moving on Israel's agenda: withholding arms sales from Arab countries, passing resolutions forbidding U.S. officials from meeting with the PLO, passing resolutions condemning UN resolutions critical of Israel, and, of course, passing ever more monumental no-strings-attached aid appropriations for Israel.

While AIPAC and the various Jewish organizations devote considerable energy to lobbying Congress, they also devote themselves to defending Israel in other areas of public life: local politics, academia, media, the arts. In research spurred by his experience at the hands of this network, Paul Findley chronicled some of the casualties: a campaign against the Hartford (Connecticut) Seminary involving charges that its long-respected Islamic studies program was anti-Semitic and an "al-Fatah support group";[9] a shrill campaign against the Georgetown Center for Contemporary Arab Studies for having accepted funds from Arab governments;[10] a campaign against a similar program at Villanova, a Catholic university in Pennsylvania, and against Middle East Studies programs nation wide;[11] a 1980 campaign against the director of the University of Arizona's Near Eastern Center featuring charges that she was "running a pro-Arab propaganda network," forcing the resignation of both the director and her superior.[12]

A longrunning media vendetta was launched against the Very Reverend Francis B. Sayre, dean of the (Episcopalian) National Cathedral in Washington, D.C. after he preached a sermon in 1972 criticizing Israel's treatment of Palestinians under occupation. Sayre later acknowledged that the attacks truncated his career.[13] Findley also found numerous instances of intimidation campaigns against political organizations, journalists, and media outlets.

There are similar tales from every community and every aspect of public life. The successful campaign to get the Boston Symphony Orchestra to drop a performance with Vanessa Redgrave in 1982 made national headlines. Others make only a local stir, destroy careers, and then slip unnoticed into history.

Local elections are a focus of intense activity, particularly where black candidates are involved. Because they have been among the most stalwart supporters of Palestinian rights, and because they have access to one of the largest voting blocs in the Democratic Party, black politicians experience particularly heavy pressure from pro-Israel activists. There is a history of friction, over the Middle East and affirmative action, between black and Jewish leaders, dating back to the Black Power movement and intensifying with the campaign around the Bakke anti-affirmative action case and the forced resignation of the Carter Administration's UN Ambassador Andrew Young for meeting with a representative of the PLO.[14] Pro-Israel activists have scarcely concealed their interest in helping to determine which black politicians come to national prominence.[15] Thus candidates for local offices as unrelated to foreign policy as county supervisor are judged on their positions on Israel. Some are pressured privately and others are asked to endorse a sort of "loyalty oath," often reflecting such extremist Israeli positions as rejection of negotiations with the PLO.[16]

The climate has been well prepared for such pressure tactics. There was little protest, except from American-Arab organizations and organizations working on Middle East-related issues, when both AIPAC and the ADL published and circulated "enemies of Israel" lists.[17]

Most insidious is the constant barrage of Arab-as-terrorist propaganda loosed on Israel's behalf. It has become perfectly acceptable for candidates for office to refuse the donations of Arab Americans. The Mondale 1984 campaign declared it had a policy of returning such donations.[18] In 1986, Joseph Kennedy, Jr. returned a $100 donation to his congressional campaign from family friend and former U.S. Senator James Abourezk.

It should not be surprising that, after failing to win a conclusive victory in its persecution of the sanctuary movement,[19] when the Reagan Administration next decided to move against domestic dissent its target was eight Palestinian resident aliens and the Kenyan wife of one of them. They were arrested on January 27, 1987 after a full-blown FBI investigation. However, as the investigation failed to turn up any evidence of "terrorism," they were held for deportation on a violation of the McCarthy-era McCarran-Walters act—specifically for disseminating literature advocating the goals of "world communism."[20] There was an immediate outpouring of support from the civil liberties community and also from those concerned with the rights of immigrants and refugees. A strong defense committee was formed. It is still not clear whether the lesson of the administration's attempt to take advantage of the outsider status of the Palestinian movement has been fully absorbed by the left.

That Los Angeles was the scene of this testing of the water could not have been more ironic. Slightly more than a year before the arrests Alex Odeh, the Southern California regional director of the American-Arab Anti-Discrimination Committee (ADC), had been assassinated in nearby Santa Ana by a bomb rigged to go off when he opened the door to the ADC office.[21] The FBI has continued to maintain that it is investigating that murder—but it has not yet been solved.

Odeh had been interviewed on television the previous night, commending the efforts of Egypt and PLO Chairman Yasir Arafat to negotiate an end to the hijacking of the cruise ship Achille Lauro.[22] An earlier bomb attempt at the Boston ADC office resulted in the death of a police officer as he tried to defuse it. Other officers of ADC have been threatened, as have a number of individuals who speak out against Israel.[23]

If this organized intimidation was all there was to the Israeli defense system abroad it would be formidable. But there is more. A recent investigation revealed the existence of an organized campaign to influence the coverage given Israel by the U.S. media. Called the *Hasbara Project*— *Hasbara* being Hebrew for propaganda—the project has enjoyed the participation of leading lights of the U.S. corporate media. Israeli diplomats are trained through apprenticeships at Madison Avenue advertising agencies and public relations firms. They are taken to meet "top editors and executives at the *New York Times*, the *Washington Post*, and the network evening news shows," as well as editors and broadcasters around the country. They sit in on editorial conferences. Thus they develop both the contacts and techniques for getting a story killed or shaded. Often their efforts are buttressed by pressure from U.S. Jewish groups, which have succeeded in killing some television programs outright, intimidating the advertisers of others, and getting advertisements for opponents' causes canceled.[24]

Stephen Rosenfeld of the *Washington Post* observed:

> They want 100 percent. They don't want fairness; they want unfairness on their side, and when they don't get it they accuse the press of being unfair. Most journalists get so much uninformed, unfair whining from the organized Jews that Jewish organizations—and ultimately Israel—may lose their credibility.[25]

That day is far off. For now, the executive producer at *Nightline* admits that Israel is "overrepresented" on the show, and that the PLO is excluded—because it is not considered a "counterpoint to Israel."[26]

Underlying these efforts are the covert activities of Israeli agents of Mossad and possibly other intelligence services. Mossad, according to one

U.S. intelligence expert, "[has] penetrations all through the U.S. government. They do better than the KGB."[27] It is well known that Israel regularly monitors U.S. government communications (in order to be able to respond in a timely manner to any contemplated new policy directions.) "We have to assume that they have wire taps all over town," said a senior State Department official.

Mossad also, according to a 1979 CIA study, "acquires data for silencing anti-Israel factions in the West." According to this study, Mossad uses domestic pro-Israeli groups in its work as well as highly-placed figures in a variety of walks of life.[28] Some activists suspect Israeli involvement in COINTELPRO, the CIA program of the 1960s and 1970s that targeted domestic dissidents.

It is because these organizations and their methods have been allowed to proceed unchallenged for so long that they now appear so menacingly invincible. It is unlikely that they will melt like the Wicked Witch of the West with the first bucket of water. Nonetheless, insiders are aware that the juggernaut has little depth. "You have an underlying fragility that was only overcome by political fear," remarked a Defense Department official, in an attempt to describe a sudden outpouring of negativity toward Israel among government bureaucrats following the arrest of Jonathan Jay Pollard for spying for Israel.[29]

Of particular concern to Jews who have never felt that the pro-Israel network represented them, its actions only confirm the old shibboleths of anti-Semites: that Jews control the media; that they conspire to control the government. Some worry that an anti-Semitic backlash is inevitable. The vehement champions of Israel have no answer to this dilemma. They have been riding high for so long, it has perhaps not occurred to them that they have created something of a monster, with at least the potential capacity to inflict harm on its creator as well as its intended victim.

For the moment, however, it is the progressives who are facing the monster—or would be, if they only dared to look. The fight will have to be waged where the challenge is: in the Congress and electoral politics; and in political and cultural life on a local level. The costs of blindness and passivity, in the long run, are apt to be even higher than a head-on confrontation.

In Congress

Although it seems all but impossible to present a counterweight to the pro-Israeli lobby, there is already evidence that issues concerning Israel's behavior outside the Middle East are a key point of vulnerability. This suggests that it will be easier to persuade both activists and legislators to deal with Israeli intervention outside the Middle East than with anything Israel does within its own bailiwick. This is a tactical rather than a moral question. Israel's lobby is armed to the teeth on issues relating to brutalization of the Palestinians under occupation, Israel's use of Lebanon for target practice and spare water, and its strange assortment of strategies, alliances and enemies among the regional actors.

The lobby is weaker where Israeli dealings with oppressor regimes outside the Middle East are concerned. Israel's ludicruous denials of any involvement with the contras after the Iran-contra scandal broke demonstrated two things: there is an absolute lack of excuses for such behavior; Congressional Democrats are offended by these activities,[30] although they are too well disciplined to squawk about them. AIPAC doesn't have much to say either, at least nothing suitable for publication.

Particularly hot potatoes have been issues dealing with Israel's relations with South Africa. The Jewish rank and file is also profoundly disturbed, preferring not to try to talk about why Israel must continue selling arms to South Africa.[31]

Everything Congress has ever done on this subject has been awkward, like children trying to get the cookie jar back on the shelf before being noticed. If anti-apartheid organizations had not been so delicate about avoiding discussion of Israel's support of the white regime, on at least two occasions Congress might have been left with no recourse but to do the right thing and apply pressure on Israel to halt its dealings with South Africa.

Had there been a presence by representatives of anti-apartheid organizations when Rep. John Conyers (D-MI) proposed legislation on South Africa's nuclear weapons, things might have gone differently indeed. This is a supersensitive issue—not the nuclear arsenal of South Africa *per se* but its nuclear mentor, Israel—which, if Congress faced, might result in cutting off aid to Israel. U.S. law calls for cutting off aid to a client which shares nuclear technology with a non-signer of the Nuclear Nonproliferation Treaty. (Neither Israel nor South Africa has signed the treaty.)

When Rep. Conyers attempted to amend the 1985 foreign aid bill with an amendment, which he said was "a very simple prohibition that provides that no foreign assistance, military or economic, may be provided to any country having a nuclear relationship with South Africa," the following dialogue occurred in the Africa subcommittee of the Foreign Affairs Committee:

> Conyers: All this amendment does, and it names no countries and it indicts no nations, is that we say that, any nation from this point on...having anything to do with developing nuclear capability with South Africa could be prohibited from receiving assistance from the United States...
>
> [Howard] Wolpe [(D-MI), Chair of the subcommittee]: I have some concerns about the amendment as it has been drafted, if I understand it correctly it could result in the cutoff of cash sales, military equipment to some U.S. allies and NATO, for example, France for example, if they have a nuclear relationship.
>
> I think, though, this is an issue that needs to be explored. I would suggest that this matter be further explored in committee hearings...[32]

Wolpe persuaded Conyers to withdraw the amendment on the promise of considering the issue during hearings on nuclear proliferation. That was in 1985—Conyers had just released a report on the 1979 nuclear test conducted by South Africa and Israel—and those hearings have never been held, largely through lack of expressed constituent interest, according to some congressional insiders.

Another such scene played itself out in the Senate the following year, again without any activist input. This time, fortuitously, the results were better. But lack of constituent action has almost totally vitiated what could have been a real victory. Together with Sen. Dan Evans (R-WA), Sen. Charles Mathias (R-MD)—he was retiring and had nothing to lose—amended anti-apartheid legislation to penalize U.S. aid recipients which had military dealings with the apartheid regime. This section of the Evans-Mathias amendment caused great consternation among Democrats on the Senate Foreign Relations Committee.

The committee retreated behind closed doors where, according to a staff member, the implications for Israel were openly discussed. Three votes were taken on the amendment. On the first vote Senator Alan Cranston (D-CA) joined rightist Republicans Helms, Boschwitz, Pressler and Murkowski in the minority. On a move for reconsideration, a 9-8 victory was wrested by Israel's friends, who on that pass included Democrats Pell, Biden, and Dodd as well as Cranston. A third vote, occasioned by a change of heart on the part of Sen. Christopher Dodd (D-CT) affirmed the amendment by a vote of 10-7. Of the committee's

Democrats, Cranston and Claiborne Pell remained in the minority with Jesse Helms and company.

Although Sen. Pell's seniority would shortly boost him into the chair of the Foreign Relations Committee, the Rhode Island Democrat had never put himself forward as a national leader. Quite the reverse was true of Cranston, who in 1984 ran for the Democratic nomination for President and portrayed himself as the candidate of the nuclear disarmament movement. Also in 1984, Cranston had led the pack in an outcry over the administration's efforts to transfer nuclear energy technology to the Peoples Republic of China. Acting on a briefing from the Israeli embassy, he worked to block the China sale for a year on the grounds that China might transfer the technology to Pakistan for its "Islamic bomb."[33] Cranston also styled himself one of the Senate's most adamant oponents of apartheid. Prior to his votes with Jesse Helms in the Foreign Relations Committee, he had introduced to the Senate the very exemplary bill against apartheid authored by Rep. Ronald V. Dellums (D-CA) that was passed by the House.[34]

Interestingly, this was AIPAC's one notable failure in several years. It let this language, which became Section 508 of the Comprehensive Anti-Apartheid Act of 1986, slip into law. AIPAC had no chance to knock it out, as the bill was never debated before being passed by the Senate and the House, and then passed again by both houses over the President's veto. However, just before the report mandated by Section 508 on U.S. allies dealing weapons to South Africa was due to be submitted to Congress, Israeli leaders worked out a gesture acceptable to Congress and the administration: a March 18 cabinet decision to phase out existing arms contracts and refrain from signing new ones. No mention was made of nuclear cooperation. Moreover, it was reported in Israel that during a January visit to South Africa, Defense Minister Rabin had signed new long-term contracts,[35] thus making the March 18 decision utterly—and insultingly—meaningless.

Immediately after the Israeli Cabinet announcement, representatives of AIPAC, the American Jewish Committee, the American Jewish Congress, the Religious Action Center of the Reform movement and U.S. Reps. Barney Frank (D-MA), Sander Levin (D-MI), Martin Frost (D-TX), and Howard Berman (D-CA) met with members of the Congressional Black Caucus and offered support for increased U.S. aid to Africa in exchange for silence on the contents of the report.[36] According to an extremely well-informed source, pressure on caucus members was very intense. Congressional sources said heavy constituent pressure would be needed to force Congress to break its silence and to act.[37]

In February 1987, a follow-up sanctions bill sponsored by Rep. Dellums was introduced. It also contained language barring U.S. aid to allies with a military relationship with South Africa, but that language was withdrawn in March after pressure from pro-Israeli partisans.

In the Democratic Party

The battle lines in the Democratic Party arena have already been sketched out—by the money men and bosses—to include the Middle East. This became apparent during Jesse Jackson's campaign for the 1984 Democratic presidential nomination. A wedge was driven into the left and it was partly immobilized by debate over whether Jackson was "anti-Semitic." Anti-Semitism was not the real question, of course. It was Jackson's independent position on the Middle East, mild as it may have been, but threatening enough as an example to call forth a shrill and hysterical campaign against Jackson as an "enemy of Israel."

Pro-Israel activists play up—indeed, often overplay—the fact that a great deal of the early money that plays such a determinative role in the candidate selection process in the Democratic Party comes from Jews. Candidates for Senate are very likely to have been prescreened by Israel's friends before they are presented to the voters. Presidential candidates—always with the lockstep Middle East position, along with the standard issue Cold War interventionism—are habitually shoved down the throats of the prime constituencies of the party, minorities, progressives, peace activists. (Sometimes this gets out of hand, when too many pass muster. There was an unseemly competition before the 1984 New York primary, with several Democratic presidential candidates striving to be seen as the most ardent supporter of a bill mandating the move of the U.S. embassy in Israel from Tel Aviv to Jerusalem,[38] despite warnings from U.S. diplomats that this would lead to worldwide protests against the U.S.[39])

The result of all this is an incapacitating dishonesty between activists and legislators who have carved out their turf on a specific area of concern. In this respect, Alan Cranston is the shining exemplar. In his 1986 race for reelection, Cranston received more money from pro-Israel PACs than any other candidate running that year. He also received support from peace, anti-intervention, environmental and social justice activists, who performed the crucial phone-banking and precinct-walking that resulted in his victory by the narrowest of margins. He is now shared, much like a vacation condominium, by groups with diametrically opposing interests.

But Cranston is not the only one. Howard Berman, for example, champions liberal causes and then sits down with representatives of the Israeli Embassy and U.S. AID to determine where Israeli government experts will work in Central America[40] and with his black colleagues to persuade them not to object to the carnage inflicted by Israel on struggling South Africans. A survey in late 1985 found not one instance where a member of Congress had alerted organizations fighting contra aid that that year's contra aid package had been attached by the House leadership to two bills carrying aid to Israel. In 1985, $27 million in contra aid flowed from congressional coffers.

This situation is replicated many times with never a confrontation, although obviously part of this problem could be remedied simply by holding legislators' feet to the fire, giving them cause to resist the pressures of the pro-Israeli forces. There are very specific and reasonable demands to which lawmakers could be forced to respond. For instance: Congressional action against Israeli military and nuclear dealings with South Africa; as part of a broader campaign against U.S. funding of Vietnam-style pacification in Central America, a clear opposition to funding Israel to collaborate on the programs.

All the usual tactics should be used: visits to district offices of Congressional representatives; letter writing (which is more effective when a written response is requested); individuals or organizations can call radio talk shows and write "op ed" pieces. Occasional phone calls to congressional offices and media editors are also helpful. Calls should be made *after* votes, as well as before them, expressing either agreement or disagreement with the position taken. This conveys a continuing interest in the issue.

In pressuring legislators there is an obvious problem to be overcome. Progressives, even when they are organized around one issue, are not "single issue," the way the pro-Israeli forces are. Instead, for the best of reasons, their interest is more than single issue. Thus, organizations and individuals concerned with the Middle East and with Israel's support of bloody oppressors are likely to settle for candidates like Cranston, because they are "good" on so many other vital issues. And everybody takes it as a given that if a candidate or serving member of Congress begins to talk meaningfully about Israel, Israel's lobby will blow her or him out of the water.

It is worth trying anyway, especially on members of the House of Representatives. There are several dozen members of the 100th Congress (elected in 1986) who would probably respond (gratefully) to constituent pressure to bar Israel from Central America and from military deals with South Africa. Perhaps more would take advantage of any opening created for them to abandon the hypocrisy that has prevailed until now.[41]

To Gain the Advantage

To avail themselves of this opening and to create others, organizations will first have to open up the issue of Israel's military, economic and political support of South Africa and its actions in Central America. While some anti-apartheid organizations have discussed it, others, have shied away for fear of losing Jewish support and being marginalized by charges of anti-Semitism.

Local organizations rather than their national offices are probably better positioned to initiate discussion of Israel's impact on their area of concern. National organizations often come under intense pressure which can involve loss of funding or loss of access to members of Congress. One very prominent national human rights organization has been concerned about Israeli activities in Guatemala for several years. It has felt compelled, however, to limit its expression of concern to private communications with Israeli officials.

Local organizations often are not constrained by the need to fund paid positions. They don't depend on elite cocktail parties. They can demand that Israeli complicity in murder—and Israeli violations of Palestinian human and national rights—be halted. Their determination to end Israel's undercutting of positive U.S. foreign policy positions can be expressed directly to Congress or used to fortify the resolve of national organizations, which can then report that grassroots sentiment is making discussion imperative. Local action should also, of course, be conveyed to the local media and put forward in coalitions.

Organizations have many means, through the media or through public education campaigns, to communicate their demands. The International Fellowship of Reconciliation approached the Israeli government directly, in an open letter "To the People of Israel and their Government" which appeared in the weekly supplement of *Al Hamishmar* (the Mapam-linked daily). The letter was a direct and respectful plea that Israeli aid to the government of Rios Montt cease. The Fellowship called attention to Israeli military and "pacification" assistance to Guatemala and concluded:

> We respect the Jewish desire for the right to self determination of
> a people, based on its tradition, beliefs, and values. We therefore

believe that you can understand the need of the people of Central America to decide the future of their nations without outside interference. We request of you not to stand in their way.[42]

Coalitions which come together to put on a major demonstration frequently debate the inclusion of a demand concerning the Middle East. Sometimes these efforts are successful, sometimes not. But each time the subject of Israel—its intervention outside the Middle East, its crimes against the Palestinian people, or its position in U.S. military doctrine—is discussed, valuable work has been done. Fear is conquered, the issue is legitimized, some layers of self-delusion and hypocrisy about the realities of Israel's role in world affairs are stripped away.

U.S. activists often receive an education in solidarity work when they learn that the South Africans or Central Americans that they support have strong and well developed bonds with the PLO. Many are surprised to learn how great the PLO's contribution to Nicaragua's development has been. Speakers from the ANC have made it a point to mention the links of solidarity between their organizations and the PLO; they have done much to educate U.S. activists on the justice of the Palestinian cause.

Unfortunately solidarity workers have been slow to communicate what they have learned to the larger U.S. progressive community. And until broad sectors of the U.S. left come to grips with their isolation from the international movements for peace and justice, they will face impediments to the creation of a truly mature and effective movement, one that is reflective of the extra responsiblity we bear as the opposition in the world's prime international offender.

Some Success Stories

Several organizations have raised and acted on issues of Israel's overseas activities. None has suffered undue consequences.

The Board of Trustees of the Unitarian Universalist Association passed a motion calling on the governments of the U.S. and Canada to "withhold foreign aid to any government which is aiding in the development of nuclear weapons for South Africa, or which is sending military or 'security' equipment or advisers to the Union of South Africa."[43] The National Conference of Black Lawyers has condemned the overall Israeli-South African relationship. At its fall 1986 national convention the Coalition of Black Trade Unionists considered a resolution condemning

Israel's ties with South Africa, and later passed a milder version which did not name Israel.

The Council on Hemispheric Affairs conducted a study of Israeli-Nicaraguan relations and not only published the results, but conducted a media campaign to publicize its report.[44]

New Jewish Agenda investigated the allegations of Nicaraguan "anti-Semitism" and published pamphlets refuting the charges, as well as supporting the sanctuary movement and dealing with Israel's role in Central America. One pamphlet concluded, "As Jews concerned about Israel's security and well-being, we believe that the Israeli government can find ways to support itself economically without losing sight of its moral vision."[45]

There has even been a demonstration against Israel's ties to South Africa and its involvement in Central America—in San Francisco in June 1985. Sponsored by a wide *ad hoc* coalition of Central America, anti-apartheid, Middle East, and human rights organizations, the demonstration got press coverage and no one reported suffering attacks from pro-Israeli activists.

San Francisco anti-apartheid activists also worked actively to defeat a contract between the city and Israel's national shipping line, Zim. There was no ultimate victory: even after it was proven that Zim did business with South Africa (and thus was in violation of the city's anti-apartheid ordinance) the Board of Supervisors voted to lease port space to the line. But the struggle drew headlines for weeks, as well as editorials in the city's major dailies. Moreover, despite the strongarm tactics one supervisor charged had been applied to the Board, not one of the several organizations involved reported a loss of members, funds, or community standing.[46]

Numerous forums and discussions on Israel's foreign policy have been held at campuses and in communities across the country. Occasionally these programs have been disrupted by pro-Israeli activists, but many have been well attended and have received favorable press coverage. In 1986, the November 29 Committee for Palestine organized a tour which included speakers from the ANC. This was especially successful in educating people on the political implications of Israeli-South African relations.

These are only a few instances. Doubtless there are others where the pro-Israel juggernaut was confronted and reduced in its legendary dimensions. It would be good if they were known about. It would be better if they were multiplied across the country.

Until the message is received in Washington that an end to Israel's foreign activities is an integral part of the progressive agenda, Israel's ability to take on the rejected fragments of U.S. policies will remain a problem with profound consequences for politics and foreign policy decisions in this country. For Israel's victims in Central America, Southern Africa and elsewhere, the consequences will be fatal.

Footnotes ....

Introduction

1. "Pretoria Unveils Updated Jet Fighter," Reuters, *International Herald Tribune,* July 17, 1986.

2. Radio South Africa (Johannesburg) External Service "Africa Today" program, 0100 GMT, July 17, 1986.

3. *Ibid.*

4. "Revealed: the secrets of Israel's nuclear arsenal," *Sunday Times,* October 5, 1986.

5. Stephen Green, *Taking Sides: America's Secret Relations with a Militant Israel,* William Morrow & Company, New York, 1984, pp. 148-169.

6. "France admits it gave Israel A-bomb," *Sunday Times,* October 12, 1986.

7. James Adams, *The Unnatural Alliance,* Quartet, London, 1984, pp. 154-157.

8. "Revealed: the secrets of Israel's nuclear arsenal" (see note 4), quotes a retired U.S. official as confirming this, the latest of many such reports.

9. Martin Bailey, "The Blooming of Operation Flower," *The Observer* (London), February 2, 1986; an earlier report of this collaboration by Claudia Wright appeared in the *New Statesman* on August 23, 1985. See also "Iran: The Flower and the Fixer," *Israeli Foreign Affairs,* March 1986.

10. "Vanunu Brought from Rome," *Israeli Foreign Affairs,* January 1987 and "Support Builds for Vanunu," *Ibid.,* March 1987.

11. Jonathan Marshall, Peter Dale Scott, and Jane Hunter, *The Iran-Contra*

Connection: Secret Teams and Covert Actions in the Reagan Era, South End Press, Boston, 1987.

12. James Brooke, "A cryptic call launched Guatemala coup," *Miami Herald,* March 28, 1982; Rios was initially head of a 3-man junta, but he soon muscled his two partners out of the way and dissolved the triumvirate in June 1982.

13. *Ma'ariv* (Tel Aviv), cited by Ignacio Klich, "Caribbean boomerang returns to sender," *The Guardian* (London), August 27, 1982.

14. "Guatemalan Army Topples President in a Brief Battle," *New York Times,* August 9, 1983.

15. *Davar* (Tel Aviv), February 14, 1984, translated in *Israeli Mirror* (London), No. 679, February 27, 1984.

16. "The Israeli Connection," *Economist,* November 5, 1977.

17. After the 1977 UN Arms Embargo, the Boers were able to continue building weapons systems of several European countries, most notably France, under license. Also, at one time or another, weapons technology—and occasionally weapons—were obtained from the U.S., Italy, Britain, West Germany and other European countries. None of these deals provided South Africa with such a consistent and vital flow of weapons and technology as it got from Israel.

18. Cheryl A. Rubenberg, *Israel and the American National Interest,* University of Illinois Press, Urbana, 1986, pp. 23-31 contains a summary of the history of the period leading up to and immediately after the adoption of the partition plan.

19. Yoram Peri and Amnon Neubach, *The Military-Industrial Complex in Israel,* International Center for Peace in the Middle East, Tel Aviv, January 1985, p. 31.

20. Edwin Black, *The Transfer Agreement,* MacMillan, New York, 1984, pp. 4-5, 13 and *passim.*

21. *Ibid.,* pp. 104-109 and *passim.*

22. *Ibid.,* p. 13. A protest statement sent to a planning committee said, in part, "The American Jewish Committee and B'nai B'rith are conviced that the wisest and the most effective policy for the Jews of America to pursue is to exercise the same fine patience, fortitude and exemplary conduct that have been shown by the Jews of Germany. This is not a time further to inflame already overwrought feelings, but to act wisely, judiciously and deliberately.".

23. *Ibid.,* pp. 41-46.

24. *Ibid.,* p. 104 and *passim.*

25. *Ibid., passim.,* David S. Wyman, *The Abandonment of the Jews,* Pantheon, New York, 1984, *passim.*

26. Jozef Garlinski, (Auschwitz historian) Letter to *The Sunday Times,* August 30, 1981.

27. This was the Biltmore Program, subscribed to by most of the major Jewish organizations. It vested diplomatic and political authority in the Jewish Agency. Rubenberg, *Israel and the American National Interest,* pp. 25-26.

28. Wyman, *Abandonment of the Jews,* p. 175. A special American Jewish

Commission set up in 1981 analyzed the performance of the major organizations during the pre-war and war years. (Walter Goodman, "U.S. Jews' response to Holocaust," *New York Times,* in *Oakland Tribune,* March 21, 1984).

29. Rubenberg, *Israel and the American National Interest,* pp. p. 33.

30. Green, *Taking Sides...,* pp. 123-147.

31. Paul Findley, *They Dare to Speak Out,* Lawrence Hill, Westport, CT, 1985, p. 117.

32. *Ibid.,* p. 116.

33. *Ibid.,* p. 119. See also Green, *Taking Sides...,* p. 25.

34. Rubenberg, *Israel and the American National Interest,* p. 91.

35. Green, *Taking Sides...,* pp. 180-214. It was in this war that Israel attacked and almost sank the U.S.S. Liberty, an unarmed intelligence ship. Evidence strongly suggests that the Israeli attack was deliberate, intended to keep the U.S. from learning about its plan to invade Syria. James M. Ennes, Jr., *Assault on the Liberty,* Random House, NY, 1979, presents documents and other material in support of this position, which Israel has strongly denied, insisting the attack was an accident.

36. *Information Please Almanac 1985,* Houghton Mifflin Company, Boston, 1985, p. 212.

37. Green, *Taking Sides...,* p. 246.

38. *Ibid.,* pp. 248-50.

39. Findley, *They Dare to Speak Out,* 122.

40. Eli Eyal, "Waiting for a Signal," *Ma'ariv,* June 21, 1974 in *SWASIA,* August 2, 1974.

41. Wolf Blitzer, *Between Washington and Jerusalem,* Oxford University Press, New York, 1985, pp. 14-15.

42. *Ibid.*

43. Grace Halsell, *Prophecy and Politics, Militant Evangelists on the Road to Nuclear War,* Lawrence Hill & Co., Westport CT, 1986.

44. Wolf Blitzer, *End of the Honeymoon,* Jerusalem Post Magazine, January 16, 1987.

45. Findley, *They Dare to Speak Out,* p. 140.

46. Rubenberg, *Israel and the American National Interest,* pp. 330-376.

47. In his book *The Fateful Triangle, The United States, Israel & the Palestinians,* South End Press, Boston, 1983, Noam Chomsky chronicles many occasions on which Israel, backed by the U.S., has turned its back on an opportunity for peace. Without a doubt there are cynics in both legislative and executive branches who knowingly work to sustain a state of constant tension. Congress' role is to passively support that status quo, rather than to create or devise a strategy that might lead to peace. While it is questionable that most of the members of Congress who adamantly support Israel understand anything at all about the Middle East, the complaisance of their "team spirit" contributes to Israel's ability to "hang tough."

48. Aaron Klieman, *Israel's Global Reach: Arms Sales as Diplomacy,* Pergamon-Brassey's, Washington, London, N.Y., 1985, pp. 16 and 26

(footnote 7).

49. Leonard Slater, *The Pledge,* Simon & Schuster, N.Y., 1970, *passim,* recounts the varied means of arms procurement the Zionists employed.

50. Klieman, *Israel's Global Reach,* pp. 17-19 and *passim.*

51. Andrew J. Pierre, *The Global Politics of Arms Sales,* Council on Foreign Relations, Princeton University Press, 1982, p. 161.

52. Klieman, *Israel's Global Reach,* p. 20.

53. *Ibid.,* p. 23.

54. Bishara Bahbah, *Israel and Latin America: The Military Connection,* St. Martin's Press, New York, & Institute for Palestine Studies, Washington, 1986, pp. 38-53.

55. Richard Deacon, *Israel's Secret Service,* Taplinger, New York, 1977, pp. 208-209.

56. Klieman, *Israel's Global Reach,* p. 23.

57. Pierre, *The Global Politics of Arms Sales,* p. 161.

58. "Israel is Trying to Increase Weapons Sales Abroad," *New York Times,* January 12, 1976; John Yemma, "Israel guns for worldwide arms market," *Christian Science Monitor,* December 27, 1982; Yoram Shapira, and Joel Barromi, *Israel-Latin American Relations,* Transaction Books, New Brunswick, NJ, pp. 104-108.

59. Dan Fisher, "Stung by Criticism, Israel Reviews Its Arms Industry," *Los Angeles Times,* September 18, 1986.

60. Peri and Neubach, *The Military-Industrial Complex in Israel,* p. 68.

61. Pierre, *The Global Politics of Arms Sales,* p. 125.

62. Peri and Neubach, *The Military-Industrial Complex in Israel,* p. 81.

63. Fisher, "Stung by Criticism, Israel Reviews Its Arms Industry."

64. Citing SIPRI which gave Israel a ranking of 7th for 1982, Peri and Neubach, *The Military-Industrial Complex in Israel,* p. 68.

65. Klieman, *Israel's Global Reach,* p. 22.

66. Peri and Neubach, *The Military-Industrial Complex in Israel,* p. 68.

67. Klieman, *Israel's Global Reach,* p. 57.

68. Bahbah, *Israel and Latin America: The Military Connection,* Table 3, p. 34.

69. List compiled from lists in Klieman, *Israel's Global Reach,* pp. 135-142, with addition of Cameroon, Sri Lanka, Iran, South Africa, the European countries and other changes by author.

70. Teodoro Ducach, "America Latina, Mercado Fundamental Para las Armas Israelies," *Excelsior,* May 8, 1986.

71. Fisher, "Stung by Criticism, Israel Reviews Its Arms Industry."

72. It is not clear whether Bokassa, or President Hastings Banda of Malawi ever bought arms from Israel, but they did receive Israeli training for various military and pre-military youth forces, as noted by Israel Shahak, *Israel's Global Role, Weapons for Repression,* Association of Arab-American University Graduates, Inc., Belmont, MA, 1982, pp. 22-23.

73. Fisher, "Stung by Criticism, Israel Reviews Its Arms Industry."

74. Klieman, *Israel's Global Reach,* p. 99. For several years Ariel Sharon has

been Israel's minister of trade and industry.

75. Quoted from Peri and Neubach, *The Military-Industrial Complex in Israel*, p. 4; the term "security establishment lobby" from p. 53; the relative strengths of foreign ministry and export aparatus from p. 81. Klieman makes much the same argument.

76. *Ibid.*, p. 81.

77. Ignacio Klich, "Nouveaux debouches en Chine pour Israel," *Le Monde Diplomatique*, March 1985.

78. "Israel and Ethiopia," *Israeli Foreign Affairs*, May 1985.

79. "The Israeli Connection" (see note 16).

80. *Ha'aretz*, August 25, 1981 in Jane Hunter, *No Simple Proxy, Israel in Central America*, Washington Middle East Associates, Washington DC, 1987, pp. 79-80.

Part I: Israel & South Africa
History

1. "Into Africa via The Back Door," *Time,* April 26, 1976.

2. Naomi Chazan, "Israeli Foreign Policy Towards South Africa," *African Affairs*, Summer, 1983, p. 171.

3. *Ibid.*, p. 199.

4. Noam Chomsky, *The Fateful Triangle, passim,* details both the bankruptcy of many of Israel's "doves" and of Americans, liberals and many leftists, so corruptly eager to adulate not only the Israeli "doves" but much of the Israeli political spectrum. Dr. Israel Shahak, a concentration camp survivor who provides English-language translations of the Hebrew press goes further, challenging the "myth" "that the [organized] American Jewish community is especially devoted to human, or civil rights, to democracy and to other 'good causes.'" In an article in *Middle East International,* "The U.S. Israel lobby: fact and myth," November 9, 1984, Shahak points out that because of organized Judaism's "totalitarian or Stalinist support for the state of Israel," its motives in supporting other struggles are suspect: "Can we...believe that a community, as expressed by its organizations, which denies the concept of equality of rights in Israel and the territories occupied by it, supports it in Alabama?" Shahak also points out that part of the exceptional influence of the organized Jewish community (see conclusion) derives from its associations with civil rights struggles. Many black observers have long pointed out that this association was patronage, rather than partnership.

5. Aharon Klieman, *Israeli Arms Sales: Perspectives and Prospects,* Jaffee Center for Strategic Studies (Tel Aviv University), Paper No. 24, February 1984, p. 37.

6. Eric Rosenthal, "Jews in South African Trade and Commerce," *South African Jewry 1965*, Johannesburg, 1965, pp. 141-153, in Richard P. Stevens & Abdelwahab M. Elmessiri, *Israel and South Africa, The Progression of a*

Relationship, New World Press, New York, 1976, p. 72.

7. Gideon Shimoni, *Jews and Zionism: the South African Experience (1910-1967),* Oxford University Press, Cape Town, 1980, pp. 3, and Chapter 2, "The Communal Ascendancy of Zionism," pp. 27-60. The South African Jewish population has been fairly constant since early in the century, at about 110,000.

8. *Ibid.,* pp. 42-47.

9. Memorandum on Africa, Weizmann to Smuts, February 26, 1948, in Stevens and Elmessiri, *Israel and South Africa,* pp. 91-94.

10. Shimoni, *Jews and Zionism,* pp. 47-49. (Those were the days when South Africa was admitted to international organizations.)

11. "For love and money," *Israel. A survey. Supplement to Financial Mail,* (Johannesburg), May 11, 1984, p. 41; Ami Raz, "Africa-Israel Ltd. where did all the profit come from?" *Jerusalem Post,* November 5, 1986.

12. Quote from *Ha'aretz,* August 20, 1986 transl. in *Israleft,* #287; other details in David Lipkin and Rafael Man, "South African Jews invested millions in Israel, *Ma'ariv,* January 27, 1987 translated by Israel Shahak, in *Collection: Israel, South Africa and the U.S.A.*

13. Adams, *The Unnatural Alliance,* p. 7.

14. Shimoni, *Jews and Zionism,* pp. 203.

15. Adams, *The Unnatural Alliance,* pp. 3-5.

16. Shimoni, *Jews and Zionism,* p. 207.

17. *Ibid.,* p. 237.

18. Adams, *The Unnatural Alliance,* quoted from p. 9, preceding material from pp. 6-9.

19. Shimoni, *Jews and Zionism,* p. 210.

20. *Transvaler,* December 1, 1946, *Ibid.,* pp. 203-204.

21. Quotation from *Rand Daily Mail,* May 11, 1956 in AFP (Agence France-Presse), *Africa South of the Sahara Bi-weekly Interafrican News Survey,* Paris, May 11, 1956, June 15, 1956.

22. Rita E. Hauser, "Israel, South Africa and the West," *South Africa International,* October 1980 (reprinted from *Washington Quarterly,* Summer 1979).

23. Chazan, "Israeli Foreign Policy..." (see note 2).

24. Abdelkader Benabdallah, *L'Alliance Raciste Israelo-Sud-Africaine,* Les Editions Canada-Monde-Arabe, Montreal, 1979, pp. 83.

25. Chart from information provided by Israel's Division of International Cooperation in Shimeon Amir, *Israel's Development Cooperation with Africa, Asia, and Latin America,* Praeger, New York, 1974, p. 113.

26. Figures from Israeli Foreign Ministry 1971 in Samuel Decalo, "Afro-Israeli Technical Cooperation: Patterns of setbacks and success," Curtis and Gitelson, eds., *Israel in the Third World,* Transaction, New Brunswick, NJ, 1976, p. 93.

27. Akiva Eger, "Histadrut: Pioneer and Pilot Plant for Israel's International Cooperation with the Third World," in Curtis and Gitelson, *Israel in the Third World,* pp. 75-81.

28. Babcock, *Washington Post*, June 15, 1986. For more details of Israel's development assistance in Africa see Jan Nederveen Pieterse, *Israel's State Terrorism and Counterinsurgency in the Third World*, Near East Cultural and Educational Foundation of Canada and International Center for Research and Public Policy, Washington DC, 1986; Hilmi Yousuf, *African-Arab Relations*, Amana Books, Brattleboro, VT, 1986.

29. Quote from South African Zionist Federation, "Minutes of Boards of Hon. Officers of the Federation and Board, March 21, 1962," in Shimoni, *Jews and Zionism*, p. 319. Chapters entitled "South Africa and Israel: Strained Relations," and "Coping with the Crisis," pp. 305-353 provide an extremely valuable view of the dynamics governing Israeli-South African relations *vis-a-vis* the South African Jewish community.

30. *Ibid.*

31. Chazan, "Israeli Foreign Policy..." (see note 2).

32. *Ibid.* The contribution was rejected.

33. Yousuf, *African-Arab Relations*, p. 56 and *passim*.

34. C.L. Sulzberger, "Strange Nonalliance," *New York Times*, April 28, 1971, in Stevens and Elmessiri, *Israel and South Africa*, pp. 130-131.

35. *Rand Daily Mail*, October 10, 1967, in Rosalynde Ainslee, *Israel and South Africa: An unlikely alliance?* United Nations Centre Against Apartheid, July 1981, (Document No. A/Ac.115/L.396)

36. Adams, *The Unnatural Alliance*, pp. 12-13.

37. "The Israeli connection," *The Economist*, November 5, 1977.

38. Shimoni, *Jews and Zionism*, p. 356.

39. Citing various dates of *Rand Daily Mail*, in Ainslee, *Israel and South Africa: An unlikely alliance?* p. 3.

40. Hirsh Goodman, "International hypocrisy," *Jerusalem Post*, January 23, 1987.

41. Willie J. Breytenbach, "Isolation and Cooperation," *Africa Report*, November-December 1980.

42. *Rand Daily Mail*, May 10, 1969, in Ainslee, *Israel and South Africa: An unlikely alliance?* p. 6; *Sechaba* (Journal of the African National Congress), April 1970.

43. Shimoni, *Jews and Zionism*, p. 357.

44. *Sunday Times*, October 10, 1976 in Ainslee, *Israel and South Africa: An unlikely alliance?* p. 8.

45. C.L. Sulzberger, "Strange Nonalliance," (see note 34).

46. Adams, *The Unnatural Alliance*, p. 114.

47. *Sunday Times*, October 10, 1976; *The Star* (Johannesburg), May 25, 1973 in Benabdallah, *L'Alliance Raciste Israelo-Sud-Africaine*, p. 180.

48. C.L. Sulzberger, "Strange Nonalliance," (see note 34).

49. *Rand Daily Mail*, September 11, 1971, in Ainslee, *Israel and South Africa: An unlikely alliance?* p. 8.

50. Susan A. Giltelson, "Israel's African Setback in Perspective," Curtis and Gitelson, eds., *Israel in the Third World*, pp. 182-199 and Yousuf, *African-Arab Relations*, Chapter 5, "The African Drive for Peace in the Middle East,"

pp. 78-94 offer interesting (and contrasting) discussions of this period. Figure of 22 derived from chart, "Black African states which severed Diplomatic Relations with Israel, 1967-1973," on p. 94.

51. Shimoni, *Jews and Zionism*, p. 357.

52. *South Africa Digest*, Week ending October 19, 1973 in Stevens and Elmessiri, *Israel and South Africa*, p. 132.

53. *Cape Times*, October 12 and 17, 1973, in Ainslee, *Israel and South Africa: An unlikely alliance?* p. 9; also *Africa News*, November 8, 1973, citing *The Daily Telegraph*, (n.d.) in Stevens and Elmessiri, *Israel and South Africa*, p. 133.

54. Adams, *The Unnatural Alliance*, p. 15.

55. Hauser, "Israel, South Africa and the West" (see note 22).

56. *Cape Times*, October 12 and 17, 1973; *Jewish Chronicle* (London), June 28, and August 2, 1974, in Ainslee, *Israel and South Africa: An unlikely alliance?* p. 9.

57. These visits, each with its reference to the daily press of the time, are enumerated in Ainslee, *Israel and South Africa: An unlikely alliance?* pp. 7 and 8.

58. Breytenbach, "Isolation and Cooperation."

59. Adams, *The Unnatural Alliance*, p. 43.

60. *Ibid.*, p. 17.

61. Wolf Blitzer, "Washington and Jerusalem," *Jerusalem Post*, June 13, 1975, in *SWASIA*, June 27, 1975.

62. "The Israeli connection" (see note 37).

63. *The Guardian*, July 8, 1975 in *Jerusalem Post*, July 10, 1975 summarized in *SWASIA*, July 25, 1975.

64. "The Israeli connection."

65. Adams, *The Unnatural Alliance*, pp. 15-16.

66. *Ibid.*, pp. 131-133.

67. *Ibid.*; Murray Waas, "Destructive Engagement: Apartheid's 'Target U.S.' Campaign, *The National Reporter*, Winter 1985.

68. *Ibid.*; Adams, *The Unnatural Alliance*, p. 133 mentions the $100 million.

69. Louis Rapoport, "Mystery Milchan," *Jerusalem Post Magazine*, February 21, 1986.

70. Adams, *The Unnatural Alliance*, p. 16.

71. Jonathan Bloch and Andrew Weir, "The Adventures of the Brothers Kimche," *The Middle East*, April, 1982; Rapoport, "Mystery Milchan,".

72. Dov Alfon, "Israel—South Africa: Business (almost) as usual," *Koteret Rashit*, June 25, 1986, translated by Dr. Israel Shahak, in *South Africa and Israel*.

Arms Industry

1. "A Very Welcome Visit," *South Africa Digest,* April 16, 1976.

2. Terrence Smith, "Vorster Visit to Israel Arouses Criticism," *New York Times,* April 18, 1976.

3. "Vorster: Man on a Wagon Train," *Time,* June 28, 1976 in Stevens and Elmessiri, *Israel and South Africa,* p. 69.

4. Benjamin Pogrund, "Israel's South African Ties," *Jerusalem Post,* April 20, 1976 in *SWASIA,* May 7, 1976.

5. Felix Kessler, "Israel Takes on an Odd New Ally, *Wall Street Journal,* April 23, 1976; Sharm El-Sheikh: Rabin lauds South Africa's Detente Bid," *Jerusalem Post Weekly (sic),* April 13, 1976, in Stevens and Elmessiri, *Israel and South Africa,* pp. 152-153. In Rabin's pretty words can be construed an endorsement of South Africa's attempts to impose a *pax africana* on the continent, to continue "creating coexistence" by warehousing blacks in bantustans, and to continue to defy international pressure to dismantle apartheid.

6. "Mount of Olives and Sharm El-Sheikh."

7. "Vorster Visit to Israel Arouses criticism" (see note 2).

8. Chazan, "Israeli Foreign Policy..."

9. Adams, *The Unnatural Alliance,* p. 17 and *passim.*

10. "Hands Across Africa," South African Digest, April 23, 1976, in Stevens and Elmessiri, *Israel and South Africa,* pp. 149-150.

11. "Need unites," *The Economist,* December 20, 1980.

12. Major Gerald J. Keller, U.S. Marine Corps, "Israel South African Trade: An Analysis of Recent Developments," *Set and Drift, Naval War College Review,* Spring 1980.

13. "Revealed: the secrets of Israel's nuclear arsenal;" Adams, *The Unnatural Alliance,* pp. 180-181 (see note 4, introduction).

14. "France admits it gave Israel A-bomb" (see note 6, introduction).

15. "Revealed: the secrets of Israel's nuclear arsenal" (see note 4, introduction).

16. Interview with Theodore Taylor (a protege of Robert Oppenheimer) by Noah Adams, *All Things Considered,* National Public Radio, October 6, 1986, transcript courtesy of Charles R. Denton.

17. Shai Feldman, *Israeli Nuclear Deterrence, A Strategy for the 1980s,* Columbia University Press, New York, 1982 discusses all of these themes— and also what the possible Western reaction to a declared Israeli nuclear posture would be.

18. Adams, *The Unnatural Alliance,* pp. 147-148.

19. David Horovitz, "Israel reportedly urged India to join attack on Pakistan nuke plant," *Jerusalem Post* Foreign Service, in *Northern California Jewish Bulletin,* February 27, 1987.

20. "France admits it gave Israel A-Bomb" (see note 6, introduction).

21. Keller, "Israeli-South African Trade..."

22. *Washington Post,* February 16, 1977 in Dr. Ronald Walters, *The September 22, 1979 Mystery Flash: Did South Africa Detonate a Nuclear Bomb?* Washington Office on Africa Educational Fund in cooperation with Congressman John Conyers, the Congressional Black Caucus Foundation and the World Campaign Against Military and Nuclear Collaboration with South Africa, May 21, 1985.

23. Washington Office on Africa, *Stop the Apartheid Bomb,* pamphlet, February 1983.

24. AFP, *Le Monde,* September 17, 1985, cited an article in the South African magazine *Optima* by a South African diplomat formerly attached to the International Atomic Energy Agency.

25. There was considerable discussion at the July 1986 meeting of the OAU of a military offensive against apartheid. Except for ten rifles offered by President Thomas Sankara of Burkina Faso, (AFP, 0807 GMT, August 3, 1986 in FBIS Middle East and Africa, August 5, 1986, p. P-3) the force is still at the talking stage. "Spotlight on apartheid," *West Africa,* August 4, 1986 gives a sense of the debate that is now going on.

26. *SIPRI Yearbook 1985,* p. 322.

27. Jonathan Kwitny, "Nigeria Considers Nuclear Armament Due to South Africa," *Wall Street Journal,* October 6, 1980 and "Africans are Advised to Develop Atom Arms," *New York Times,* June 10, 1983 in Leonard S. Spector, *The New Nuclear Nations,* Vintage Books, New York, 1985, p. 213.

28. *Stop the Apartheid Bomb* (see note 23).

29. Maps shown to author by an ANC London representative, October 1986.

30. Walter Pincus, "S. Africa Uranium Plant Reported Ready," *Washington Post,* in *Los Angeles Times,* October 2, 1986, also Andre Payenne, "La bombe atomique est une realite au pays de l'apartheid," *Le Journal de l'Economie Africaine,* October 1985.

31. This gambit is suggested in *Stop the Apartheid Bomb* (see note 23).

32. Adams, *The Unnatural Alliance,* p. 170.

33. Speech to South African Institute of International Affairs, Johannesburg, September 13, 1986, *Ibid.,* p. 171.

34. *Ibid.,* pp. 180-181 and p. 195, which names the journalists as Eli Teicher and Ami Dor-on and their government sources.

35. "Halting Pretoria's A-test," *Newsweek,* September 5, 1977.

36. "A Friend in Need".

37. Walters, *The September 22, 1979 Mystery Flash,* p. 1.

38. *Ibid.,* p. 5.

39. *Ibid.,* p. 16.

40. *Ibid.,* p. 1.

41. Jack Anderson, "U.S. Knew in Advance of Mystery Blast," *Washington Post,* April 26, 1985 and another columns in *Washington Post,* September 14, 1980, *Ibid.,* p. 12.

42. Thomas O'Toole, "South Africa Ships in Zone of Suspected N-Blast," *Guardian,* January 31, 1980, *Ibid.,* p. 12.

43. Stephen Talbot, "The Case of the Mysterious Flash," *Inquiry*, April 21, 1980, *Ibid.*, p. 16.

44. Executive Office of the President, Office of Science and Technology, *Ad Hoc Panel Report on the September 22 Event*, July 15, 1980, *Ibid.*, p. 5.

45. Thomas O'Toole, "Neutron Bomb Suspected in Africa Blast," *Washington Post*, March 9, 1980, *Ibid.*, p.7 and *passim*.

46. Thomas O'Toole and Milton Benjamin, "Officials Hotly Debate Whether African Event was Atom Blast," *Washington Post*, January 17, 1980, *Ibid.*, p. 14.

47. *Ibid.*, p. 15.

48. Stephen Talbot, "The Case of the Mysterious Flash," *Inquiry*, April 21, 1980, *Ibid.*

49. "Evidence shows S. Africa tested A-bomb in '79," Reuter, *Jerusalem Post*, May 22, 1985.

50. Judith Miller, "2 in House Withdraw Atom Curb," *New York Times*, December 9, 1981 in Feldman, *Israeli Nuclear Deterrence*, p. 226.

51. Walters, *The September 22, 1979 Mystery Flash*, p. 2.

52. *Ibid.*, p. 17.

53. *Congressional Record—House*, July 11, 1985, p. H 5469.

54. David Taylor, "Israel-South Africa Nuclear Link Exposed," *The Middle East*, April 1981.

55. David K. Willis, "How South Africa and Israel are maneuvering for the bomb," *Christian Science Monitor*, December 3, 1981.

56. Judith Miller, "Nuclear Contacts Quietly Widened by Israel, Taiwan and South Africa," *New York Times*, June 28, 1981. Reference is made in this article to Taiwan, with which both Israel and South Africa have had some nuclear cooperation.

57. Walters, *The September 22, 1979 Mystery Flash*, p. 3.

58. Author's interview with Robin Morgan, head of *Sunday Times* Insight Team, October 19, 1986. Insight Team produced the *Sunday Times* reports cited above (October 5 and 12, 1986.)

59. BBC TWO TV *Newsnight*, 2250 GMT, July 11, 1985, transcript courtesy of Palestine Liberation Organization, London.

60. Martin Bailey, "South Africa's Island Bombshell," *The Observer*, (London), December 28, 1986.

61. Interview, January 1987.

62. *Jewish Telegraphic Agency Bulletin*, January 26, 1970, in Abdelwahab M. Elmessiri, "Israel and South Africa: A Link Matures," in Stevens and Elmessiri, *Israel and South Africa*, pp. 67.

63. C.L. Sulzberger, "Strange Nonalliance."

64. Adams, *The Unnatural Alliance* devotes a chapter (pp. 38-71) to the complicated series of ruses by which South Africa gained the SRC gun, bringing to public view the results of several government investigations and an investigation by the *Burlington Free Press* (Vermont). These and other sources are summaried in his notes, pp. 206-207.

65. Hyam Corney, "Israel helped CIA get arms to S. Africa—TV report,"

Jerusalem Post, October 21, 1980.

66. Adams, *The Unnatural Alliance,* pp. 38-71.

67. Taylor, "Israel-South Africa Nuclear Link Exposed."

68. *Rand Daily Mail,* January 30, 1979 in *Policies of Apartheid of the Government of South Africa, Special Report of the Special Committee against Apartheid on recent developments in the relations between Israel and South Africa,* November 2, 1979, UN Document 79-28658.

69. Adams, *The Unnatural Alliance,* pp. 105-107.

70. "Pistol Shipment now to go to South Africa via Israel," *Arbeiter-Zeitung* (Vienna), June 29, 1983, in FBIS Western Europe, July 6, 1983, p. E-1.

71. "A Friend in Need".

72. Hauser, "Israel, South Africa and the West."

73. William E. Farrell, "Israeli Tours South Africa As Arms-Trade Furor Grows," *New York Times,* February 10, 1978.

74. Bernard D. Kaplan, "South Africa's enemies are also Israel's enemies," *San Francisco Examiner,* July 11, 1976. These were said to be part of the arms Israel captured during the 1973 war. They might have been, but they might also have been weapons Israel obtained on the international arms market (or perhaps even fabricated). A former CIA officer has told the author that Israel is the second biggest dealer, after the USSR, of East-bloc weaponry. The same would hold true regarding arms Israel would ship to Iran and to the contras, all of which were said to have been captured in Lebanon.

75. *The Economist Foreign Report,* March 26, 1980 in Ainslee, *Israel and South Africa: An unlikely alliance?* p. 13.

76. Johathan Broder, "Israel Grows Sensitive over Links to South Africa," *Chicago Tribune,* April 2, 1977.

77. Dial Torgerson, "Weizman Reportedly Visited South Africa," *Los Angeles Times,* March 20, 1980.

78. *Defense and Foreign Affairs Daily,* March 16, 1983 in Peter L. Bunce, "The Growth of South Africa's Defence Industry and its Israeli Connection," *Journal of Royal United Services Institute,* London, June 1984.

79. Cited in William E. Farrell, "Israeli Tours South Africa As Arms-Trade Furor Grows," *New York Times,* February 10, 1978.

80. Broder, "Israel Grows Sensitive over Links to South Africa" (see note 76).

81. The low number comes from the contention of Naomi Chazan (to *Le Monde,* August 14, 1985) that sales to South Africa represent "only" 5 percent of Israel's military exports. The high figure from *New York Times,* March 19, 1987.

82. *SIPRI Yearbook 1981,* p. 84, 86.

83. The loyalty and enforcement to maintain the blanket of silence is apparently so complete that Israelis were literally shocked that Mordechai Vanunu would reveal the workings of the Dimona nuclear plant.

84. *Economist Foreign Report,* November 2, 1977 in Adams, *The Unnatural Alliance,* p. 93.

85. *Ibid.*, p. 93.

86. "I saw homeland police and members of the SADF laugh and joke as they hurled teargas canisters into buses full of cheerful, chanting people in KwaNdbele yesterday," wrote a reporter on the front page of the Johannesburg Star. (*Johannesburg Star,* May 15, 1986 in FBIS Middle East and Africa, May 19, 1986, p. U-23; *New York Times,* May 15, 1986 has a picture of this incident in which two youths were killed.)

"A one-year-old baby fainted after inhaling teargas fumes when security forces fired at mourners in the Port Elizabeth township of Kwazakhele during a funeral of unrest victims," reported the South African radio. (SAPA, Johannesburg, 1932 GMT, March 8, 1986 in FBIS Middle East and Africa, March 10, 1986, p. U-10.)

"Four Saulsville children had to be treated by a local doctor after teargas had been sprayed into their home on Saturday." (SAPA, 1107 GMT, March 17, 1986 in FBIS Middle East and Africa, March 18, 1986 p. U-9.)

"President of the World Alliance of Reformed Churches, Dr. Allan Boesak, is considering laying charges after a teargas canister was lobbed into his car at a church service in Elsies River today." (SAPA, 2130 GMT, July 20, 1986 in FBIS Middle East and Africa, July 21, 1986, p. U-6.)

"In February 1987 white government authorities acknowledged 20 instances in which teargas was used against prisoners since the declaration of the 1985 state of emergency." (SAPA, 1620 GMT, February 10, 1987, in FBIS Middle East and Africa, February 11, 1987, p. U-6).

87. For more details see Jane Hunter, "The Tel Aviv-Pretoria Arms Link," *Israeli Foreign Affairs,* February 1986.

88. "Spy Plane Had Israeli Patent," *Tanzanian Daily News,* June 3, 1983; Joseph Hanlon, "South Africa Adopts Israeli Military Tactics," *New African,* August 1983.

89. *Al-Safir* (Beirut), April 26 and May 13, 1986, in FBIS Middle East & Africa, and confidential sources. For complete account and analysis see Jane Hunter, "Copters for Pretoria," and "Zaire: Way Station to Iran," *Israeli Foreign Affairs,* June 1986 and January 1987, respectively. It is possible that part of this shipment was involved in the Iran-contra affair, in which South Africa's role has barely begun to be explored, but in which it seems fairly clear, money and materiel were shifted around from one band of US-backed mercenaries to another, as well as to Iran.

90. *Sunday Telegraph* (London), November 16, 1987 cited by South Africa Press Association, 1340 GMT, November 16, 1986 in FBIS Middle East & Africa, November 19, 1986, p. U-12.

91. Martin Streetly, "Israeli airborne SIGINT systems," *Jane's Defence Weekly,* December 27, 1986; The *SIPRI Yearbook 1984,* p. 243, lists " B-707-320B Transports sold to South Africa," with the notation that this aircraft is also designated B-707-344C.

92. Interview with Martin Streetly, December 1986. See also Jane Hunter, "More Military Deals With South Africa," *Israeli Foreign Affairs,* February

1987.

93. Adams, *The Unnatural Alliance, passim.*, Bunce, "The Growth of South Africa's Defence Industry and its Israeli Connection."

94. Adams, *The Unnatural Alliance*, pp. 106.

95. "The Israeli Connection."

96. Adams *The Unnatural Alliance*, p. 122; Norman L. Dodd, "African Navies South of the Sahara," *Proceedings of the U.S. Naval Institute*, vol. 109, no. 3, pp. 53-54, in Bunce, "The Growth of South Africa's Defence Industry and its Israeli Connection."

97. "A Friend in Need".

98. *Jane's Infantry Weapons 1982-83*, p. 167 in Bunce, "The Growth of South Africa's Defence Industry and its Israeli Connection."

99. Adams, *The Unnatural Alliance*, pp. 122-123.

100. BBC World Service, 0606 GMT, June 6, 1986 in "'Israeli' Missile Sinks Ship," *Israeli Foreign Affairs*, July 1986.

101. Adams, *The Unnatural Alliance*, pp. 122-123.

102. "The Israeli Connection."

103. *Aviation and Marine International*, February 1980, *Strategy Week*, November 24:30 1980, and *Armada International*, January 1980 in Adams, *The Unnatural Alliance*, p. 123.

104. Christopher Coker, "Botha's Threat from the West," *The Independent* (London), October 8, 1986.

105. *Ibid.*

106. Charles R. Denton, "Submarines for Israel," *Israeli Foreign Affairs*, February 1986.

107. "W. German sub plans sold to S. Africa," AP, *San Francisco Examiner*, December 11, 1986.

108. Mark Daly, "South Africa's Cheetah Mirage update," *Jane's Defence Weekly*, July 26, 1986.

109. Denton, "Submarines for Israel" (see note 106).

110. Charles Babcock, "How U.S. Came to Underwrite Israel's Lavi Fighter Project," *Washington Post*, August 6, 1986.

111. Richard Witkin, "U.S. Plane Deal Spurs Drive in Israel to Build Own Jet," *New York Times*, May 21, 1978.

112. John Fialka, "Israel Bucks Big Leagues in Arms Sales," *Wall Street Journal*, June 22, 1984.

113. "House Panel Votes Amendment Clearing U.S. Funds for Lavi," *Aviation Week and Space Technology*, March 25, 1985. These concessions amounted to $250 million in 1984, and $200 million in 1985 and 1986.

114. Broder, "Israel Grows Sensitive over Links to South Africa" (see note 76).

115. Jerusalem Domestic Service, 1105, 1200 and 1900 GMT, March 19, 1980, FBIS Middle East and Africa, March 19, 1980, p. I-1.

116. Adams, *The Unnatural Alliance*, p. 109. This information has been repeated many times, most recently by Michael Hornsby, "Pretoria Shows off its Military Might, *The Times of London*, September 14, 1984; Dial Torgerson,

"Weizman Reportedly Visited South Africa," also mentions Weizman's secret trip.

117. Yossi Melman and Dan Raviv, "Has congress Doomed Israel's Affair With South Africa?" (Editorial Section) *Washington Post*, February 22, 1987.

118. Babcock, "How U.S. Came to Underwrite Israel's Lavi Fighter Project."

119. "Strangers and Brothers," *Sunday Times* of London, April 15, 1984—article based on James Adams' *The Unnatural Alliance*.

120. "Lavi Contracts With U.S. Companies Detailed," *Aviation Week & Space Technology*, January 21, 1985.

121. "Decrease in U.S. Aid to Israel May Force Halt in Lavi Program," *Ibid.*, June 9, 1986.

122. "Lavi - IAI seeks U.S. partner," *Flight International*, May 3, 1986.

123. Rita E. Hauser, "Israel, South Africa and the West."

124. Hirsh Goodman of *Jerusalem Post* quoted by *Oakland Tribune* editorial "Dog fighter or dog of a fighter?" August 22, 1986.

125. Daniel Snyder, "Japan Eyes U.S. For Fighter," *Defense Week*, May 27, 1986.

126. Fialka, "Israel Bucks Big Leagues in Arms Sales" (see note 112).

127. Charles Babcock, "How U.S. Came to Underwrite Israel's Lavi Fighter Project,".

128. "Northrop Halts Work on F-20 Fighter Plane," AP, *Los Angeles Times*, November 18, 1986.

129. "Decrease in U.S. Aid to Israel May Force Halt in Lavi Program" (see note 121).

130. Leonard Silk, "Military Costs An Israeli Issue," *New York Times*, June 4, 1986.

131. "House Leaders: Release Lavi Funds," *Defense News*, July 21, 1986.

132. "Dog fighter or dog of a fighter?"

133. Fialka, "Israel Bucks Big Leagues" (see note 112).

134. "The Israeli connection," *Military Technology, MILTECH 20*, pp. 26-36 in Adams, *The Unnatural Alliance*, pp. 110-111.

135. *Ibid.*, p. 110.

Arms Sales & Policy

1. Adams, *The Unnatural Alliance*, p. 123

2. *Ibid.*, pp. 112-113; collaboration also noted by Broder, "Israel grows sensitive..."

3. Judy Siegel, "Plans launched for absorbing South African Jews," *Jerusalem Post*, August 20, 1985

4. Farrell, "Israeli Tours South Africa..." (see note 78, chapter 3).

5. *Yediot Aharonot*, February 15, 1981, translator unknown.

6. Luanda Domestic Service, 1430 GMT, May 29, 1985, FBIS Middle East and Africa, May 30, 1985, p. U-1. The commando also explained that his groups' orders had been to make the attack appear as if it had been perpetrated by UNITA, the South African- and U.S.-backed mercenaries pitted against Angola.

7. PANA (Pan African News Agency, Dakar) 0901 GMT, November 10, 1986 in FBIS Middle East and Africa, November 13, 1986, p. U-5; SAPA, Johannesburg, 1735 GMT, October 28, 1986 and *Ilanga* (Durban Zulu language publication), October 27-29, 1986, in FBIS Middle East & Africa, October 29, 1986, p. U-10.

8. SAPA, 1143 GMT, January 22, 1987 in FBIS Middle East & Africa, January 23, 1987, p. U-1.

9. Michael Parks, "Black Neighbors Say S. Africa Risks War in Region, Blame Pretoria in Death of Machel," *Los Angeles Times,* October 30, 1986. The day before Machel was killed there were reports from Mozambique of great fear and expectations of a South African attack to overthrow the Frelimo government (*Observer,* October 19, 1986). Zambia had just discovered and broken up a Unita supply route (*West Africa,* October 20, 1986).

10. National Public Radio, *All Things Considered,* October 24, 1986.

11. "Samora Machel's Last Flight: Fake Racist Beacon Downed Plane," *The Herald* (Harare), October 28, 1986, in FBIS Middle East and Africa, November 5, 1986, p. U-13.

12. SAPA, 1722 GMT, January 22, 1987 in FBIS Middle East & Africa, January 23, 1987, pp. U-1-2.

13. Jim Fish, "Last day of a president," *The Guardian* (London), October 21, 1986.

14. *Quarterly Economic Review of Zaire, Rwanda, and Burundi,* No. 4, 1985.

15. SAPA, Johannesburg, 1735 GMT, October 28, 1986, in FBIS Middle East and Africa, October 29, 1986, p. U-10.

16. Paul Fauvet, "Machel's Plane May Have Been Lured Off Course," *Guardian* (New York), February 4, 1987.

17. Station commentary on Johannesburg Domestic Service, 0500 GMT, December 12, 1984 in FBIS, Middle East and Africa, December 20, 1984, p. U-4.

18. Jonathan Kapstein, "Armed Confrontation Builds in South Africa," in *Proceedings of the U.S. Naval Institute,* December 1981, p. 32, in Bunce, "The Growth of South Africa's Defence Industry and its Israeli Connection."

19. W. Andrew Terrill, "South African Arms Sales and the Strengthening of Apartheid," *Africa Today,* 2nd Quarter, 1984.

20. This section is based on author's interviews and *Setting U.S. Policy Toward Apartheid,* Senate Report 99-370, Calendar No. 775, 99th Congress, 2nd Session, August 6 (legislative day, August 4) 1986. For more extensive coverage of the legislation and reactions to it, see issues of *Israeli Foreign Affairs* for September and October, 1986 and January, February and March 1987.

21. Thomas L. Friedman, "Israelis Reassess Supplying Arms To South Africa," *New York Times,* January 29, 1987.

22. Benny Morris, "Israel to keep status quo with SA," *Jerusalem Post,* January 28, 1987.

23. Melman and Raviv, "Has Congress Doomed Israel's Affair With South Africa?"

24. Friedman, "Israelis Reassess Supplying Arms To South Africa" (see note 19).

25. *Newsweek,* February 2, 1987.

26. Melman and Raviv, "Has Congress Doomed Israel's Affair With South Africa?" (see note 116, chapter 2).

27. Dan Fisher, "Israel to End Arms Sales to S. Africa," *Los Angeles Times,* February 12, 1987.

28. *Ibid.* The only promises Israel has kept with any regularity are its vows to mount military attacks every time it experiences what it perceives as a "terrorist" attack within the territory it occupies.

29. Asher Wallfish, "Israel's [sic] won't 'play tricks' over Pretoria," *Jerusalem Post,* January 28, 1987.

30. Adams, *The Unnatural Alliance,* p. 125.

31. Melman and Raviv, "Has congress Doomed Israel's Affair With South Africa?"

32. UN Doc. A/33/22/Add. 2, paras. 17, 19 in Ainslee, *Israel and South Africa: An Unlikely Alliance?* p. 13.

33. *South Africa Digest,* March 30, 1979 and *The Star* (weekly airmail ed., Johannesburg), June 16, 1979 in *Special Report of the Special Committee against Apartheid...,* p. 4.

34. *Guatemala!* Guatemala News and Information Bureau, (Oakland CA.), September-October 1986.

35. *The Star,* no date given, cited by Jerusalem Domestic Service, 1700 GMT, May 24, 1982 in FBIS Middle East and Africa, May 25, 1982, p. I-4.

36. *SIPRI Yearbook 1986,* p. 399.

37. "Is Israel Still Selling Arms to Iran?" *Israeli Foreign Affairs,* February 1985; "Iran Mystery Plane," *Ibid.,* November 1985 (this turned out to be one of the joint U.S.-Israeli shipments that came to light when the Iran-contra affair broke) "The Great Iran Arms Sale Plot," *Ibid.,* June 1986; "Israel's Peccadillos," *Ibid.,* October 1986.

38. Martin Sieff, "S. Africa barters arms for oil; Iran, Iraq get same weapons," *Washington Times,* December 23, 1986.

39. *Ibid.*

40. "Fib of the Month," *Israeli Foreign Affairs,* August 1986.

41. Simon Malley, "Le contrat Hassan II-Peres," *Afrique-asie,* week ending September 21, 1986 and "Ifrane's Hidden Agenda," *Israeli Foreign Affairs,* November 1986.

42. Klieman, *Israel's Global Reach,* p. 140

43. "Des officiers israeliens sur le 'mur,'" *Afrique-asie,* week ending October 19, 1986.

44. *Al-Sh'ab* (Cairo), January 20, 1987 in FBIS Middle East & Africa.

45. W. Andrew Terrill, "Potential Global Responses to South African

Arms Export Policies," *Africa Today*, 2nd Quarter, 1984 makes this argument in urging that the UN embargos on arms sales to South Africa and arms purchases from South Africa be upheld.

46. "The strong alliance between Israel and South Africa derives from their similarity of condition—both are settler colonial states which see themselves as outposts of Western civilization in 'a sea of barbarism.' Though the South Africans quite openly acknowledge this affinity, the Israelis find it more a source of embarrassment than pride." Alfred Moleah, "The Unholy alliance," *Palestine Focus*, August 1983. "One thing that brings them together is their total opposition to the right to self-determination for the indigenous people of South Africa and for the Palestinian people. Of course, there are other parallels: the use of religion as a basis, or spiritual rock...the claim of predestination, or divine right; and the view of Palestine and South Africa as 'promised lands.'" Mfanafuthi (Johnny) Makatini, director of International Affairs Department and Chief Representative to the United Nations of the ANC, Interview in Geneva, September 1983 in Steve Goldfield, *Garrison State*, Palestine Focus Publications, San Francisco/EAFORD, London and New York, 1985, p. 65.

47. Kenneth Adelman, "The Club of Pariahs," *Africa Report*, November-December 1980

48. Kaplan, "South Africa's enemies are also Israel's enemies."

49. Paul Moorcraft quoted by Paul Van Slambronck, "South Africa and Israel: birds out of favor flock together," *Christian Science Monitor*, June 6, 1983.

50. *Sunday Express*, no date or place given, quoted in "The Israeli-South Africa Axis—a Treat to Africa," *Sechaba* (official organ of the African National Congress), April 1970.

51. Broder, "Israel Grows Sensitive..."

52. Adams, "Israel and the Fortification of South Africa," Chapter 5 in *The Unnatural Alliance*, pp. 73-101.

53. *Ibid.*, p. 80.

54. Howard Taylor, Jr. and John Flinn, "Tutu tells clergy he's troubled by reported Israeli ties to S. Africa," *San Francisco Examiner*, January 22, 1986.

55. Roy Isacowitz, "S. Africa blacks want ties with groups here," *Jerusalem Post*, July 26, 1985.

56. Jerusalem Domestic Service, 0700 GMT, August 11, 1985, in FBIS-Middle East and Africa, August 13, 1985, p. I-7.

57. Jewish Telegraphic Agency, in *Northern California Jewish Bulletin*, April 11, 1986.

58. Letter signed by L. Hlongwane to *City Press*, November 10, 1985.

59. Adams, *The Unnatural Alliance*, p. 93, citing Israeli intelligence sources and Israeli and South African diplomatic sources (note, p. 208).

60. Yoram Peri, "Les relations d'Israel avec l'Afrique du Sud ne sont ni morales ni rentable," *Davar*, July 9, 1978, translation from Hebrew into French from unknown source.

61. Drew Middleton, "South Africa Needs More Arms, Israeli Says," *New York Times*, December 14, 1981.

62. Uri Dan, "The Angolan Battlefield," *Monitin,* January, 1982, translated by Dr. Israel Shahak, Shahak Collection, early 1982.

63. For a full account of South Africa's brutal occupation of Namibia see John Ya-Otto, *Battlefront Namibia,* Lawrence Hill & Co., Westport CT, 1981.

64. "Namibia Offer Merely Diplomatic 'Cheap Shot,'" *Rand Daily Mail,* June 8, 1984 in FBIS Middle East and Africa, June 8, 1984, p. U-5.

65. Johannesburg Domestic Service, 1500 GMT, June 11, 1984, FBIS Middle East and Africa, June 12, 1984, p. U-3.

66. "Israel to Provide Development Aid," *The Windhoek Advertiser,* April 22, 1985, in JPRS (U.S. Govt. Joint Publications Research Service) Sub-Saharan Africa, June 13, 1985.

67. "Benefits of Ministers' Visit to Israel Reviewed," *Windhoek Observer,* July 26, 1986 in JPRS.

68. Hillel Schenker, "Facing the Third World," *Israel Horizons,* March-April 1986.

69. SWAPO representative Hidipo Hamutenya interviewed by Tom Foley ("SWAPO leader: Namibia is held hostage by U.S.") *Peoples Daily World,* September 23, 1986.

70. Adams, "Strangers and Brothers."

71. Quoting Def. Minister Magnus Malan, Johannesburg Domestic Service, 0600 GMT, May 13, 1985 in FBIS Middle East and Africa, May 13, 1985, p. T-5.

72. Joseph Hanlon, "South Africa adopts Israeli military tactics," *New African,* August 1983.

73. Chomsky, *The Fateful Triangle,* pp. 217-228.

74. Maputo in English to Southern Africa, 1800 GMT, October 17, 1985 in FBIS Middle East and Africa, October 21, 1985, p. U-1.

75. As reported by BBC World Service, 1025 GMT, January 7, 1986, taped from relay broadcast by KXLR-AM, San Francisco.

76. "South African Defends Raids on Neighbor Nations," *New York Times,* May 21, 1986.

77. Asher Wallfish, "Sharon on Attacking 'Terrorist' HQ in Jordan," *Jerusalem Post,* July 30, 1985 in FBIS, Middle East and Africa, July 30, 1985.

78. Frank J. Prial, "Israeli Planes Attack P.L.O. in Tunis, Killing at Least 30; Raid 'Legitimate,' U.S. Says," and Bernard Gwertzman, "As U.S. supports Attack, Jordan and Egypt Vow to Press for Peace," *New York Times,* October 2, 1985; John Bulloch, "PLO Victims were Mossad Agents," *Daily Telegraph* (London), October 3, 1985.

79. For an account of that attack see "'Israeli' Missile Sinks Ship," *Israeli Foreign Affairs,* July 1986.

80. Richard Hall, "Angola worried by Israelis next door," *Observer,* January 23, 1983.

81. Alan Ben-Ami, "U.S., Israel involved in Angolan arms affair, too," *Jerusalem Post,* December 19, 1986.

82. Hall, "Angola worried by Israelis next door."

83. James Brooke, "CIA said to Send Rebels in Angola Weapons via

Zaire," *New York Times,* February 1, 1987.

84. EFE (Spanish News Agency, Madrid), 1300 GMT, January 16, 1983 in FBIS Middle East and Africa, January 19, 1983, p. I-5.

85. Eliezer Strauch, "Israel Seeks Contact with Former Portuguese Colonies in Lisbon," *Espresso* (Lisbon), February 16, 1985, JPRS SubSaharan Africa, March 29, 1985.

86. Quoted in *West Africa,* November 12, 1984.

87. Jonathan Bloch, "Israel's new openings in Africa," *The Middle East,* January 1985 and author's confidential sources.

88. Kinshasa Domestic Service, 1130 GMT, February 10, 1984, citing *Jornal de Angola,* in FBIS Middle East and Africa, February 13, 1984, p. S-2.

89. "Israelis 'aiding MNR rebels,'" *Africa Analysis* (London), November 28, 1986.

90. *The Independent* (London), November 29, 1986. For an excellent analysis of Israel's activities in Africa see Bloch, "Israel's new openings in Africa."

91. Gerald Nadler, "4 Nations Plan Swap of Political Prisoners," *Miami Herald,* February 26, 1978; author's source.

92. "Released Israeli tells of interrogation in Mozambique," *Jerusalem Post,* February 21, 1983.

Economy

1. Yosef I. Abramowitz, *Jews, Zionism & South Africa,* B'nai B'rith Hillel Foundations, no date, p. 17, which equivocates: "even if the IMF statistics do not tell the whole story, as some people maintain, Israel's trade would still be marginal compared to the major industrialized Western countries." The only other significant commodity of trade between Israel and South Africa is the indirect purchase of diamonds through London." This work denies Israeli arms sales to South Africa and carries an apology wrested from Sen. William Proxmire, (D-WI) who had read some figures about that arms trade from the work of Aaron Klieman. See *Israeli Foreign Affairs,* May 1985.

2. *Financial Mail* (Johannesburg), September 14, 1979, in "Policies of Apartheid," p. 5; this estimation has since been repeated by Adams and others.

3. The figure given for the 11 months ending in November 1986 was $1.56 billion. Simon Louisson, "Diamond industry sees downturn ahead," *Jerusalem Post,* January 9, 1987.

4. *Ibid.*

5. Originally noted in "For Love and Money," its existence was verified by reporter Jeffrey Blankfort in April 1986

6. Barry Sergeant, "Embattled Israel draws SA investors," *Sunday Times, Business Times,* September 9, 1984.

7. Avi Temkin, "Israel Seeking Increased South African Aid," *Jerusalem*

Post, February 4, 1983 in FIBS Middle East and Africa, February 4, 1983, p. 1-11.

8. Michael Yudelman, "Who buys what from whom," *Jerusalem Post*, July 11, 1986.

9. Sergeant, "Embattled Israel draws SA investors;" "Israel and S. Africa tighten trade ties," *Financial Times*, December 15, 1980; Chazan, "Israeli Foreign Policy Towards South Africa;" Malcolm Fothergill, "Aid reform plans, urges Hersov," *The Star* (Johannesburg), November 21, 1983.

10. Ethan Nadelman, "Israel and Black Africa: a rapprochement?" *Journal of Modern African Studies*, No. 19, 1981, p. 191 in Chazan, "Israeli Foreign Policy Towards South Africa."

11. These are detailed in Chazan, "Israeli Foreign Policy Towards South Africa, fn 39.

12. Yitzhak Rabi, "Free Trade Area agreement boosts Israeli trade to the U.S.," JTA in *Northern California Jewish Bulletin*, December 26, 1986.

13. "For love and money," p. 41.

14. Friedman, "Israelis Reassess Selling Arms to South Africa."

15. "For love and money," p. 41.

16. "Israel and S. Africa tighten trade ties."

17. "For love and money," p. 41.

18. *Ha'aretz* (Tel Aviv), August 18, 1982 in in FBIS Middle East and Africa, August 20, 1982, p. I-11.

19. *Ibid.*; Chazan, "Israeli Foreign Policy Towards South Africa;" Raz, "Africa-Israel, Ltd..."

20. "For Love and Money..."

21. "For Love and Money;" Adams, *The Unnatural Alliance*, p. 26. Under both EEC (European Economic Community) and U.S. rules a minimum amount of value added must be added to products for reexport. Enforcement takes the form of a complaint by an injured competitor to trade authorities and/or the civil courts.

22. Zoram Shapiro, *A Study of Some of the Factors Influencing the Use of Israel as a Springboard for South African Exports* (Unpublished MBA thesis), University of Cape Town, 1979, p. 142.

23. *Israel supplement to Financial Mail*, September 14, 1979, in "Policies of Apartheid..." p. 7.

24. Temkin, "Israel Seeking Increased South African Aid."

25. Ainslee, *Israel and South Africa...*, p. 22.

26. *The Star* (Johannesburg), April 19, 1980, *Ibid.*, p. 23.

27. Shapiro, *op. cit.*, p. 18.

28. Ainslee, *Israel and South Africa...*, p. 22

29. *Financial Mail*, September 14, 1979, *Ibid.*, p. 19; Shapiro, *op. cit.*, pp. 22-23.

30. Dan Fisher, "Israel Needs Time on S. Africa," *Los Angeles Times*, February 21, 1987.

31. *Ha'aretz*, December 31, 1981 (sic, probably 1980) in *Israeli Mirror*, February 2, 1981.

32. According to Dr. Israel Shahak the kibbutzim are quite deeply involved with South Africa (correspondence with author).

33. "U.S.-Israeli Trade Pact Benefits SA Exporters," *Business Day* (Johannesburg), September 23, 1985 in JPRS SubSaharan Africa, November 7, 1985.

34. "Exports to Israel," *South African Digest,* November 29, 1985.

35. BBC World Service, 0503 and 0603 GMT, November 4, 1985, relayed on KXLR-AM, San Francisco.

36. *Business Day,* June 3, 1985.

37. *The Star,* December 19, 1985 in FBIS Middle East and Africa, December 20, 1985, p. U-4. The decline of the rand after Western banks refused to roll over South Africa's loans also played a part in this surge.

38. John Tilston, "SA exports R1,3 bn up in first 2 months," *Business Day,* April 16, 1986.

39. *Jerusalem Post,* June 8, 1986 in FBIS Middle East and Africa, June 11, 1986, p. I-4.

40. The South African bureau of trade and industry urged censorship of trade statistics, which "could easily be used by our adversaries..." (Johannesburg SAPA, 1650 GMT, August 6, 1986 in FBIS Middle East and Africa, August 7, 1986, p. U-4).

41. "Liat: Israeli-South African Firm Moves in on Sierra Leone," *Israeli Foreign Affairs,* Feb. 1987.

42. Julie Fredericks, *Morning Edition,* National Public Radio (NPR), April 3, 1985; also, "Is There Life After Sanctions," *Economist,* July 26, 1986.

43. Peter Allen-Frost, "SA aid in Israeli rail line possible," *The Star,* July 12, 1984.

44. Slomo Avineri, "A timely delay," *Jerusalem Post,* Nov. 12, 1985.

45. "Sanctions busting SA-style," Reuter, *Jerusalem Post,* Oct. 10, 1986.

46. "Advert by 'Israel firm' offers to bust sanctions," *Ibid.,* Nov. 17, 1986.

47. Roy Isacowitz, "Embassy closure upgrades image," *Ibid.,* June 17, 1986.

48. IDF Radio, 1400 GMT, June 16, 1986, in FBIS Middle East and Africa.

49. Andrew Whitley, "Israeli delegation set for trade talks with S. Africa," *Financial Times,* Aug. 6, 1986.

50. *Jerusalem Post,* Aug. 8, 1986 in FBIS Middle East and Africa, Aug. 8, 1986, p. I-3.

51. *All Things Considered,* NPR, Aug. 13, 1986.

52. Whitley, see note 49; reference to increased trade in a Reuters report cited by Washington *Jewish Week,* "Israel Talks Trade with South Africa," Aug. 28, 1986.

53. *All Things Considered,* NPR, Aug. 13, 1986; also typical was the BBC "Newsreel" report broadcast several times on Aug. 13-14, 1986.

54. Reuters, "Pretoria holds talks to increase trade ties with Israel," *Jerusalem Post,* Aug. 14, 1986.

55. Avi Temkin, "S. Africa investments deal renewed," *Ibid.,* Aug. 18,

1986.

56. See, for instance, David Landau, "Towards a science-based economy," *Jerusalem Post*, Independence Day Supplement, April 24, 1985, typical of a spate of articles (which have not yet produced the desired trend).

57. *U.S. Assistance to the State of Israel, GAO Uncensored Draft Report*, American-Arab Anti-Discrimination Committee, Washington DC, 1983, p. 55. "Mexico Deal," *Israeli Foreign Affairs*, September 1985. Israel currently obtains most of its oil from Mexico.

58. Quentin Peel, "Israel and S. Africa in Major Coal Deal," *Financial Times*, Jan. 16, 1979.

59. "The Israeli Connection," *op. cit.*

60. "Israel Moves Toward More Coal Use," *Journal of Commerce*, Feb. 12, 1986.

61. *Ha'aretz*, June 20, 1984, in Klieman, *Israel's Global Reach*, pp. 152, 164-165.

62. Avraham Dishon, "Israeli investors set up industries in South Africa, *Yediot Ahronot*, June 21, 1984, trans. Israel Shahak, *Collection: Israel and South Africa*, summer 1984.

63. UPI in *San Francisco Examiner*, Aug. 20, 1985.

64. Michael Parks, "Under Threat of Sanctions, S. Africa Prepares for Siege," *Los Angeles Times*, Sept. 15, 1986 lists this eventuality among a number of other medium-term consequences of sanctions.

65. Macabee Dean, "South African blacks and whites all in the same boat," *Jerusalem Post*, Oct. 24, 1985.

66. Johannesburg Domestic Service, 1700 GMT, March 3, 1983, in FBIS Middle East and Africa, March 4, 1983, p. U-4.

67. *Computer Mail*, supplement to *Financial Mail*, January 31, 1986.

68. "Closer Scientific Ties with South Africa Planned," *Ha'aretz*, April 26, 1984, in FBIS Middle East and Africa, April 26, 1984, p. I-5.

69. Yossi Melman, "Secret S. African-Israeli Pact," *Jane's Defence Weekly*, Feb. 23, 1985. Aquva Eldar, "Cooperation Agreement Reported Signed with Sout Africa," *Ha'aretz*, Feb. 14, 1985, FBIS Middle East and Africa, Feb. 15, 1985, p. I-4.

70. Whitley, "Israeli delegation set for trade talks with S. Africa."

71. "Closer Scientific Ties with South Africa Planned."

72. "Technion 'no' to spending cut," *Jerusalem Post International Edition*, July 2-8, 1984.

73. Jean-Pierre Langellier, "La visite du chef de la diplomatie sudafricaine illustre les relations etroite entre les deux pays," *Le Monde*, Nov. 6, 1984.

74. Advertisement for Afitra, in *Supplement to Financial Mail, op. cit.*, p. 35.

75. "For love and money," p. 42.

Bantustans

1. *New African* (London), in *Africa Diary,* May 21-27, 1982.

2. Jerusalem Domestic Service, 0500 GMT, March 4, 1983 in FBIS Middle East and Africa, March 10, 1983, p. I-6.

3. Roy Isacowitz, "Aridor involvement in Ciskei 'likely to harm Israel,'" *Jerusalem Post,* June 20, 1984.

4. *The Sowetan,* March 10, 1983; Johannesburg Radio, and Israeli Radio for March 4, 1983, in *SWB/Monitoring Report* ME7274/ii, March 5, 1983.

5. The same sources as footnote 4, above, but cited by *Africa Report,* May-June, 1983.

6. Elazar Levin, "Foreign Investments/Awakening Africa. Ciskei— Another Israeli Speculation," *Koteret Rashit,* February 13, 1985, translated by Dr. Israel Shahak, *Collection: Israel and South Africa.*

7. *Keesing's Volume XXX,* February 1984, p. 32661.

8. Roy Isacowitz, "Government leery of MKs' Ciskei Jaunt," *Jerusalem Post,* April 7, 1985.

9. Akiva Eldar, "Milo's law office deals with a Ciskei representative," *Ha'aretz,* June 29, 1984, in Shahak, *Collection: Israel and South Africa, op. cit.* Isacowitz, "Government leery of MKs' Ciskei Jaunt."

10. Isacowitz, "Government leery of MKs' Ciskei Jaunt."

11. Joshua Brilliant, "Ciskei president at West Bank twinning," *Jerusalem Post International Edition,* Week ending November 10, 1984; Levin, "Foreign Investments/Awakening Africa."

12. Hyam Corney, "SA upset by Israel ties with black homelands," *Jerusalem Post,* July 2, 1984.

13. Levin, "Foreign Investments/Awakening Africa."

14. Roy Isacowitz, *Jerusalem Post,* August 11, 1985.

15. Roy Isacowitz, "Israelis linked to Ciskei corruption," *Jerusalem Post,* July 31, 1985.

16. *Ibid.*

17. *Ibid.*; Roy Isacowitz, "Ciskeian legal team was in Israel to investigate corruption charges," *Jerusalem Post,* August 1, 1985.

18. Isacowitz, "Israelis linked to Ciskei corruption."

19. Isacowitz, "Aridor involvement in Ciskei 'likely to harm Israel'"; *The Argus ,* September 8, 1983, from ANC *Briefing.*

20. Isacowitz, "Israelis linked to Ciskei corruption."

21. Isacowitz, "Ciskeian legal team was in Israel to investigate corruption charges."

22. Isacowitz, "Israelis linked to Ciskei corruption."

23. *Davar,* August 19, 1984, in FBIS Middle East & Africa, August 21, 1984, p. I-16; also *Keesings, op. cit.* which says the bantustan "defense minister" confirmed the purchase of aircraft.

24. *Sunday Times* of London cited in "Pretoria upset by Israel ties with black homelands," *Jerusalem Post International Edition,* July 8-14, 1984.

25. *Ibid.*

26. *Private Eye,* No. 640, June 27, 1986.

27. *Rand Daily Mail,* December 15, 1981, in Adams, *Unnatural Alliance,* p. 96.

28. Barry Streek, "Israel woos SA homelands," *Guardian* (London), October 15, 1983.

29. *Sowetan,* June 22, 1984, ANC *Briefing.*

30. "South African Homeland Opens an Office in Israel," Reuters, *New York Times,* June 5, 1985.

31. AP, in *Washington Times,* August 29, 1985.

32. *Keesing's, op. cit.*

33. ITIM (Tel Aviv), 1950 GMT, October 30, 1984, in FBIS Middle East & Africa, October 31, 1984, p. I-6.

34. Earlier a PFP spokesman had noted that the "Indaba," or gathering, at which the plan had been drawn up, had been touted by South Africa's ambassadors as proof of liberalization—Johannesburg SAPA, 0913 GMT, November 18, 1986, in FBIS Middle East and Africa, November 20, 1986, p. U-10. For background on Buthelezi and a full discussion of his dealings with Israel see Jane Hunter, "Israel and the Bantustans," *Journal of Palestine Studies,* Spring 1986.

35. "Survey South Africa," *Economist,* September 19, 1981.

36. Michel Bole-Richard, "L'autre facon de combattre apartheid," *Le Monde,* July 10, 1986.

37. Christine Abdelkrim, "Pretoria: le montage Buthelezi," *Afrique-Asie,* No. 358, October 7, 1985.

38. SAPA, 1139 GMT, June 26, 1986, in FBIS Middle East and Africa, June 26, 1986, p. U-4.

39. "South Africa Waives Ban to Let Moderate Zulu Chief Hold Rally," *New York Times,* June 30, 1986.

40. SAPA 1505 and 1733 GMT, December 6, 1986 in FBIS Middle East and Africa, December 8, 1986, p. U-10.

41. Alan Cowell, "Violence Erupts at Black's Rites in a 'Homeland,'" and "Violence and Apartheid," *New York Times,* August 15, 1985 and August 12, 1985 respectively.

42. Wolf Blitzer, "Unclear on Apartheid," *Jerusalem Post,* August 16, 1985. During the same period South Africa was sending emissaries to the U.S. Jewish community, reminding them of South Africa's exceptional support for the Jewish state and urging them to "rethink traditional attitudes"—Sanford Ungar, "South Africa's Lobbyists," *New York Times Magazine,* October 13, 1985.

43. Jerusalem Domestic Service, 1600 GMT, August 5, 1985, in FBIS Middle East and Africa, August 6, 1985, p. I-1; "Peres: Israel totally rejects apartheid," *Jerusalem Post,* August 6, 1985.

44. Daniel J. Elazar, "Ideas for Pretoria," *Jerusalem Post,* August 16, 1985.

45. Jerusalem Domestic Service, 0700 GMT, August 11, 1985, in FBIS Middle East and Africa, August 13, 1985, p. I-7.

46. Roy Isacowitz and David Richardson, "More help to South Africa's blacks likely after Zulu chief's visit," *Jerusalem Post*, August 15, 1985; Thomas Friedman, "Zulu Leader Sets Primary Demands," *New York Times*, August 14, 1985.

47. David Richardson and Roy Isacowitz, "Focus" (Interview with Buthelezi), *Jerusalem Post*, August 16, 1985.

48. Isacowitz and Richardson, "More help to South Africa's blacks..."

49. Isacowitz and Richardson, "Israelis to study aid projects for Zulus," *Jerusalem Post*, August 23, 1985.

50. Isacowitz and Richardson, "More help to South Africa's blacks likely after Zulu chief's visit."

51. Abdelkrim, "Pretoria: le montage Buthelezi."

52. "Focus on Africa," BBC World Service, 1515 GMT, March 19, 1986, in FBIS Middle East and Africa, March 26, 1986, p. U-7.

53. *Israel Magazine*, heard August 18, 1985 on KQED-FM, San Francisco.

54. *Near East Report*, August 19, 1985.

55. This is used repeatedly in handouts distributed by pro-Israeli activists and appears in Yosef I. Abramowitz, *Jews, Zionism & South Africa*, B'nai B'rith Hillel Foundations, Washington DC, no date, but first appeared in summer 1985, p. 17. This book defines its task as "expos[ing] the inappropriateness and destructive nature of anti-Zionism and in particular, its irrelevance to the anti-apartheid movement," p. 6.

56. The Israeli mission to the UN was first to report and shrilly protest the meeting. Its source, according to news accounts at the time, was intelligence provided by Mossad (Paul Findley, *They Dare to Speak Out*, Lawrence Hill & Company, Westport, CT, 1985, p. 148, based in part on an interview with Young; and Robert G. Weisbord and Richard Kazarian, Jr., *Israel in the Black American Perspective*, pp. 121-133, who argue against this construction, but end up giving it even more credence).

57. Charley Levine, "South African Zulu Chief is Ardent Supporter of Israel," JTA, in Washington *Jewish Week*, July 10, 1986. Buthelezi also confided that some of his best white friends were Jewish. The entire piece has a whiff of South African money: for one thing, KwaZulu is treated by Levine as a legitimate entity, never identified as a bantustan (although JTA datelines it "Ulundi, Kwazulu (sic) South Africa"). Levine is identified as a "public affairs analyst and journalist based in Jerusalem."

58. *Ibid.*

59. N. Perlmutter and D. Evanier, "The African National Congress, A Closer Look," *ADL Bulletin*, May 1986. Perlmutter is the National Director of the organization. The article contained such earthshaking revelations as: "*Sechaba*, the ANC magazine, is printed in Communist East Germany"; and "In 1982, seven members of the ANC national executive committee were identified in sworn testimony before the U.S. Senate Subcommittee on Security and Terrorism as SACP [South Africa Communist Party] members. The 30-member national executive committee now has 12 to 15 members said to be affiliated with SACP." Sen. Denton, whose committee elicited that exciting

testimony, was apparently too far to the right even for the good citizens of Alabama, and he was defeated in the 1986 elections.

60. *Ibid.*

61. See also Jane Hunter, "Attempts to Defame the ANC," *Israeli Foreign Affairs*, September 1986, from which this section was adapted.

62. *Washington Times*, June 18, 1986.

63. Charley Levine, "Arab Terrorists Aid South African Groups," Washington *Jewish Week*, July 10, 1986. In dwelling on the connections between the ANC and the South African Communist Party, Levine seems to be transfixed by the role of Joe Slovo, the white Jewish chairman of the SACP, and also commander of Umkhonto We Sizwe, the ANC's military wing.

Political and Cultural Ties

1. Tom Tugend, "Centre forward," *Jerusalem Post*, April 18, 1986.

2. Author's investigation.

3. Tugend, "Centre forward."

4. Roy Isacowitz, "S. Africa blacks want ties with groups here," *Jerusalem Post*, July 26, 1985.

5. Tugend, "Centre forward."

6. Dan Fisher, "S. African Blacks See Israel Training as Aid for Future," *Los Angeles Times*, April 8, 1986.

7. Jonathan Broder, "Israelis investing in South Africa's future," *Chicago Tribune*, March 16, 1986.

8. Tugend, "Centre forward."

9. William Claiborne, "Black S. Africans Train in Israel," *Washington Post*, April 8, 1986.

10. Hugh Orgel, "Histadrut Seeking Links with South African Black Unionists," JTA January 22, 1986.

11. Interview with aide to Tom Hayden.

12. Tugend, "Centre Forward."

13. "Hayden reveals his CIA role during Vietnam War," AP, *San Francisco Examiner*, June 21, 1986.

14. Jon Wiener, "Tom Hayden's New Workout," *The Nation*, November 29, 1986.

15. Claiborne, "Black S. Africans Train in Israel."

16. Gideon Remez, "Pressure Mounts in Israel to Dissociate from South Africa," Washington *Jewish Week*, July 10, 1986.

17. *Policies of Apartheid of the Government of South Africa, Special Report of the Special Committee against Apartheid on Recent Developments in the Relations between Israel and South Africa*, General Assembly Thirty-fourth session, Agenda item 28, 79-28658, November 2, 1979.

18. "Suspension tactique des rencontres sportives," *Yediot Aharonot*,

January 22, 1979 (French translation of unknown origin); *Jersualem Post*, January 23 & 24, 1979 in *Policies of Apartheid of the Government of South Africa*, p. 8.

19. Jerusalem Radio, January 30, 1979 in *Policies of Apartheid of the Government of South Africa*.

20. *Los Angeles Times*, September 30, 1986.

21. Jack Leon, "S. Africa may be kept out of Maccabiah," *Jerusalem Post*, June 9, 1985.

22. *Ibid.*

23. Jack Leon, "S. Africa Maccabiah visa ruse?" *Jerusalem Post*, July 17, 1985.

24. Jack Leon, "Facing up to the Maccabiah problems," *Jerusalem Post*, July 12, 1985 and letter to the *Jerusalem Post* from Hanna Foighel, whose information on the 1984 meeting came from members of the Danish Maccabiah team, August 25, 1985.

25. Jack Leon, "Israel's top 3 to play in South African Open," *Jerusalem Post*, November 13, 1986.

26. "Shadow on Amos' glory," *Jerusalem Post*, November 26, 1986. When interviewed by South African television—a most important part of the exercise is for the South Africans to demonstrate for the home and overseas audiences that foreign athletes are not only willing to play in South Africa, but enjoy it—Mansdorf disingenuously noted that "The crowd is very fair, they are not influenced by partiality to local players." Dudley Kessel, "Amos marches to S.A. final," *Jerusalem Post*, November 23, 1986.

27. "Shadow on Amos' glory," a comment which ends by suggesting that the tennis players could make things right by "assert[ing] their loathing of apartheid."

28. Jack Leon and Benny Morris, "Israeli tennis players did not break rules," *Jerusalem Post*, November 26, 1986.

29. *Jerusalem Post*, November 26, 1986.

30. *Register of Entertainers, Actors and others who have performed in Apartheid South Africa*, UN Centre Against Apartheid Notes and Documents, 86-11227, April 1986.

31. *The Star* (Johannesburg, weekly airmail ed.), April 8, 1985 in *Recent Developments Concerning Relations between Israel and South Africa, Special Report of the Special Committee Against Apartheid*, General Assembly, Fortieth Session, 85-28121 1609n (E), October 14, 1985, p. 11.

32. *Ha'aretz*, July 6, 1986, in FBIS Middle East and Africa, July 7, 1986, p. I-6.

33. *Israel Magazine*, heard August 17, 1986 on KQED-FM, San Francisco.

34. *The Star* (Johannesburg), September 19, 1984, *Recent developments concerning relations between Israel and South Africa*, .

35. Interview with Barry Streek, April, 1986.

36. Michal Yudelman, "Travel in a Troubled Paradise," *Jerusalem Post*, December 2, 1985, Supplement on South African Tourism.

37. Haim Shapiro, "Israelis visit South Africa as others begin to shun it,"

Jerusalem Post, October 29, 1985.

38. *The Star,* May 20, 1986, in FBIS Middle East and Africa, May 22, 1986, p. U-12.

39. *Jerusalem Post,* September 24, 1986, October 17, 1986.

40. *Ha'aretz,* October 16, 1986 in FBIS Middle East and Africa, October technology to South Africa is being violated."
who actually decide to take up residence in Israel have lately been very small.

40. *Jerusalem Post,* September 24, 1986, October 17, 1986.

41. Alex Berlyne, the author of these pieces, tried to use a zippy style and convey a sense of good fun, but his credentials as a judge of "reform" in South Africa are a bit shaky, as he could not resist throwing in such material as this limerick: "His daughter's name is Wong Wong/ And she sure is yellow all right/ Her boyfriend belongs to the Royal Marines/ But two Wongs don't make a white." Of course it was the "complexity" of the white government's problem with the black majority that Berlyne was supposed to explain away.

42. "Israeli Left Attacks South Africa; Israeli Rightists Defend It," INB, *Jewish Press,* August 22, 1986. This, even though, according to the article, at least ten of the kibbutzim associated with Mapam had "active business links" with South Africa and the one kibbutz which in 1986 decided to sever its links with the apartheid state required three meetings to arrive at a vote to stop shipping their machinery products to South Africa.

43. "Israeli Left Attacks South Africa..." notes that one of the organizers of a demonstration outside a cabinet meeting on South Africa was Stanley Goldfoot. Goldfoot, originally from South Africa and jailed in connection with the 1947 murder of Count Bernadotte, received money from the U.S. religious right on behalf of Jewish criminals plotting to blow up the Dome of the Rock in Jerusalem. The Lifta gang was rounded up by Israeli authorities prior to the deed and many members were jailed for earlier attacks on Palestinians. (Michael and Barbara Ledeen, "The Temple Mount Plot," *The New Republic,* June 18, 1984.)

44. JTA, November 15, 1985. The government actually did decide to delay dispatching its legate, but it was never clear whether the decision was prompted by the protests or the desire to keep a low profile until after that autumn's UN session on South Africa had been held.

45. *Jerusalem Post,* December 8, 1985.

46. *Morning Edition,* National Public Radio, January 13, 1986.

47. *Ma'ariv,* October 21, 1984 in FBIS Middle East & Africa, October 22, 1984, p. I-12.

48. Roy Isacowitz, "Ministry to consider EEC decision on S.A. sanctions," *Jerusalem Post,* September 18, 1986.

49. Section 508 (a) says "The President shall conduct a study on the extent to which the international embargo on the sale and exports of arms and military technology to South Africa is being violated.

508 (b) says, "Not later than 179 days after the date of enactment of this Act, the President shall submit to the Speaker of the House of Representatives and the chairman of the Committee on Foreign Relations of the Senate a report

setting forth the findings of the study required by subsection (a), including an identification of those countries engaged in such sale or export, with a view to terminating United States military assistance to those countries." The section was numbered 505 in earlier versions of the bill.

50. Roy Isacowitz, "Why Israel is Unlikely to Opt for Sanctions," *Jerusalem Post,* July 11, 1986.

51. "Cameroon Renews Diplomatic Ties," *Israeli Foreign Affairs,* October 1986.

52. *Ha'aretz,* August 28, 1986, in FBIS Middle East and Africa, August 29, 1986, p. I-1.

53. Isacowitz, "Ministry to consider EEC decision on S.A. sanctions."

54. Roy Isacowitz, "What's good for the Jews of South Africa?" *Jerusalem Post,* November 22, 1986.

55. Shlomo Avineri, "South Africa, a Zionist emergency," *Jerusalem Post,* February 2, 1986.

56. "No wish to join sanctions on SA," *Jerusalem Post,* February 4, 1987.

57. Hauser, "Israel, South Africa and the West."

58. "Israel Moves to Block Congress, Save South African Arms Sales," *Israeli Foreign Affairs,* April 1987.

Part II: Israel & Central America
El Salvador

1. "Dear Colleague" letter circulated with the draft legislation, HR 5424, June 1984.

2. Testimony of Jeffrey A. James, adjunct professor at American University, before House of Representatives Foreign Affairs Committee Subcommittee on Europe and the Middle East, on HR5424, June 7, 1984 (typed copy). James also said: "Israel has made great strides since 1948 to give her considerable credibility as a developmental role model and as a donor of technical assistance. The communial [sic] organizational structures and idealogy [sic] have seemed particularly appropriate for the Third World nations also preemenently [sic] concerned with nation building through consensus politics."

It did not occur to James to mention that, in most countries where Israel works, the consensus is between the forces of reaction there and in the U.S., and most often the military.

3. Jewish Telegraphic Agency, November 29, 1985. Contrary to the original rationale for CDR, with the exception of Ghana, all the projects were in nations with longstanding ties with Israel.

4. "Development Aid to Central America," *Israeli Foreign Affairs,* June 1986. This article is based on contracts and other U.S. AID documents relating to the three projects.

5. Inter-Hemispheric Resource Center Bulletin, (Box 4506 Albuquerque, NM 87196), no date—received May 1986; and Sara Miles, "The Real War,

Low-Intensity Conflict in Central America," NACLA *Report on the Americas,* April-May 1986. Both outline the Reagan Administration's attempts to translate into military technique its vicious fantasies of reversing liberation struggles.

6. "Development Aid in Central America."

7. Ignacio Klich, "Israel Arms the Dictators," drawing on information from *Jane's Fighting Ships, SIPRI Yearbooks* and *Strategy Week* in *Middle East International,* December 23, 1982; Penny Lernoux, "Who's Who of Dictators Obtain Arms from Israel," *National Catholic Reporter,* December 25, 1981.

8. Edy Kaufman, Yoram Shapira, and Joel Barromi, *Israel-Latin American Relations,* Transaction, New Brunswick, NJ, 1979, p. 105.

9. Interview with Guerra y Guerra, February 1983. Guerra was one of the reformist "young officers" who overthrew President Romero in 1979 and were driven out in their turn in 1980 by more conservative (U.S.-backed) military officers.

10. Chris Hedges, "Salvadoran colonel who mutinied is back in war," *Christian Science Monitor,* September 26, 1984.

11. Julia Preston, "Ochoa, A Good Fighter but Too Independent for Salvador Army?" *Christian Science Monitor,* January 13, 1983. For a full profile of this hard-line officer see, "Israel's Salvadoran Protege," *Israeli Foreign Affairs,* April 1985.

12. This premise already had the support of Congress, which in 1976 had passed legislation linking U.S. aid to human rights practices (*Journal of Commerce,* March 18, 1977). In actual practice during the Carter Administration, the aid going to big violators, e.g. South Korea and the Philippines, was not cut off because they were strategically important. Only Argentina, Chile, Nicaragua, El Salvador, and Guatemala were affected by the policy.

13. Department of Defense figures show that between 1950 and 1980, 2097 Salvadorans, 3334 Guatemalans, 3834 Hondurans and 5679 Nicaraguans had participated in U.S. IMET (International Military Education and Training) training programs, *DOD Foreign Military Sales and Military Assistance Facts,* December 1980 in Arnon Hadar, *The United States and El Salvador: Political and Military Involvement,* U.S.-El Salvador Research & Information Center, Berkeley, CA, 1981, p. 126.

14. Tom Barry, Beth Wood, and Deb Preusch, *Dollars and Dictators,* Grove Press, 1983, is an excellent examination of the interplay between U.S. government and U.S. corporate influence on Central America.

15. Hadar, *The United States and El Salvador,* p. 20.

16. Alan Nairn, "Behind the Death Squads," *Progressive,* May 1984.

17. Carolyn Forche and Philip Wheaton, "History and Motivations of U.S. Involvement in the Control of the Peasant Movement in El Salvador: The Role of AIFLD in the Agrarian Reform Process, 1970-80," in James Dunkerley, *The Long War, Dictatorship & Revolution in El Salvador,* Verso, London, 1982 (reprinted 1983), p. 98.

18. "El Salvador Rejects U.S. Arms Aid," AP, *Washington Post,* March 19, 1977.

19. Dunkerly, *The Long War*, pp. 110-111.

20. Hadar, *The United States and El Salvador*, Appendix 13, p. 127.

21. In the shadowy world of arms sales it is very difficult to track the smaller items, which are not as carefully tracked as the "big ticket" items by such organizations as SIPRI; thus the sources for the small items in the accompanying chart are more anecdotal.

22. "Leftist Says Salvadoran Troops Are Being Trained by the Israelis," Reuters, *New York Times*, October 10, 1979.

23. Interview with Guerra, February 1983.

24. Interview with Ramos, January 1983.

25. Hadar, *The United States and El Salvador*, Dunkerly, *The Long War*, *passim*. Guerra y Guerra relates that Carter Ambassador Frank Devine actively worked to bring out of the first 1979 junta the exceedingly conservative and brutal 1980 government controlled by Col.'s Garcia and Gutierrez, which, in its ultimate version, was fronted by Jose Napoleon Duarte.

26. *International Herald Tribune*, December 31, 1979, in Ignacio Klich, "Les choix de Jerusalem en Amerique centrale," *Le Monde Diplomatique*, October 1982.

27. Jeffrey Heller, "Salvadoran guerrilla denies attacks on Israeli Targets," *Jerusalem Post*, May 13, 1982. It would not be surprising if one of the guerrilla groups had carried out the bombing. However, several journalists have spoken to this author about the deep and abiding anti-Semitism of the Salvadoran officer corps.

28. *This Week in Central America and Panama*, February 25, 1980.

29. Dunkerley, *The Long War*, *passim*.

30. Karen DeYoung, "State's Latin Bureau Urges Resumption of Arms Aid to Salvador," *Washington Post*, January 10, 1981.

31. Karen DeYoung, "Carter Decides to Resume Military Aid to El Salvador," *Ibid.*, January 14, 1981. The Salvadoran far right began a reign of terror coinciding with the election of Ronald Reagan, an attempt, thought some, to establish "facts" that Reagan would be most likely to support.

32. *Davar*, January 3, 1982, translator unknown. According to the article, Israel's economic attache in Washington, Danny Halperin confirmed the transaction.

33. *Latin America Weekly Report*, December 17, 1982.

34. *SIPRI Yearbook 1982*, p. 213 in Bishara Bahbah, *Israel and Latin America, The Military Connection*, St. Martin's Press (New York) and Institute for Palestine Studies (Washington), 1986, p. 79.

35. "Napalm: Made in Israel, Used in El Salvador," *Israeli Foreign Affairs*, December 1984. The need for napalm was supposedly obviated when the Salvadoran government began bombing and strafing the civilian population from A-37 aircraft obtained from the U.S.

36. Heller, "Salvadoran guerrilla denies..." and "Salvadoran envoy blasts MKs' talks with 'terrorist,'" *Jerusalem Post*, May 14, 1982.

37. "Latin America's relations with Israel and the Arab World," *Special Report*, Latin American Newsletters, November 1985.

38. *Ha'aretz,* November 12, 1981, in Klich, "Les Choix de Jerusalem ..."

39. Bahbah, *Israel and Latin America,* p. 152, was given this estimate in 1982 by a PLO representative and told by the international relations department of the FMLN in Managua that same year that Israeli advisers were involved with the Salvadoran intelligence services. In late 1982 Arnaldo Ramos, U.S. representative of the FDR, gave the author those same numbers and said that many Israelis were working on a secret military base near San Salvador.

40. *Davar,* May 3, 1984, in FBIS Middle East and Africa, May 4, 1984, p. I-6.

41. Juan O. Tamayo, "Want to buy a fully trained SWAT team?" *Miami Herald,* September 4, 1986. This article is datelined Jerusalem and so must have been passed by the Israeli censors.

42. "El Salvador returns embassy to Jerusalem," *Jerusalem Post International Edition,* April 22, 1984.

43. Radio Venceremos, 0000 GMT, April 25, 1984 in FBIS Latin America, April 26, 1984, p. P-9.

44. "U.S. Denies Latin Aid Role for Israel," AP, *New York Times,* April 22, 1984.

45. "Salvadorans Talk of More Israeli Aid," AP, *New York Times,* April 21, 1984.

46. ACAN, Panama City, 2228 GMT, April 23, 1984, in FBIS Latin America, April 24, 1984, pp. P-1,2.

47. Reuters, *New York Times,* April 21, 1984; ironically, the rupture hit Costa Rica harder than El Salvador, which did not have much of an international reputation to lose.

48. Doyle McManus, "Demos vying hard to lure wary Jewish voters," *Los Angeles Times,* April 2, 1984 in *San Francisco Chronicle.*

49. "Egypt Warns U.S. on Moving Israel Embassy," UPI, *San Francisco Chronicle,* May 2, 1984.

50. "Israel Dara Mayor Respaldo en Armamentos," *Excelsior* (Mexico City), April 21, 1984.

51. Teodoro Ducach, "Busca el Gobierno Salvadoreno la Asistencia de Militares Israelies," *Excelsior,* August 4, 1983.

52. Edward Cody, "El Salvador, Israel Set Closer Ties," *Washington Post,* August 17, 1983.

53. Ducach, "Busca el Gobierno Salvadoreno ..."

54. Arthur Allen, "Say Israel, El Salvador to Strengthen Ties," AP, 0642, August 17, 1983. Prior to the agreement, El Salvador had voted with the vast majority of UN members in support of the PLO.

55. Cody, "El Salvador, Israel Set Closer Ties."

56. Author's confidential sources.

57. Allen, "Say Israel, El Salvador to Strengthen Ties."

58. See Edward S. Herman and Frank Brodhead, *Demonstration Elections,* South End Press, Boston, 1984. In the Reagan lexicon the term "democratic elections" covers a vast galaxy of fraud and venality, whereas the 1984 elections

in Nicaragua have been dismissed (only by the Reagan Administration) as phony and fraudulent.

59. Craig Pyes, "Salvadoran Rightists: The Deadly Patriots," *Albuquerque Journal*, December 18, 1983. This was the first of a series of articles that ran until December 22.

60. "Si hay golpe en El Salvador, se retirara toda ayuda belica de EU," *El Dia* (Mexico City), April 5, 1984.

61. Robert Leikin, "Ochoa's gambit," *Miami Herald*, January 16, 1983.

62. Joanne Omang, "CIA admits funding Salvadoran elections," *Washington Post*, May 11, 1984 in *Oakland Tribune*. The CIA also pumped some money into Jose Guerrero's Conciliation Party, which proceeded to surprise observers by staying neutral, rather than throwing its support to D'Aubuisson.

63. San Salvador Radio Cadena YSKL, 0025 GMT, June 4, 1984 in FBIS Latin America, June 5, 1984, p. P-4.

64. "U.S. Officials Cheered by Salvador Arms Aid," *New York Times*, August 13, 1984.

65. In 1985 Duarte himself told Reuters that he was indeed interested in having Israel provide military training to the Salvadoran forces.

66. Robert Block, "Israel to Aid El Salvador in Areas tied to Counterinsurgency," Reuters North European Service, February 22, 1986.

67. Author's confidential sources.

68. San Salvador Radio Cadena YSU, 1200 GMT, May 21, 1985 in FBIS Latin America, May 23, 1985, pp. P-3-4.

69. *El Diario De Hoy* (San Salvador), July 20, 1984, in FBIS Latin America, July 23, 1984, p. P-5.

70. *Enforprensa*, May 17, 1985.

71. Clifford Krauss and Tim Carrington, "U.S. Effort to Win 'Hearts and Minds' Gains in El Salvador," *Wall Street Journal*, September 8, 1986.

72. Clifford Krauss, "Salvador Pacification Off to a Shaky Start," *Wall Street Journal*, July 18, 1984.

73. James LeMoyne, "Salvador Air Role in War Increases," *New York Times*, July 18, 1985.

74. Jeruslam Domestic Service, 1100 GMT, April 13, 1984, in FBIS Latin America, April 13, 1984, p. I-6.

75. San Salvador, *El Mundo*, February 23, 1985 in FBIS Latin America, February 27, 1985, p. P-4.

76. Dan Williams, "Comunidades Fortificadas del Proyecto Piloto de Achichilco," translated from the *Los Angeles Times* in *Excelsior*, February 8, 1985.

77. Chris Hedges, "Salvador plans to resettle 500,000 displaced persons," *Christian Science Monitor*, September 28, 1984.

78. Williams, "Comunidades Fortificadas del Proyecto Piloto de Achichilco."

79. Hedges, "Salvador plans to resettle 500,000 displaced persons."

80. Williams, "Comunidades Fortificadas del Proyecto Piloto de Achi-

chilco."

81. Madrid, EFE 0427 GMT, August 29, 1985, in FBIS Latin America, September 4, 1985.

82. Williams, "Comunidades Fortificadas del Proyecto Piloto de Achichilco."

83. Tamar Kaufman, "Salvadoran Jew to discuss U.S. policy in Latin America," Northern California Jewish Bulletin, September 12, 1986.

84. Block, "Israel to Aid El Salvador."

85. *Ibid.* The program would have to be propped up like Lazarus.

86. "Asistencia Technologia de Israel a El Salvador," *El Dia*, July 3, 1986, which cites *Davar*.

87. James LeMoyne, "El Salvador's Refugees: The Many Peasants Who Get Caught," *New York Times*, July 1, 1986. This unpleasant business has been going on for years. Dr. Charles Clements, who tended patients on Guazapa Volcano in 1982 and 1983, spoke frequently on his return of military raids in which the army would take care to smash every dish a family owned.

88. James LeMoyne, "Salvador War Recovery Plan is Announced by Army Chief," *New York Times*, July 30, 1986.

89. Dunkerley, *The Longest War,* p. 29 and *passim.*

90. Interview with Guerra y Guerra.

Guatemala

1. So vicious was the Guatemalan military in its anti-popular war that such stalwarts of the Reagan policy in Central America as Henry Kissinger, and Langhorne Motley and Thomas Enders, both formerly Assistant Secretary of State for Inter-American Affairs, noted its brutality and either affirmed or did not contest U.S. distance from Guatemala. Milton Jamail and Margo Gutierrez, *It's No Secret: Israel's Military Involvement in Central America,* AAUG Press, (556 Trapelo Rd., Belmont, MA 02178), 1986, p. 51.

2. Allan Nairn, "Terror with a Human Face," *Village Voice,* November 5, 1985. Other estimates run between 30,000 and 100,000. See also Marjorie Miller, "Indians' Culture Torn by Guatemalan Political Strife," *Los Angeles Times* November 29, 1985.

3. Frank del Olmo, "In Guatemala, Fusiles y Frijoles," *Los Angeles Times*, February 11, 1983.

4. Opinion piece by Wayne Smith, former head of the U.S. interest section in Cuba, *New York Times,* October 12, 1982 in Jonathan Fried, Marvin E. Gettleman, Deborah T. Levenson, and Nancy Peckenham, *Guatemala in Rebellion: Unfinished History,* Grove Press, Inc., New York, 1983, p. 311.

5. "Report Bombs Set off at Israel, Other Embassies in Guatemala," JTA, January 14, 1982.

6. "Israeli embassy rocked by blast," *Miami Herald,* August 13, 1982.

7. Cheryl A. Rubenberg, "Israeli foreign policy in Central America," *Third World Quarterly,* July 1986; Kaufman *et. al., Israeli-Latin American Relations,* pp. 3 and 138.

8. Jamail and Gutierrez, *It's No Secret,* pp. 51, 52.

9. Chart from the Israeli Foreign Ministry, 1971, in Kaufman *et. al., Israeli-Latin American Relations,* p. 247; Shimeon Amir, *Israel's Development Cooperation with Africa, Asia, and Latin America,* Praeger, New York, 1974, p. 113; Curtis and Gitelson, *Israel in the Third World,* p. 399.

10. "Shopping Around for Weapons," *Central America Report,* March 28, 1977. Guatemala actually preempted the move by canceling its agreements with Washington.

11. George Black, "Israeli Connection—Not Just Guns for Guatemala," *NACLA Report on the Americas,* May-June, 1983.

12. "International Arms Transfers to Central America Since 1969," *Update* (Central American Historical Institute, Georgetown University), July 9, 1984 in Jamail and Gutierrez, *It's No Secret,* p. 53.

13. "Israel pushes aircraft at interfer," *Central America Report,* October 31, 1977.

14. Yoav Karni, "The Israel-Guatemala Connection," *Ha'aretz,* February 7, 1986, translated in *Al Fajr,* February 14, 1986.

15. Christopher Dickey, "Guatemala Uses U.S. 'Civilian' Copters in Warfare," *Washington Post,* January 23, 1982.

16. "Israel May Become Regional Arms Supplier," December 5, 1977, and "Israel Pushes Aircraft at Interfer," October 31, 1977, *Central America Report*; Bernard Debusmann, "After Embassy Flap, a Look at Israel's Latin Arms Role," Reuters, *Philadelphia Inquirer,* April 24, 1984. According to President Laugurud, five patrol boats had been ordered (*Central America Report,* December 12, 1977).

17. Guatemala City Radio Television, 0400 GM1, June 11, 1984, in FBIS Latin America, June 12, 1984.

18. Victor Perera, "Uzi Diplomacy—How Israel Makes Friends and Enemies Around the World," *Mother Jones,* July 1985.

19. "Problems From the Barrels of Israeli Guns," *Latin America Weekly Report,* May 16, 1980 and Rarihokwats, *Guatemala: The Horror and the Hope,* Four Arrows, York, PA, 1982, p. 106 in Jamail and Gutierrez, *It's No Secret,* p. 53.

20. "Arms seizure irritates Belize dispute," *Central America Report,* July 4, 1977.

21. *Central America Report,* October 17, 1977.

22. *Ma'ariv,* April 30, 1974, in Kaufman *et. al., Israeli-Latin American Relations,* pp. 107-108.

23. "Israel May Become Regional Arms Supplier"; "Israel Pushes Aircraft at Interfer"; Debusmann, "After Embassy Flap, a Look at Israel's Latin Arms Role."

24. Karni, "The Israel-Guatemala Connection."

25. Cynthia Arnson and Flora Montealegre, *IPS Resource Update,*

Washington, June 1982, in "Garrison Guatemala," *NACLA Report on the Americas,* January/February, 183, p. 25.

26. Robert Graham, "Barter Revisited: Latin America Takes a Fresh Look at Countertrade," *Financial Times* in *Houston Chronicle,* February 11, 1985.

27. Klieman, *Israel's Global Reach,* p. 135.

28. Graham Hovey, "U.S. Blocks Sale of Israeli Planes to Ecuadoreans," *New York Times,* February 8, 1977.

29. "Arms seizure irritates Belize dispute."

30. Graham, "Barter revisited: Latin America takes a fresh look at countertrade."

31. *Enfoprensa,* March 8, 1985.

32. Interview with information officer, Greek Embassy, Washington DC; *Jerusalem Post,* March 30, 1986 and *Hadashot,* April 1, 1986 in FBIS Middle East and Africa; a complete account of the seizure of the West Lion appears in *Israeli Foreign Affairs,* May 1986. Inquiries made in Greece in early 1987 determined that the case had quietly dropped out of sight.

33. CBS Evening News (Bob Simon reporting from Guatemala) February 16, 1983, in Nat Hentoff, "Should a Jewish State Arm a Christian Slaughterer?" *Village Voice,* June 21, 1983.

34. "Israeli Arms for Sale," *Time,* March 28, 1983.

35. Interview in *Moment,* June 1984.

36. "Adquirio Guatemala Aviones Militares," PL, SIAG, *Enfoprensa,* in *Excelsior,* December 6, 1983.

37. Dan Rather, CBS Evening News, February 16, 1983 in Bahbah, *Israel and Latin America,* p. 161.

38. George Black with Milton Jamail & Norma Stoltz Chinchilla, *Garrison Guatemala,* Monthly Review Press, 1984 p. 156.

39. Allan Nairn, "Controversial Reagan Campaign Links with Guatemalan Government and Private Sector Leaders," *COHA Research Memorandum,* October 30, 1980, in Black *et. al.,* *Garrison Guatemala,* pp. 147-148.

40. Greve, "Israel able to expand role as Latin military supplier."

41. Allan Nairn, "The Guatemala Connection," *The Progressive,* May 1986. This article details a number of Reagan Administration arms shipments in defiance of the congressional ban. The Reagan Administration was operating under the dual handicap of having to slip these items past both Congress and the British, which continued to object to arms sales to Guatemala (Jackson and Keatley, "Britain protests at U.S. arms sales to Guatemala," *Manchester Guardian,* January 16, 1983.) The Thatcher government has similarly blocked Israeli arms sales to Argentina through the U.S. government.

42. "Israel desarrolla una industra de guerra en Guatemala, denuncia el EGP," *El Dia,* October 11, 1983.

43. *Enfoprensa,* January 6, 1984.

44. *Latin America Regional Reports Mexico & Central America,* August 17, 1984; in a 1985 special edition, (*op. cit.*) *Latin America Newsletters* said that Austria had provided "the plant and some of the technology" and that a number

of Guatemalan officers had been to Austria for technical training. This would appear to contradict Gen. Lucas' statement that Israel provided the factory.

45. Karni, "The Israel-Guatemala Connection."

46. "Israel's Part in Central America," (II) *Central America Report,* December 14, 1984, in Jamail and Gutierrez, *It's No Secret,* p. 59.

47. "Industria Militar de Israel en Guatemala," AFP, AP, UPI, ANSA, *Enfoprensa* and SIAG, *Excelsior,* October 11, 1983.

48. Cody, "El Salvador, Israel Set Closer Ties."

49. Karni, "The Israel-Guatemala Connection."

50. U.S. Congress, House, Committee on International Relations, Subcommittee on International Organizations, *Human Rights in Nicaragua, Guatemala and El Salvador: Implications for U.S. Policy,* Hearings, 94th Cong., 2d Sess., 1976, pp. 51-52 in Delia Miller *et. al., Background Information on Guatemala, The Armed Forces and U.S. Military Assistance,* Institute for Policy Studies, June 1981, p. 6.

51. Shirley Christian, "Congress is Asked for $54 Million to Aid Latin Antiterrorist Efforts," *New York Times,* November 6, 1985.

52. Hentoff, "Should a Jewish State Arm a Christian Slaughterer?"

53. *Israeli Foreign Affairs,* November 1985 and April 1986.

54. David Gardner, "How Israelis act as surrogates for U.S. in Central America," *Financial Times,* November 27, 1986.

55. James LeMoyne, "Guatemala Crushes Rebels Its Own Way: Ruthlessly," *New York Times,* January 13, 1985.

56. *Yediot Aharonot,* February 7, 1979 in Bahbah, *Israel and Latin America,* p. 162.

57. Panama City ACAN, 2146 GMT, March 23, 1982, in FBIS Latin America, March 26, 1982 and NACLA interviews in Guatemala City, June 1982, in Black *et. al., Garrison Guatemala,* p. 123. Alvarez, as was Rios, was safe in Miami.

58. Black, "Israeli Connection—Not just Guns for Guatemala."

59. Allan Nairn and Jean-Marie Simon, "Bureaucracy of Death," *New Republic,* June 30, 1986; DPA, 2324 GMT, February 5, 1986 in FBIS Latin America, February 6, 1986.

60. John Rettie, "Israeli arms help Guatemala's fight against Guerrillas," *Manchester Guardian,* January 10, 1982.

61. "Moderna escuela de transmissiones y electronica del ejercito inaugurada," *Diario de Centro America,* (Guatemala City), November 5, 1981 in Cheryl A. Rubenberg, "Israel and Guatemala: Arms, Advice and Counterinsurgency," *Middle East Report,* May-June 1986.

62. Rettie, "Israeli arms help Guatemala's fight against guerrillas."

63. Black, "Israeli Connection—Not just Guns for Guatemala."

64. Karni, "The Israel-Guatemala Connection," This installation is thought to have been destroyed in 1984 by insurgents (David Ferreira, "Guatemala: Unholy Allies," *AfricAsia,* November 1984).

65. Nairn and Simon, "Bureaucracy of Death."

66. Luisa Frank and Philip Wheaton, *Indian Guatemala: The Path to*

Liberation, EPICA task force, Washington, 1984, gives the earliest date among a number of sources (including "Keeping Track: Israeli Computers in Guatemala and El Salvador," *Israeli Foreign Affairs,* March 1985) and Yosef Pri'el, *Davar,* August 13, 1982, the latest (autumn, 1981) in Rubenberg, "Israeli Foreign Policy in Central America."

67. Fr. Ronald Burke, a Catholic priest who had worked since 1969 in the highland department of Chimaltenango, noted that "the computerized hit lists at that time were all coordinated at the annex at the Presidential Palace. And when I checked it out with the [U.S.] Embassy people they let me know indirectly that I was on that particular national hit list, and I was advised to get out of the country, quickly." Interview with Fr. Burke by Lenard Millich, January 1985.

68. Christopher Dickey, "Guatemalan War Grows Fiercer," *Washington Post,* January 22, 1982.

69. "Pozos de tortura y trabajo forzado en las *aldeas modelo* de Guatemala," SIAG and Enfoprensa, *El Dia,* May 22, 1983.

70. "Crearan in Guatemala una tarjeta unica de identificacion personal," *El Dia,* August 22, 1986.

71. AFP, 0236 GMT, September 17, 1983 in FBIS Latin America, September 19, 1983, p. P-17.

72. Cited in *Inforpress Centroamericana,* August 30, 1984.

73. Victor Perera, "Uzi Diplomacy," *Mother Jones,* July 1985.

74. Black, "Israeli Connection - Not just Guns for Guatemala."

75. "Asesores Israelies se encuentran en Guatemala," AIP, Enfoprensa and Salpress in *El Dia,* June 23, 1983.

76. Nancy Peckenham, "Bullets and Beans," *Multinational Monitor,* April 1984.

77. Marlise Simons, "Guatemalans Are Adding A Few Twists to 'Pacification,'" *New York Times,* September 12, 1982.

78. "Habra en Toda Guatemala Aldeas Modelo: Mejia V.," *Excelsior,* January 2, 1984.

79. Black *et. al., Garrison Guatemala,* p. 155.

80. Alan Riding, "Government-Backed Cooperatives in Guatemala Aid Indians," September 13, 1975, and "Guatemala Opening New Lands but the Best Goes to Rich," April 5, 1979, *New York Times;* Stanley Meisler, "Guatemalan Co-ops Attract 'Red' Label," *Los Angeles Times,* February 1, 1976.

81. Black, "Israeli Connection."

82. *Ibid.*

83. Peckenham, "Bullets and Beans."

84. *Ibid.*

85. Victor Perera, "The Lost Tribes of Guatemala," *The Monthly* (Berkeley, CA.) November 1985.

86. Peckenham, "Bullets and Beans."

87. "Transforming the Indian highlands," *Latin America Regional Reports Mexico & Central America,* May 6, 1983.

88. Perera, "The Lost Tribes of Guatemala."

89. Mary Jo McConahay, "Guatemalan town gets a road," Pacific News Service, *Oakland Tribune,* July 21, 1985.

90. "Transforming the Indian highlands." See also Douglas Foster, "Guatemala: On the Green Path," *Mother Jones,* November-December 1985.

91. Peckenham, "Bullets and Beans"; Christian Rudel, "Pacification Violente au Guatemala," *Le Monde Diplomatique,* August, 1985.

92. Peckenham, "Bullets and Beans."

93. Rudel, "Pacification Violente au Guatemala."

94. *Ibid.*

95. *Guatemala: A Nation of Prisoners,* Americas Watch, New York, January 1984, p. 82.

96. Marjorie Miller, "Indians' Culture Torn by Guatemalan Political Strife."

97. Rudel, "Pacification Violente au Guatemala."

98. *El Dia,* November 12, 1983.

99. Nancy Peckenham, "Campos de reducacion para los indigenas," *unomasuno,* February 12, 1984.

100. The Spanish is patrullas auto-defensas civilas.

101. Simons, "Guatemalans Are Adding A Few Twists to 'Pacification.'"

102. In 1983 the National Workers Central (CNT) charged that under Rios Montt torture chambers were built in some of the model villages and that peasants who refused to participate in the patrols were punished in these. ("Pozos de tortura y trabajo forzado...")

103. Perera, "The Lost Tribes of Guatemala."

104. Rubenberg, "Israeli Foreign Policy in Central America."

105. Guatemala City Cadena de Emisoras Unidas, 0050 GMT, June 9, 1984 in FBIS Latin America, June 12, 1984, p. P-13.

106. Peckenham, "Bullets and Beans"; *Guatemala: A Nation of Prisoners,* pp. 85-86.

107. del Olmo, "In Guatemala, Fusiles y Frijoles."

108. "Civil Defense Is Fact of Life In Guatemala, *New York Times,* Marcy 4, 1984.

109. U.S. Department of State, Bureau of Public Affairs, *Sustaining A Consistent Policy in Central America: One Year After the National Bipartisan Commission Report,* Special Report No. 142, Washington, DC, April 1985, p. 12, in Jamail and Gutierrez, *It's No Secret,* p. 58.

110. "Guatemala Asks Arms' Release," *Washington Post,* December 27, 1983; *Latin America Regional Report, Mexico & Central America,* January 13, 1984 says that U.S. officials said the rifles were Remingtons, while Israeli sources said they were Mausers; Bishara Bahbah (p. 161) says Israel has sold Guatemala "German-made bolt-action Mauser rifles from 1948 purchases from Czechoslovakia."

111. "Guatemala Claims Rifles Seized by U.S. Customs," *Washington Post,* December 25, 1983.

112. Guatemala City Cadena de Emisoras Unidas, 1230 GMT, December 24, 1983 in FBIS Latin America, December 27, 1983, p. P-13. The antiquated weapons are in keeping with the reluctance of Guatemalan authorities to arm the population—in marked contrast to the Nicaraguan government's practice of distributing rifles.

113. SIAG (Guatemalan Information and Analysis Service), Mexico City, April, 1984.

114. "Pozos de tortura y trabajo forzado..."

115. Loren Jenkins, "Guatemala turns to 'model villages' in its battle against guerrilla rebels," *Washington Post* in *Philadelphia Inquirer,* January 13, 1985.

116. Rudel, "Pacification Violente au Guatemala."

117. Moreover, because it occurs in a global economic system, the exploitation of the Guatemalan peasants creates additional victims. A strike of food workers against several Watsonville, California processing plants which account for 80 percent of the frozen broccoli and cauliflower (among other vegetables) sold in the U.S. and abroad (Antonio Garcia, "Big chill in frozen food industry," *People's World,* August 31, 1985)—it began in the fall of 1985 and was still in progress in February 1987—over employer efforts to reduce the base wage from $7.06 to $4.25 an hour is directly related to what is happening in Guatemala, named as one of the countries where workers do not make that much in a day. (Robert Lindsey, "New Food Patterns Affect Strike in West," *New York Times,* January 1, 1986.)

118. Jamail and Gutierrez, *It's No Secret,* p. 57.

119. *Guatemala: A Nation of Prisoners,* pp. 85-86.

120. It is the method proposed by Kach party leader Meir Kahane—expulsion of Palestinians and recommended laws to prevent intermarriage and the accompanying thuggery—to which other Israeli factions and U.S. Jewish organizations object, not the ultimate objective of reducing the Palestinian population of pre-1967 Israel and the occupied territories.

121. Elizabeth Gray, Report on *Sunday Morning,* Canadian Broadcasting Company, heard March 10, 1985, KALW-FM, San Francisco.

122. Rubenberg, "Israeli Foreign Policy in Central America."

123. *Ma'ariv,* in Shahak, *Israel's Global Role,* p. 48.

124. Christopher Dickey, "Religious Rivalries Complicate Conflict Among Guatemalans," *Washington Post,* January 6, 1983. One interesting point made in this article is that the fundamentalists had a tendency to split and that the proliferation of churches tended to disorganize communities and diffuse opposition to the government.

125. *Ibid.*

126. "Este Acto Injustificable Hiere a la Iglesia Catolica, Dice el Nuncio Apostolico," *Excelsior,* November 13, 1983. In November 1983, shortly after Rios was deposed, the Army chief of staff admitted that a number of Roman Catholic catechists had been detained at the Puerto Barrios military base after having been captured that August "for investigation to determine if they are actual participants in the subversion." (*El Dia,* November 12, 1983.)

127. Shelton H. Davis, "Guatemala: The Evangelical Holy War in El Quiche," *The Global Reporter*, March 1983.

128. Tom Pratt, "Falwell: Israel Needs U.S. Support," *Tyler Courier-Times-Telegraph*, (Texas) February 6, 1983, in Alan Dehmer, *Unholy Alliance*, ADC Issue Paper #16, Washington, DC, April 1984.

129. CBN, *700 Club*, June 9, 1982, *Unholy Alliance*.

130. *Ibid.*

131. Off-record interview with House Foreign Affairs Committee Western Hemisphere Subcommittee staff member, July 1, 1985.

132. *Ibid.*; Jenkins, "Guatemala turns to 'model villages'..."

133. Letter to *New York Times*, January 24, 1984.

134. The military also passed a decree granting amnesty to its members for any crimes they may have committed between 1982 and 1986. Decrees listed by number in *Update on Guatemala*, (publication of Nattional Committee in Solidarity with the People of Guatemala, 225 Lafayette St., Room 212, New York, NY 10012) January-March 1986.

135. Guatemala City Radio-Television Guatemala, 0040 GMT, March 12, 1986, in FBIS Latin America, March 17, 1986, p. P-10.

136. *Boletin International* (publication of Guatemala Human Rights Commission [CDHG], Mexico City), March 1986.

137. *Economist*, September 7, 1985; *Diario Las Americas*, September 8, 1985.

138. James LeMoyne, "In Guatemala, the Army's Retreat May be Good Politics," *New York Times*, August 11, 1985.

139. Clifford Krauss, "Guatemala Will Elect A Civilian, but Will He Control the Military?" *Wall Street Journal*, October 30, 1985.

140. Piero Gleijeses, "The Guatemalan Silence, *New Republic*, June 10, 1985.

141. *All Things Considered*, National Public Radio, June 25, 1986.

142. AGN (Guatemala News Agency [Managua]) January 18, 1985; not exactly the kind of speech Solarz, a liberal by reputation, would be making in his own Brooklyn district.

143. Heard extensively on RTF (Radio France International) and Spanish radio stations during the week of October 14, 1986.

144. Guatemala City Cadena de Emisoras Unidas, 0050 GMT, September 19, 1986 in FBIS Latin America, September 19, 1986, p. P-8. Following the restoration of relations with Britain in late 1986, Guatemala expected to receive aid from the EC itself.

145. Letter to the Editor from Ramiro Gereda Asturias, *Jerusalem Post*, July 24, 1986. In his letter, a reply to a statement by the prime minister of Belize, Geredo insisted that Guatemala "does not buy defensive weapons" from Israel "because it produces its own."

146. Dial Torgerson, "Tactics Shifting to All-Out War in Guatemala," *Los Angeles Times*, January 25, 1982.

147. Stephen Kinzer, "Guatemala Chief Confronts Crisis," *New York Times*, April 13, 1985; Guatemala City Cadena de Emisoras Unidas, 2350

GMT, June 6, 1985, in FBIS Latin America, June 10, 1985, p. P-10.

148. ITIM (Tel Aviv) 1818 GMT, June 15, 1982 in FBIS Middle East and Africa, June 16, 1982, p. I-21.

149. Black, "Israeli Connection."

150. Joel Millman, "Waist Deep" (Book review) *Present Tense*, Spring 1985.

151. Perera, "The Lost Tribes of Guatemala."

152. *Central America Report*, December 2, 1983.

153. Dan Rather, CBS Evening News, February 16, 1983, in Bahbah, *Israel and Latin America*, p. 163.

154. Gil Kesary, "Pesakh Ben-Or: Business in Darkness," *Ma'ariv*, December 13, 1985, translated by Dr. Israel Shahak, *Collection: More about Israeli weapons trade, and the way it influences Israeli politics.*

155. Gardner, "How Israelis act as surrogates for U.S. in Central America."

156. Juan Tamayo, "Want to buy a fully trained SWAT team?" *Miami Herald*, September 4, 1986; Simon Louisson, "How to build a bodyguard empire," *Jerusalem Post*, January 23, 1987.

157. "Foreign Policy Put to the Test," *Guatemala!* (Publication of Guatemala News and Information Bureau, P.O. Box 28594, Oakland, CA. 94604), September-October 1986.

158. Author's sources; David Ferreira, "Guatemala: Unholy Allies"; Rudel, "Pacification Violente au Guatemala."

159. "Foreign Policy Put to the Test."

160. Cerigua and Enfoprensa, *El Dia*, August 8, 1986.

161. Ignacio Klich, "Caribbean boomerang returns to sender," (London) *Guardian*, August 27, 1982.

162. Kesary, "Pesakh Ben-Or: Business in Darkness"; Juan O. Tamayo, "Dealers: Israel sent rebels arms," *Miami Herald*, December 1, 1986.

163. "Israel and Central America," *Latin America Regional Report Mexico and Central America*, February 14, 1986.

164. Kesary, "Pesakh Ben-Or: Business in Darkness."

165. *Ibid.*

166. *Ibid.*

167. Perera, "The Lost Tribes of Guatemala"; Teodoro Ducach, "America Latina, mercado Fundamental Para las Armas Israelis," *Excelsior*, May 8, 1986.

168. *Enfopresna* April 19, 1985.

169. "Early friends take distance," *Latin America Newsletters, Special Report*, November 1985; Israel seems to be firmly convinced that in the field of diplomacy, at least its pariah variety, examples generate momentum which generates results.

170. "Cardamom Exports Will Resume, *This Week in Central America and Panama*, September 15, 1980. However, Dr. Israel Shahak says he has observed an active Guatemalan diplomatic office in Jerusalem.

171. Kesary, "Pesakh Ben-Or: Business in Darkness."

172. Ducach, "America Latina, Mercado Fundamental Para las Armas Israelies."

173. Kesary, "Pesakh Ben-Or: Business in Darkness."

174. Stephen Kinzer, "Guatemalan Voters Will Get a Clear Choice," *New York Times,* December 1, 1985.

175. Perera, "The Lost Tribes of Guatemala."

176. Margaret Hooks, "Guatemala's new president is ready for challenge," *Miami Herald,* January 16, 1986.

177. "Israel and Central America."

178. Ducach, "America Latina, mercado Fundamental Para las Armas Israelies."

179. Guatemala City Radio-Television Guatemala, 0400 GMT, May 6, 1986 in FBIS Latin America, May 7, 1986, p. P-2; Juan O. Tamayo, "Israel won't assist contras, Shamir says after Latin tour," *Miami Herald,* May 10, 1986.

180. Karni, "The Israel-Guatemala Connection."

181. ACAN, 0011 GMT, February 19, 1986 in FBIS Latin America, February 20, 1986, p. P-5.

182. "Israel increases its presence," *Latin America Regional Reports Mexico & Central America,* January 10, 1986.

183. Stephen Kinzer, "Guatemala Gets Help in Rebuilding Its Police," *New York Times,* May 18, 1986.

184. *Jerusalem Post,* July 17, 1986.

185. Milton Jamail, "Links with Belize," *Israeli Foreign Affairs,* July 1985.

186. Jerusalem Domestic Service, 1400 GMT, July 9, 1986 in FBIS Middle East & Africa, July 10, 1986, p. I-10.

187. *El Grafico,* (Guatemala City), July 25, 1986 in FBIS Latin America.

188. ACAN (Panama City), 2200 GMT, July 31, 1986 in FBIS Latin America.

189. Guatemala City Cadena de Emisoras Unidas, 0050 GMT, July 10, 1986 in FBIS Latin America.

190. *El Graphico,* (Guatemala City) May 7, 1986 in FBIS Latin America, May 12, 1986, p. P-9.

191. Tamayo, "Israel won't assist contras, Shamir says after Latin tour."

192. "Demandan los trabajadores municipales de Guatemala, la renuncia del alcalde," Cerigua and IPS, *El Dia,* April 6, 1986; *Central America Report,* February 21, 1986 and report the same day from SIAG.

193. John M. Goshko, "Controversy Looms Over Bid to Aid Guatemala," *Washington Post,* March 11, 1979.

194. James LeMoyne, "Guatemala Fights Its Bad-Guy Image, *New York Times,* December 25, 1984.

195. *Latin America Regional Report,* Mexico and Central America, May 4, 1984.

196. Stephen Schlesinger and Stephen Kinzer, *Bitter Fruit,* Anchor Books, Garden City, NY, 1983, provides an account of the destruction of Guatemala in the interest of "anti-communism" and the United Fruit Company.

197. Black *et. al.*, *Garrison Guatemala*, pp. 21-24.

198. Nairn and Simon, "Bureaucracy of Death."

199. Alexander Cockburn, "Sharing Responsibility for Guatemalan horrors," *Wall Street Journal*, February 24, 1983. He adds that "investors have hastened to take advantage of tax incentives, a cowed and ill-paid work force and plans for military reorganization of the entire fabric of the countryside."

Nicaragua Under Somoza

1. Slater, *The Pledge*, pp. 257-259

2. Anastasio Somoza Debayle, *Nicaragua Betrayed*, Western Islands, Belmont MA 1980, p. 12. (The publisher of this autobiography is a John Birch Society subsidiary.)

3. *Ibid.*, p. 173. Kaufman *et. al.*, *Israel-Latin American Relations*, pp. 118, 204.

4. Kaufman *et. al.*, *Israel-Latin American Relations*, pp. 107-205.

5. Alan Riding, "Nicaragua Tries Economic Cure," *New York Times*, November 27, 1979. "Nicaraguan Debt Obligations Emerge as a Key Pointer of Junta Policy Direction," *Business Latin America*, October 10, 1979.

6. *SIPRI Yearbook 1980*, p. 96. The remaining two percent came from Argentina and a private dealer in Miami.

7. *Jerusalem Post*, February 8, 1974 in Kaufman *et. al. Israel-Latin American Relations*, p. 108.

8. Chart derived from *Jane's Fighting Ships, SIPRI Yearbooks, The Military Balance, Strategy Week,* in Ignacio Klich, "Israel arms the Dictators," *Middle East International*, December 23, 1982.

9. William R. Long, "Somoza Still Has the Firepower; Can Mass Uprising Topple Him?" *Miami Herald*, September 17, 1978.

10. "Israeli-Made Weapons Helped Save the Somoza Dynasty," London Observer Service, *Miami Herald*, October 18, 1978.

11. *Davar*, November 13 1979 in Israel Shahak, *Israel's Global Role: Weapons for Repression*, Association of Arab-American University Graduates, Belmont, MA 1982, p. 17.

12. Citing an OAS report of November 1978, James Nelson Goodsell, "OAS raps Nicaraguan ruler," *Christian Science Monitor*, November 20, 1978.

13. *Davar*, November 14, 1979 in Shahak, *Israel's Global Role*, p. 17.

14. Robert B. Cullen, "U.S. Won't Attempt to Prevent Israeli Arms Sales to Somoza," AP, *Miami Herald*, November 18, 1978.

15. "Nicaragua: Somoza's Guernica," *Latin America Political Report*, June 29, 1979.

16. Somoza, *Nicaragua Betrayed*, p. 260.

17. "Nicaragua: destruction with honour," *Latin America Political Report*,

July 6, 1979.

18. Alan Riding, "Reporters Notebook: Somoza Fighting On as Aides Panic," *New York Times*, June 28, 1979.

19. Alan Riding, "Nicaragua After Somoza," *New York Times*, February 3, 1980.

20. "Israel Agrees to Suspend Nicaraguan Arms Deliveries," *Washington Post*, July 1, 1979.

21. Somoza, *Nicaragua Betrayed*, p. 239-240.

22. "Begin Peace Prize Called 'Tainted,'" *Miami Herald*, November 13, 1978.

23. Alan Riding, "Both Sides Prepare for Bloodletting in Nicaragua," *New York Times*, November 19, 1978.

24. Cullen, "U.S. Won't Attempt to Prevent Israeli Arms Sales to Somoza".

25. "Israel Agrees to Suspend Nicaraguan Arms Deliveries."

26. James Bock, "Israel's role in Central America quiet, longstanding," *Baltimore Sun*, December 5, 1986.

27. Alan Riding, "Nicaragua Tries Economic Cure."

28. Jean-Pierre Langellier, "Israel au sud du rio Grande," *Le Monde*, Weekly International Edition, week ending December 7, 1986.

29. Jerusalem Domestic Service, 0900 GMT, August 6, 1982 in FBIS Middle East and Africa, August 6, 1982, p. I-9.

Israel & the Contras

1. "Israel-Contras Link Goes Back Years, According to Israeli," AP, *San Francisco Chronicle*, December 5, 1986.

2. Jerry Meldon, "The Contra Connection May Go Back As Far As 1979," *Boston Globe*, November 30, 1986. This article is based on sources of Daniel Sheehan of the Christic Institute, which filed a racketeering suit against a number of network operatives and U.S. officials after two journalists were injured in the attempted assassination of Eden Pastora in 1984. EATSCO was the Egyptian American Transport Services Company.

3. Ben Bradlee, Jr., "Ex-agent says U.S. shielded 4 tied to contras," *Boston Globe*, January 25, 1987.

4. Meldon, "The Contra Connection May Go Back As Far As 1979."

5. Christopher Dickey, *With the Contras*, Simon & Shuster, NY, 1985, pp. 112, 119, 123-4, 145-6, 155-6.

6. Testimony of Hector Francis, a defecting Argentine contra trainer, to Latin American Federation of Journalists, Mexico City, published in *Barricada*, (Managua) December 2, 1982, translated by Carmen Alegria in *Black Scholar*, March-April, 1982.

7. Dickey, *With the Contras, op. cit.*

8. *Ha'aretz*, December 5, 1986 in FBIS Middle East & Africa, December 5, 1986, p. I-4. This story cites *Foreign Report*, which it does not further identify but might be the report by that name produced by the intelligence unit of the *Economist*. The story also details an earlier attempt by Iran, under Israeli pressure, to bomb the Osirak reactor.

9. Jerusalem Domestic Service, 0900 GMT, August 6, 1982 in FBIS Middle East and Africa, August 6, 1982, p. I-9.

10. Stephen Engelberg, "Official Says Contacts by Israelis on Arming of the Contras Date from '82," *New York Times*, February 8, 1987. Israel captured a great stock of arms in Lebanon in 1982. However intelligence sources say that since it captured East bloc arms in its 1967 war, Israel has been trading in them and is perhaps the second biggest trader in these wares, after the USSR.

11. *Newsweek* December 6, 1986. "America's Secret Warriors," *Ibid.*, October 10, 1983.

12. Jeff McConnell, "How Israel came to deal with the contras," *Boston Sunday Globe*, January 18, 1987.

13. "Israeli arms sales in Latin America," *Le Monde* (in *Manchester Guardian*) 5/6/84; Philip Taubman, "Israel Said to Aid Latin Aims of U.S.," *New York Times*, July 21, 1983.

14. Edy Kaufman, "The View from Jerusalem," *Washington Quarterly*, Fall, 1984.

15. Jacques Lemieux, "Le role d'Israel en Amerique centrale," *Le Monde Diplomatique*, October 1984.

16. *Washington Post*, December 7, 1982; Ignacio Klich, "Israel et L'Amerique Latine," *Ibid.*, February 1983.

17. *Latin America Weekly Report*, December 17, 1982.

18. *SIPRI Yearbook 1984*, p. 238.

19. Danny Goodgame, "Israel Asks U.S. to Finance Sales to Latin America, *Miami Herald*, December 13, 1982.

20. *Ibid.*; *U.S. Assistance to the State of Israel*, pp. 43-45.

21. M. Torres, "La Influencia de Estados Unidos en la formulacion de la Politica Exterior de Honduras," *Boletin Informativo Honduras*, Centro de Documentacion de Honduras, Tegucigalpa, March 16, 1985.

22. Undelivered speech by Sharon, published in *Ma'ariv*, December 18, 1981, transl. in *Journal of Palestine Studies*, No. 43, Spring 1982.

23. Gid'on Samet, "Superman Must Take it Easy," *Ha'aretz*, December 3, 1986, in FBIS Middle East & Africa, pp. I-3-4.

24. Charles R. Babcock, "U.S.-Israeli Ties Stronger Than Ever," *Washington Post*, August 5, 1986.

25. *Report of the President's Special Review Board* (Tower Commission Report), February 26, 1987, p. C-9.

26. *Der Spiegel*, July 26, 1983 in Jesus Guevara Morin/Notimex, "Israel es el principal proveedor de armas a los contrarrevolucionarios nicaraguenses," *unomasuno*, April 23, 1984.

27. "An Israeli Connection?" *Time*, May 7, 1984.

28. "Eden Pastora Unmasked as Longtime U.S. Agent," *Counterspy*

Sept.-Nov. 1983. According to Hector Francis (see above), Pastora had served as an informer for the U.S. as early as 1979, "because he was finding out that he was not going to have the degree of power that he thought he should have within the revolution."

29. Caitlin Randall, "Two U.S. journalists are cleared of libeling rancher in Costa Rica," *Miami Herald,* May 25, 1986; Jay Ducassi and Christina Cheakalos, "Journalists suit claims ring tried to kill contra," *Ibid.,* May 30, 1986; Mark Prendergast, "Pro-Contras linked to plot to assassinate Pastora, envoy," *Fort Lauderdale News and Sun-Sentinel,* in *San Antonio Light,* May 22, 1986. After further CIA pressure, Pastora retired in May 1986.

30. "The Most Dangerous Game," *Time,* October 17, 1983.

31. Joel Brinkley, "Costa Rican Aides Are Said to Take Rebel Bribes," *New York Times,* April 23, 1984.

32. Prendergast, "Pro-Contras linked to plot to assassinate Pastora, envoy." Martha Honey and Tony Avirgan, *La Penca,* San Jose, Costa Rica, draft copy, 1984, p. 72; later there would be an airstrip, drug dealing and a plot to assassinate the U.S. ambassador.

33. Juan O. Tamayo, "Mysterious donations boost Pastora's numbers and goals," *Miami Herald,* September 9, 1983.

34. *Sunday Times* (London) August 30, 1983, in Guevara, "Israel es el principal proveedor de armas a los contrarrevolu-cionarios nicaraguenses."

35. Author's source.

36. Panama City ACAN (dateline, San Jose), 0045 GMT, April 24, 1984 in FBIS Latin America, April 25, 1984, p. P-12.

37. Sonia Vargas L., Alfonso Robelo, "Pastora debe aceptar union de ARDE y FDN," *La Nacion Internacional,* (San Jose, Costa Rica) June 7-13, 1984.

38. Madrid EFE, 022 GMT, September 25, 1984 in FBIS Latin America, September 27, 1984, p. P-15.

39. "Noriega ordeno el asesinato," *Rumbo Centroamericano,* (San Jose, Costa Rica) September 26-October 2, 1985.

40. *Newsweek,* ("Periscope" section) June 30, 1986; see also "General Noriega of Panama," *Israeli Foreign Affairs,* September 1986. The Panamanian military had President Ardito Barletta, Devalle's predecessor, resign to forestall and investigation into the murder of Spadafora, which many believe would have implicated the military.

41. Jeff McConnell, "How Israel came to deal with the contras," *Boston Sunday Globe,* January 18, 1987.

42. Bob Woodward, "CIA Sought 3rd-Country Contra Aid," *Washington Post,* May 19, 1984.

43. Philip Taubman, "Nicaragua Rebels Reported to Have New Flow of Arms," *New York Times,* January 13, 1985.

44. Chris Maupin, report and report in *Nuevo Diario,* (Managua) April 1, 1985.

45. Chris Maupin, interviews in Nicaragua, March and April 1985.

46. *All Things Considered,* April 23, 1985.

47. Maupin, eyewitness report.

48. Stephen Engelberg, "Official Says Contacts by Israelis on Arming of the Contras Date from '82"; Congressional investigators "suspected" the "basic outline" of Terrell's account "to be accurate."

49. Chris Hedges, "Contra visit to Israel disclosed," *Dallas Morning News*, December 10, 1986.

50. Tom Jelton report from Miami, *All Things Considered*, National Public Radio, December 6, 1986; Jerusalem Domestic Service, 1700 GMT, February 2, 1987, FBIS Middle East and Africa, February 3, 1987, p. I-3.

51. Chris Hedges, "Contra visit to Israel disclosed," *Dallas Morning News*, December 10, 1986.

52. Jerusalem Domestic Service, 1700 GMT, February 2, 1987, FBIS Middle East and Africa, February 3, 1987, p. I-3; the Israeli press has consistently referred to Montealegre as Montenegro.

53. *Newsweek*, December 15, 1986.

54. *Newsday*, January 18, 1987 cited in Jack Colhoun, "Congress deflects gaze from contra side of scandal," *Guardian*, February 4, 1987.

55. *Newsweek*, December 15, 1986.

56. Ignacio Klich, "Israel and the Contras," *Middle East International*, April 3, 1987.

57. Stephen Engelberg, "Official Says Contacts by Israelis on Arming of the Contras Date from '82."

58. *Report on Preliminary Inquiry*, p. 50.

59. Juan O. Tamayo, "Dealers: Israel sent rebels arms," *Miami Herald*, December 1, 1986.

60. Glen Frankel, "Israeli Economy Depends on No-Questions-Asked Arms Sales," *Washington Post*, December 12, 1986.

61. Tamayo, "Dealers: Israel sent rebels arms."

62. Gil Qeysari and Yosef Walter, "Arms Traced Through Honduras to Contras," *Ma'ariv*, November 27, 1986 in FBIS Middle East & Africa, December 1, 1986, p. I-7. The original *Ma'ariv* article (Gil Kesary, "Pesakh Ben-Or—Business in Darkness," December 13, 1985, translated by Israel Shahak in *Collection: More about Israeli weapons trade, and the way it influences Israeli politics,*) which this one updates focused primarily on Ben Or's activities in Guatemala. In a telephone conversation Col. Perez confirmed the documents and verified his signature—one of undoubtedly many instances where Honduran officers acted as forwarding agents for the contras.

63. Frankel, "Israeli Economy Depends on No-Questions-Asked Arms Sales."

64. Jack Colhoun, "Contra Weapons Conduit Goes through Tel Aviv," *Guardian*, April 16, 1986.

65. Joel Brinkley, "White House Aid to Nicaraguan Rebels Reportedly Worried CIA," *New York Times*, August 10, 1985.

66. Ignacio Klich, "Pro the Contras," *Guardian*, October 11, 1985.

67. Jack Colhoun, "Contra Weapons Conduit Goes through Tel Aviv," *Guardian*, April 16, 1986.

68. A report in *Defense and Foreign Affairs* "suggests that Ben Or may have

supplied the Soviet SAM-7 missiles." (Cited in "Israel and Central America," *Latin America Regional Report Mexico and Central America*, February 14, 1986).

69. Contra sources said that when they had trouble operating the SAM-7s Gen. Singlaub arranged for a technician to fix them and train the contras to maintain them. Singlaub acknowledged the story but "refused to identify the technician or his nationality, saying, 'It would put too many people in jeopardy.'" Doyle McManus, "Contras Say They Bought Missile From Soviet Bloc," *Los Angeles Times*, December 7, 1985.

70. Kesary, "Pesakh Ben-Or—Business in Darkness," Gil Qeysari and Yosef Walter, "Arms Traced Through Honduras to Contras," *Ma'ariv*, November 27, 1986 in FBIS Middle East & Africa, December 1, 1986, p. I-7; Jack Colhoun, "Contra Weapons Conduit Goes through Tel Aviv," *Guardian*, April 16, 1986.

71. Kesary, "Pesakh Ben-Or—Business in Darkness."

72. Qeysari and Walter, "Arms Traced Through Honduras to Contras."

73. Author's source.

74. "Israel security firm denies aiding Contras," *Jerusalem Post*, January 19, 1987.

75. Klich, "Israel and the Contras."

76. "Israel security firm denies aiding Contras."

77. Frankel, "Israeli Economy Depends on No-Questions-Asked Arms Sales."

78. Klich, "Israel and the Contras."

79. James Rowen, "Rebels got weapons through theft and third-party deals," *Milwaukee Journal*, January 19, 1987.

80. *Ibid.*

81. *Ma'ariv*, February 1, 1987 in FBIS Middle East & Africa, February 2, 1987, p. I-2.

82. IDF Radio, 1405 GMT, February 1, 1987, in FBIS Middle East and Africa, February 2, 1987, pp. I-2-3.

83. "De nouveaux conseillers israeliens en Amerique centrale," *Afrique-Asie*, April 25, 1983.

84. Quoting Washington intelligence sources, ANN, ANSA, AP and EFE, "Apoyo de Israel, Brasil y Venezuela a somocistas," *unomasuno*, (Mexico City) July 1, 1983. These sources also spoke of support from Brazil and Venezuela.

85. *Davar*, cited by Latin America Regional Reports Mexico and Central America, March 23, 1984.

86. Simon Louisson, "How to build a bodyguard empire," *Jerusalem Post*, January 23, 1987.

87. *Davar*, cited by Klich, "Pro the Contras."

88. Juan O. Tamayo, "Want to buy a fully trained SWAT team?" *Miami Herald*, September 4, 1986.

89. *Ibid.*

90. Louisson, "How to build a bodyguard empire."

91. Tamayo, "Want to buy a fully trained SWAT team?"

92. Louisson, "How to build a bodyguard empire."

93. Tamayo, "Want to buy a fully trained SWAT team?"

94. Lev Bearfield, "Masters of All they survey," *Jerusalem Post Magazine*, December 19, 1986.

95. William E. Geist, "About New York—A boutique for All Your Anti-Terrorist Needs," *New York Times*, January 1, 1987.

96. Dan Fisher, "Stung by Criticism, Israel Reviews its Arms Industry," *Los Angeles Times*, September 18, 1986.

97. Jane Hunter, "The Great Iran Arms Sale Plot," *Israeli Foreign Affairs*, June 1986.

98. Asher Wallfish, "Scandals prompt change in permits to sell weaponry," *Jerusalem Post*, October 29, 1986.

99. Tel Aviv IDF Radio, 0600 GMT, December 10, 1986 in FBIS Latin America, December 10, 1986, p. P-16.

100. Michael Preker, "Anonymous Israeli tells of dealings with contras," *Dallas Morning News*, December 7, 1986.

101. *Ha'aretz* cited in "Israeli contra training reported," *Christian Science Monitor*, January 13, 1987.

102. Woodward, "CIA Sought 3rd-Country Contra Aid."

103. "Backdoor Help for Contras, Replaces Congress-Voted Aid," *This Week Central America and Panama*, September 17, 1984. Philip Taubman, "Nicaragua Victims Tied to Recruiting," *New York Times*, September 4, 1984. These figures were estimates by FDN leaders, "government officials" and "White House sources." Other givers were big U.S. corporations and the governments of Guatemala, Venezuela, Taiwan, Honduras, El Salvador and Argentina.

104. Alfonso Chardy, "Private Aid Fuels Contras in Nicaragua," *Miami Herald*, September 9, 1984.

105. AP, *Washington Post*, September 15, 1985; Bird & Holland, "Dispatches," *The Nation*, September 28, 1985.

106. Ellen Ray and William Schaap, "The Modern Mithridates: Vernon Walters: Crypto-diplomat and Terrorist," *CovertAction Information Bulletin*, Number 26, Summer 1986. Walters has played a leading role in a number of the worst episodes of U.S. intervention: Iran, Brazil, Guatemala, Chile, Argentina as well as meddling in North and Southern Africa.

107. Alfonso Chardy, "How U.S. used network to fund contras," *San Jose Mercury News*, October 28, 1986.

108. "Probes Encompass Roles of Casey and CIA," *Washington Post*, November 28, 1986.

109. Chardy, "How U.S. used network to fund contras."

110. Jack Colhoun, "Congress of cowards," *Guardian*, (NY) October 2, 1985.

111. Frank Greve, "Israel reported set to pick up U.S. role with Latins," *Philadelphia Inquirer*, May 31, 1984.

112. "Dine on 'Revolutionary Era,'" *Near East Report* (publication of AIPAC, Israel's registered lobby), April 14, 1986.

113. *Ha'aretz,* May 20, 1982 in FBIS Middle East & Africa, May 21, 1982, p. I-1.

114. *U.S. Assistance to the State of Israel,* p. 38; David Landau "Israel Gaining Closer Ties with African States," *Jerusalem Post,* December 4, 1981 in Shahak, *Israel's Global Role,* pp. 46-47; (Sharon said the the U.S. would pay interest for delaying the implementation of the MOU *Ha'aretz,* May 20, 1982 in FBIS Middle East & Africa, May 21, 1982, p. I-1).

115. Philip Taubman, "Israel Said to Aid Latin Aims of U.S.," *New York Times,* July 21, 1983; "Where the United States Needs Israel," *Ha'aretz,* November 11, 1983 in *Israel Mirror* (no date).

116. "Israel and Central America," *Latin America Regional Report Mexico and Central America,* February 14, 1986.

117. Philip Taubman, "Israel Said to Aid Latin Aims of U.S.," *New York Times,* July 21, 1983.

118. Richard B. Straus, "Israel's New Super-Lobby In Washington: Reagan and Co.," *Washington Post* (opinion piece), April 27, 1986, speaks of the open hostility to Arabs in Congress; the theme that Washington should not "cater" to Arab governments is echoed frequently by AIPAC and was the rationale of recent congressional action to block arms sales to Arab states by conditioning those sales on the willingness of Jordan or Saudi Arabia to unilaterally negotiate (i.e. abandon demands for a solution to the Palestinian issue) with Israel.

119. Charles R. Babcock, "U.S.-Israeli Ties Stronger Than Ever," *Washington Post,* August 5, 1986.

120. Interview in *Hatzofe,* December 16, 1983 in FBIS Middle East & Africa, December 19, 1983, p. I-1.

121. *Ma'ariv,* April 10, 1984 in FBIS, Middle East and Africa, April 10, 1984, p. I-2. The UN condemned it.

122. *Yediot Aharonot,* December 4, 1983, FBIS Middle East & Africa, December 6, 1983, p. I-5.

123. James McCartney, "New Reagan policy stresses Israel, firepower," *San Francisco Sunday Examiner & Chronicle,* December 4, 1983.

124. Chardy, "How U.S. used network to fund contras."

125. Richard B. Straus, "Kimche: The Missing Link Between Iran and the Contras?" Los Angeles Times, January 11, 1987.

126. "Where the United States Needs Israel."

127. Straus, "Kimche: The Missing Link Between Iran and the Contras?"

128. "Money Laundering Request," *New York Times,* November 26, 1986.

129. David K. Shipler, "Israel Was Reportedly Given Differing Signals by U.S. on Iran Arms Sales," *Ibid.,* November 27, 1986.

130. Chardy, "How U.S. used network to fund contras."

131. *Ha'aretz,* presumably another fragment of the April 4 report, cited in "Israeli Latin Role is Denied by U.S," AP, *New York Times,* April 22, 1984.

132. *Ha'aretz,* April 4, 1984, excerpt transl. in *Israleft* No. 244, May 4, 1984; other parts of article cited in *Latin America Weekly Report,* May 4, 1984.

133. Wolf Blitzer, "U.S. wants Israeli aid in Central America," *Jerusalem Post,* April 22, 1984.

134. "Israeli Reports Policy is Not to Aid Sandinista Foes," *New York Times,* April 28, 1984.

135. Bob Woodward, "Steps Toward a Disengagement in Nicaragua Are Recommended," *Washington Post,* April 13, 1984.

136. Bob Woodward, "CIA South 3rd-Country Contra Aid," *Ibid.*, May 19, 1984.

137. "Biggest Nicaraguan Rebel Group Wants Aid from Israel," *Los Angeles Times,* (in *San Francisco Chronicle* April 16, 1984).

138. Pastora Interviewed on Voice of Sandino (clandestine to Nicaragua) 2300 GMT, April 16, 1984 in FBIS Latin America, April 17, 1984, pp. P-20-21.

139. Amir Oren, "Nicaraguan Rebel Representative Calls for Aid," *Davar,* April 27, 1984 [excerpt] in FBIS Middle East & Africa, April 27, 1984, pp. I-4-5 (and repressive governments were being helped by Israel).

140. Fred Francis, NBC Nightly News, 5:30 p.m. (PDT), April 23, 1984. Transcript courtesy of November 29th Committee for Palestine, (P.O. Box 27462, San Francisco, CA 94127).

141. Jerusalem Domestic Service in English, 1800 GMT, April 25, 1984 in FBIS Middle East & Africa, April 26, 1984, p. I-5.

142. "Israeli Latin Role is Denied by U.S," AP, *New York Times,* April 22, 1984.

143. Oswald Johnston, "Israel Denies That It's Aiding Nicaragua Rebels," *Los Angeles Times,* April 28, 1984.

144. Edy Kaufman, "The View From Jerusalem," *Washington Quarterly,* Fall 1984.

145. David K. Shipler, "Israel and the U.S. Stay On Speaking Terms," *New York Times,* December 29, 1985.

146. John M. Goshko, "Israel Denies Arming Nicaraguan Contras," *Washington Post,* April 28, 1984.

147. Kathryn Ferguson report on *All Things Considered,* National Public Radio, April 27, 1984.

148. John M. Goshko, "U.S., Israel Discuss Increasing Aid to Third World Countries," *Washington Post,* April 27, 1984.

149. Senate Select Committee on Intelligence, (99th Congress), *Report on Preliminary Inquiry,* Washington, DC, January 29, 1986, p. 53 and *passim.* notes the testimony of a CIA analyst who believed that some of the profits reaped from arms sales to Iran had been used for "other projects of the U.S. and Israel."

150. The *Report on Preliminary Inquiry,* speaks of Nir as the culprit. Kimche was mentioned first, in earlier reports, e.g. *New York Times,* December 30, 1986.

151. Christopher Thomas, "Secret evidence suggests Peres originated Contra cash scheme," *Times* (London), January 12, 1987.

152. Lally Weymouth, "Khashoggi Speaks," *Washington Post*, February 1, 1987.

153. *Davar*, May 3, 1984, in FBIS Middle East & Africa, May 4, 1984, pp. I 6-7.

154. *SIPRI Yearbook 1984*, p. 526; Frank Greve, "Israel Reported Set to Pick Up U.S. Role with Latins," *Philadelphia Inquirer*, May 31, 1984.

155. *Milavnews*, July 1977.

156. Juan Tamayo, "Honduran Forces Too Sparse to Risk War with Nicaragua," *Miami Herald*, May 13, 1983.

157. Edward Cody, "Sharon to Discuss Arms Sales in Honduras," *Washington Post*, December 7, 1982.

158. John Yemma, "Israel Guns for Worldwide Arms Market," *Christian Science Monitor*, December 27, 1982.

159. Susan Morgan, "Israel selling fighter jets, tanks to Honduras?" *Ibid.*, December 14, 1982; "Alvarez looks for Israeli arms," *Latin America Weekly Report*, December 17, 1982; Juan Tamayo, "Honduras seeks to buy weapons from Israelis," *Miami Herald*, December 9, 1982.

160. Klich, "Pro the Contras."

161. ACAN-EFE (Panama City—dateline Tegucigalpa), 1925 GMT, June 21, 1984, in FBIS Latin America, June 22, 1984.

162. This was known as early as 1985 (Kesary, "Pesakh Ben-Or Business in Darkness"), and confirmed again on CBS *Sixty Minutes* February 22, 1987.

163. *Jerusalem Post*, October 23, 1986 and other sources in *Israeli Foreign Affairs*, November 1986 and December 1986.

164. Honey and Avirgan, *La Penca*.

165. *Latin America Regional Reports, Mexico and Central America*, October 29, 1982; Ignacio Klich, "Israel et l'Amerique Latine, Le pari d'un engagement accru aux cotes de Washington," *Le Monde Diplomatique*, February 1983.

166. "Monge Whistles in the Dark," *Latin America Regional Report, Central America and Mexico*, July 7, 1982; *Ha'aretz*, November 11, 1982, translated in *Israeli Mirror* (London).

167. Ignacio Klich, "Israel et L'Amerique Latine."

168. Martha Honey, "Costa Rica Declares Its Neutrality," *The Times* (London), September 19, 1983.

169. Yoav Karny, "Door is Open for Military Aid to Costa Rica," *Yediot Aharonot*, October 25, 182, in FBIS Middle East and Africa, October 27, 1982.

170. *Jerusalem Post*, January 9, 1983.

171. David Landau, "Israel to Help Costa Rica's Economy," *Jerusalem Post*, October 20, 1982; Karny, "Door is Open for Military Aid to Costa Rica."

172. Jacques Lemiuex, "Le role d'Israel en Amerique Centrale," *Le Monde Diplomatique*, October 1984; *Miami Herald*, September 13, 1983.

173. *Diario La Hora* (Guatemala), March 19, 1985 in *Inforpress Centroamericana*, March 28, 1985. Along with the U.S. and West Germany, Israel helped train the right-wing paramilitary OPEN; Leslie Gelb, "Israel Said to Step Up Latin Role, Offering Arms Seized in Lebanon," *New York Times*, December 17, 1982; *El Dia*, May 15, 1986, translated in *Israeli Foreign Affairs*,

June 1986.

174. San Jose Radio Reloj, 1330 GMT, December 4, 1983, in FBIS Latin America, December 5, 1985.

175. *Diario La Hora, op. cit.*

176. *Ha'aretz*, November 1, 1982, transl. in *Israeli Mirror; Defense Latin America*, August 1983 and *Pittsburgh Press*, March 1, 1983 in *Counterspy*, September-November 1983; *Libertad*, (San Jose) May 4-10, 1984 in FBIS Latin America, May 22, 1984; Dial Torgerson, "Frontier Area No Longer Neglected," *Los Angeles Times*, May 23, 1983; Jack Anderson, "U.S. and Israel Aim for Pinch on Nicaragua," *Washington Post*, February 14, 1983; "Costa Rica Recibe Donacion Millonaria de Estados Unidos? A Cambio de Que?" *Inforpress Centroamericana*, April 11, 1985.

A Classic Case of Disinformation

1. Everybody, save a few lonely voices, notably Rep. Ronald Dellums and other members of the Congressional Black Caucus, concurred, however, on Libya, which the administration bombed in April 1986. But Israel had also been designating Libya as an enemy for months.

2. "Where the United States Needs Israel."

3. Taubman, "Israel Said to Aid Latin Aims of U.S."

4. Jeff McConnell, "How Israel came to deal with the contras," *Boston Globe*, January 18, 1987.

5. *Latin America Regional Report, Mexico and Central America*, May 4, 1984.

6. Taubman, "Israel Said to Aid Latin Aims of U.S."

7. Dan Sudran and Robert Rubin, "In defense of Nicaragua—anti-Semitism is not evident," *Northern California Jewish Bulletin*, August 2, 1985.

8. Joseph Berger, "Nicaragua's Jews: Wide Disagreement on Status," *New York Times*, April 20, 1986.

9. Edward Cody, "Managua's Jews Reject Anti-Semitism Charge," *Washington Post*, August 29, 1983.

10. Comision Nacional de Promocion y Proteccion de los Derechos Humanos, *Resultados de una investigacion que la comision nacional...hizo en relacion a un comunicado de la "Anti Defamation League (ADL) of B'Nai B'rith" sobre una supuesta persecucion a la comunidad judia en Nicaragua,"* Managua, 1983, p. 5.

11. Franz Schneiderman, *Bending Swords into Plowshares: An Investigation of the Tensions between Israel and Nicaragua*, special report by the Council on Hemispheric Affairs, Washington DC, November 26, 1985.

12. *Ibid.*

13. Dan Sudran and Robert Rubin, "In defense of Nicaragua—anti-Semitism is not evident," *Northern California Jewish Bulletin*, August 2, 1985.

14. Walter Ruby, "NJA Mission Meets with Nicaraguans," *Genesis 2* September/October 1984.

15. Robert Weisbrot, "Dateline Managua: Anti-Semitism or Anti-climax?" *Moment*, October 1984.

16. Brickner, "Demythologizing Nicaragua," *Christian Century*, October 10, 1984.

17. Saul Sorrin, "Report from Nicaragua," *Reform Judaism*, Summer 1984.

18. *Latin America Regional Report, Mexico and Central America*, May 4, 1984.

19. Weisbrot, "Dateline Managua: Anti-Semitism or Anti-climax?"

20. Schneiderman, *Bending Swords Into Plowshares..."*

21. Robert Weisbrot, "Dateline Managua: Anti-Semitism or Anti-climax?" *Moment*, October 1984.

22. Edward Cody, "Managua's Jews Reject Anti-Semitism Charge," *Washington Post*, August 29, 1983.

23. "De Antisemitismo Accusa Moussali a Nicaragua," *Excelsior*, June 8, 1983.

24. Author's interviews.

25. *Resultados de una investigacion que la comision nacional...hizo*, p. 5.

26. George Black, "Taking Note," *Nacla Report on the Americas*, June 1986.

27. Cited from *Washington Post*, January 27, 1985, "U.S. Jews against Contras," *Jewish Currents*, June 1986.

28. Nadine Joseph, "3 dispute charges of anti-Semitism by Nicaragua," *Northern California Jewish Bulletin*, December 14, 1984. Although AK-47s are more commonly associated with the contras, they have been supplied with the Galil. Others might have preserved the rifles from their service with the Somocist National Guard.

29. Liz Balmaseda, "Nicaraguan Jews feel sting of ouster," *Miami Herald*, July 2, 1983.

30. Sorrin, "Report from Nicaragua,."

31. Robert Weisbrot, "Dateline Managua: Anti-Semitism or Anti-climax?"

32. *All Things Considered*, National Public Radio, August 24, 1984.

33. In August 1985 the State Department published a polemic entitled *The Sandinistas and Middle Eastern Radicals,* which it described as "An unclassified report on Sandinsita ties to Middle Eastern radicals, including Sandinista participation in Middle East aircraft hijacking and terrorism in 1970, [sic] and their continuing relations with these groups and states in the 1980s." For its "analysis," the Department drew on a narrow swath of rightist sources, such as Claire Sterling, the ADL, the Council for Inter-American Security, *Midstream*, the Heritage Foundation, the Cuban-American National Foundation and the Center for International Security.

34. Edward Cody, "Managua's Jews Reject Anti-Semitism Charge," *Washington Post*, August 29, 1983.

35. Weisbrot, "Dateline Managua: Anti-Semitism or Anti-climax?"

36. "Anti-Semitism Should Have No Place in the Nicaragua Debate," Letter to the *New York Times*, April 18, 1986.

37. *Mideast Observer*, April 1, 1986.

38. Tom Tugend, "American Jews split over sanctuary issue," *Jerusalem Post*, March 13, 1987.

39. "U.S. Jews Offer Sanctuary," *Israeli Foreign Affairs*, June 1985.

40. Evans & Novak, "The Missing Paragraphs," *Washington Post*, July 27, 1983.

41. Joseph Berger, "Nicaragua's Jews: Wide Disagreement on Status," *New York Times*, April 20, 1986.

42. Alexander Reid, "Jewish League Reports on Bias in Nicaragua," *New York Times*, April 5, 1986.

43. Author's source.

44. Laurie Becklund, "Sandinistas Are Anti-Semitic, Group Charges," *Los Angeles Times*, March 14, 1985.

45. "Ex-Nicaraguan Jews accuse Sandinistas of anti-Semitism," JTA in *Northern California Jewish Bulletin*, April 18, 1986.

46. Ignacio Klich, "Initiative from Nicaragua," *Jerusalem Post*, November 11, 1986.

47. *Mideast Observer*, March 15, 1986; *New York Times*, March 6, 1986.

48. Interview with Michael Saba, 1985.

49. Interview with Zehdi Terzi, Palestine Liberation Organization Permanent Representative to the United Nations, February 1985.

50. Interview with Miriam Hooker, Nicaraguan Embassy press attache, February 1985.

51. *La Prensa* (Managua), January 25, 1985 in FBIS Latin America, January 28, 1985, p. P-13; Managua Domestic Service, 2306 GMT, January 25, 1985 in FBIS Latin America, January 28, 1985, p. P-12; during the same period Iran negotiated trade agreements with Honduras, Uruguay, Brazil and Argentina.

52. In 1984 Iran and Nicaragua issued a joint communique condemning U.S. military maneuvers in Central America and the Persian Gulf, the invasion of Grenada, and the racist regime in South Africa, and declaring support for the Palestinian and Polisario causes (Havana International Service, 1600 GMT, March 18, 1984 in FBIS March 20, 1984, p. Q-9).

53. *New York Times*, March 6, 1986; "Reagan Bids Jews Support Contras," *Israeli Foreign Affairs*, April 1986.

54. *Mideast Observer*, April 1, 1986.

55. Author's source.

56. Moses Rischin, *The Promised City*, Harvard University Press, Cambridge, MA, 1962, p. 97 in Roberta Strauss Feuerlicht, *The Fate of the Jews*, Times Books, New York, 1983, pp. 93-94 and *passim*.

57. Victor Navasky, *Naming Names*, Viking, New York, 1980, pp. 97-142.

58. Nathan and Ruth A. Perlmutter, *The Real Anti-Semitism*, Arbor House, 1982, argues that fundamentalists make better allies than the more liberal Christian organizations, such as those grouped in the National Council of Churches, with their tendency to issue statements supportive of Palestinian

rights.

59. Donald E. Wagner, "Anxious for Armageddon," *All in the Name of the Bible,* edited by Hassan Haddad and Donald E. Wagner, PHRC Special Report #5, (The Palestine Human Rights Campaign, 1 Quincy Court, 220 South State St., Suite 1308, Chicago, IL 60604) April 1985, pp. 12-24; thanks also to Sara Diamond, for many illuminating explanations of premillenialism.

60. Perlmutter, *The Real Anti-Semitism,* pp. 171-172.

61. According to Sara Diamond, the focus of the leading televangelists has become more political, less "supernatural."

62. Grace Halsell, *Prophecy and Politics: Militant Evangelists on the Road to Nuclear War,* Lawrence Hill & Co., 1986. The author provides first-hand evidence of President Reagan's adherence to this superstition.

63. "U.S. Jewry no longer is Israel's lackey," *Jewish Post and Opinion,* April 3, 1985.

64. David Silverberg, "Which priority for Jews: Israel or liberal causes?" *Northern California Jewish Bulletin,* November 22, 1985.

65. "U.S. Jews against Contras," *Jewish Currents,* June 1986.

Will the Lessons Be Learned?

1. "Nicaragua: Efforts to Heal," *Israeli Foreign Affairs,* February 1985.

2. *Jerusalem Post,* November 11,1986.

3. *Ibid.,* December 4, 1986.

4. Letter to editor, *Middle East International,* December 19, 1986.

5. *Latin American Weekly Report* January 15, 1987.

6. Henry Kamm, "Israel Said to Seek Restoration of Diplomatic Ties with Nicaragua," *New York Times,* December 12, 1986.

7. *Ibid.*

8. E. Kaufman, "Israeli Involvement in Latin America," in W. Perry & P. Wehner (eds.), *The Latin American Policies of U.S. Allies,* Praeger (ca. 1984), p. 144.

9. *Genesis 2,* Sept.-Oct. 1984.

10. "Nicaragua ayuda a la OLP, acusa Israel," AP, *La Jornada,* June 19, 1986.

11. *Ha'aretz,* June 18, 1986 in FBIS Middle East & Africa, June 19, 1986, p. I-2.

12. ANSA (Italian news agency) in *La Jornada,* January 6, 1987.

13. UPI, *Houston Post,* December 6, 1986.

14. "Una derrota politica de Reagan en la ONU," *Barricada,* November 4, 1986.

Conclusion

1. Paul Findley, *They Dare to Speak Out*, Lawrence Hill, Westport CT, 1985, pp. 12-22.

2. *Ibid.*, pp. 21-22.

3. Wolf Blitzer, *Between Washington and Jerusalem*, Oxford University Press, New York, 1985, p. 116.

4. *Ibid.*, p. 115. It is striking that no pretense is made that Israel might be supported on principle!

5. Findley, *They Dare to Speak Out*, p. 35.

6. Richard H. Curtiss, *A Changing Image: American Perceptions of the Arab-Israeli Dispute*, American Educational Trust, Washington, DC, 1986, p. 270.

7. Findley, *They Dare to Speak Out*, p. 36.

8. Robert Scheer, "Israel Lobby—Clout but No Monolith," *Los Angeles Times*, April 7, 1983.

9. Findley, *They Dare to Speak Out*, pp. 187-188.

10. *Ibid.*, 194-199.

11. *Ibid.*, pp. 199-211.

12. *Ibid.*, pp. 212-241.

13. *Ibid.*, pp. 253-259.

14. Robert Weisbord and Richard Kazarian, Jr., *Israel in the Black American Perspective*, Greenwood Press, Westport, CT, 1985, chronicles black-Jewish relations from a Zionist perspective, and in so doing betrays the heavy-handed manipulativeness with which Jewish organizational leaders have dealt with black politicians and organizations.

15. Earl Raab, "Timely book deals with feelings of blacks toward Israel," *Northern California Jewish Bulletin*, June 7, 1985 reviews the Weisbord-Kazarian book and notes that "We all have a stake in which segment of [the] black elite wins the minds of the black populace." The segment of that black "elite" to be excluded was described by Charles Silberman, the influential author of *A Certain People—American Jews and Their Lives Today*, as "younger persons with higer education" who ascribe to "the political anti-Semitism that pervades the ideology of the left worldwide." (Elsa Solender, "Author says doomsayers wrong on U.S. Jewry's fate," *Ibid.*, September 27, 1985.) The "political anti-Semitism" referred to is, of course, anti-Zionism.

16. Such incidents have been reported to the author many times—as they would be to anyone who bothered to ask.

17. Rubenberg, *Israel and the American National Interest*, pp. 336-338.

18. Findley, *They Dare to Speak Out*, p. 135.

19. The administration secured a conviction of leading sanctuary activists in Arizona in 1986, but popular sentiment was so heavily against its targeting the mostly religious movement for spying and prosecution—and against its vindictive policies of returning Salvadoran and Guatemalan refugees to almost certain political execution—that it has not sought to follow up its largely

Phyrric victory.

20. The *Los Angeles Times*, has had the most complete coverage of this case, beginning on January 28, 1987.

21. "Bomb Kills Leader of U.S. Arab Group," UPI, *New York Times*, October 12, 1985.

22. Letter from James G. Abourezk, National Chairman of ADC, October 13, 1985.

23. A totally apolitical Palestinian-owned restaurant chain in suburban Chicago had one facility bombed to the ground. Others closed after a campaign against the chain featuring such tactics as posters saying "Mediterranean House food in your stomach is like Jewish blood on your hands," and "Money Spent Here Supports PLO Terrorism," applied to restaurant walls and adorned with red paint and raw liver. The excuse for the campaign was that among the radio advertising bought by the chain were spots on a Palestinian radio program. It also bought spots on Jewish programs (Findley, *They Dare to Speak Out*, pp. 290-293).

24. Robert I. Friedman, "Selling Israel to America," *Mother Jones*, Feb.-March, 1987.

25. *Ibid.*

26. *Ibid.*

27. *Newsweek*, September 3, 1979 in Findley, *They Dare to Speak Out*, p. 148.

28. *Ibid.*, pp. 149-151.

29. David K. Shipler, "Israel and the U.S. Stay on Speaking Terms," *New York Times*, December 29, 1985.

30. Wolf Blitzer, "End of the Honeymoon," *Jerusalem Post Magazine*, January 16, 1987, reveals that offense was taken; there is no public record.

31. "U.S. Jews weigh Israel—S. Africa arms deals," JTA, *Jerusalem Post*, February 20, 1987.

32. *Congressional Record*, July 11, 1985, H 5469.

33. "Reagan's China Card Trumped," *Israeli Foreign Affairs*, December 1984.

34. The Senate version of the bill was later accepted by the House, in the interests of haste.

35. *Ha'aretz*, March 20, 1987, quoted verbally by Israel Shahak, Stockholm, March 26, 1987.

36. Larry Cohler, "Black leaders agree to mute attack on Israel-S. Africa tie," Washington *Jewish Week*, in *Northern California Jewish Bulletin*, April 10, 1987.

37. Author's sources. For a full history of the moves leading up to the report see "More Military Deals With South Africa," "Arms Sales to South Africa—Four More Years," and "Israel Moves to Block Congress, Save South African Arms Sales," *Israeli Foreign Affairs*, February, March and April 1987.

38. Doyle McManus, "Demos vying hard to lure wary Jewish voters," *Los Angeles Times*, (in *Oakland Tribune* April 2, 1984).

39. *New York Times*, (in *San Francisco Chronicle*, March 12, 1984).

40. Interview with Berman aide, "Israeli Development Aid to Central America."

41. It is also within the realm of possibility for activists, especially in coalition with unions or some other group with access to minimal funding, to put together a winning primary campaign in some congressional districts. In the aftermath, there would, naturally, be a struggle to get party support for an independent candidate, progressive across the board and willing as well to confront Israel, but in his first race for mayor of Chicago Harold Washington demonstrated that similar problems could be overcome (to the shame of those who caused them).

42. March 18, 1983.

43. The January 31, 1986 press release announcing the resolution—and another condemning anti-Arab racism in the U.S.—said that the resolution was passed "with the full understanding that Israel was the military supplier that receives the most American aid."

44. This is the report cited above. Unfortunately, except for a very positive column by Colman McCarthy, the COHA report was largely ignored.

45. *Jews and Central America: the Need to Act,* New Jewish Agenda, New York, 1985. Also *Jews and the Sanctuary Movement.*

46. "Zim Sails On," *Israeli Foreign Affairs,* November 1986.

Index ....

Michell Curry
Cont